היסטוריה

The ArtScroll History Series®

Rabbi Nosson Scherman / Rabbi Meir Zlotowitz
General Editors

The

Published by
Mesorah Publications, ltd

Chazon Ish

The Life and Ideals of Rabbi Avraham Yeshayah Karelitz

by
Rabbi Shimon Finkelman

FIRST EDITION
First Impression . . . April, 1989

Published and Distributed by
MESORAH PUBLICATIONS, Ltd.
Brooklyn, New York 11232

Distributed in Israel by
MESORAH MAFITZIM / J. GROSSMAN
Rechov Harav Uziel 117
Jerusalem, Israel

Distributed in Europe by
J. LEHMANN HEBREW BOOKSELLERS
20 Cambridge Terrace
Gateshead, Tyne and Wear
England NE8 1RP

**THE ARTSCROLL HISTORY SERIES®
THE CHAZON ISH**
© Copyright 1989, by MESORAH PUBLICATIONS, Ltd.
4401 Second Avenue / Brooklyn, N.Y. 11232 / (718) 921-9000

No part of this book may be reproduced
in any form without **written** permission from the copyright holder,
except by a reviewer who wishes to quote brief passages in connection with a review
written for inclusion in magazines or newspapers.

THE RIGHTS OF THE COPYRIGHT HOLDER WILL BE STRICTLY ENFORCED.

ISBN:
0-89906-496-5 (hard cover)
0-89906-497-3 (paperback)

Typography by CompuScribe at ArtScroll Studios, Ltd.
4401 Second Avenue / Brooklyn, N.Y. 11232 / (718) 921-9000

Printed in the United States of America by Noble Book Press Corp.
Bound by Sefercraft, Quality Bookbinders, Ltd. Brooklyn, N.Y.

Table of Contents

Preface	7
Chapter 1: For Its Sake Alone	13
Chapter 2: The Early Years	22
Chapter 3: Marriage, Authorship, and Uprooting	31
Chapter 4: In Lithuania's Jerusalem	43
Chapter 5: Bnei Brak	60
Chapter 6: The Hidden Leader	80
Chapter 7: Master of Halachah	102
Chapter 8: The Date-Line Controversy	120
Chapter 9: Wisdom and Approach	129
Chapter 10: Emunah and Bitachon	145
Chapter 11: Servant of Hashem	161
Chapter 12: An Angel Among Mortals	176
Chapter 13: Everyone's Father	192
Chapter 14: Apple of His Eye	213
Chapter 15: The Chazon Ish and the Steipler	229
Chapter 16: The State	237
Chapter 17: Final Days	256
Glossary	266
Bibliography	271

◆§ Preface

Soon after this project began, I met an acquaintance whom I had not seen for some time. In the course of our conversation, I made mention of this book. My acquaintance advised me: "Whatever there is to say about the Chazon Ish has already been said." He did not elaborate and I did not pursue the comment. Interestingly, I have since heard similar comments from others. It would seem proper to use this preface as a means to convey what the publication of this book hopes to accomplish.

The basic outline of the Chazon Ish's life is well known. He studied almost all his life in virtual solitude, lived according to the most stringent standards of *Halachah*, wrote voluminously, and was instrumental in reviving proper observance of *mitzvos* relating specifically to *Eretz Yisrael*. He was a leader in the struggle to forge a strong Torah community despite the opposition of a secularist government, in the years immediately following the founding of the State of Israel. He shunned the limelight in a way that was unusual even among *gedolei Torah*, while offering counsel to the multitudes that streamed to his simple apartment in Bnei Brak.

There is much, however, that is not well known. While his halachic standards and unbending commitment to undiluted Torah *hashkafah* against all opposition suggest a stern, unyielding fighter, the Chazon Ish was, in fact, a man of warmth, love, and unbridled concern for virtually anyone who sought his assistance. While his halachic opinions suggest someone searching for stringencies, the Chazon Ish could be lenient when others would not dare, if he felt that such leniency had firm basis in *Halachah*. While his struggles against those opposing the Torah camp are well known, his disciplined, careful approach to conducting such struggles is not.

Literally thousands of people sought the Chazon Ish's counsel during the last twenty years of his life. Of the fraction of these encounters that have been preserved, some convey fundamental points of *hashkafah*, while others illustrate the all-embracing wisdom inherent in Torah and those who are living Torah Scrolls. Though every second was a treasure to him, his accessibility to old and young of every possible background was a marvel of the age.

The Chazon Ish's collected letters, *Kovetz Igros Chazon Ish*, and his *Emunah U'Vitachon* (both of which were published by his family, posthumously), are treasuries of Torah *hashkafah* (outlook) on a wide variety of themes. This book draws heavily from these sources. The reader is urged to study these works; no translation can do adequate justice to the warmth, lyric beauty and power of the Chazon Ish's writings.

I would like to express particular gratitude to the renowned author and bibliographer Rabbi Aharon Sorasky, who graciously permitted extensive use of his *HaChazon Ish B'Dorosav* and his five-volume *Pe'er HaDor*, which was edited by the Chazon Ish's disciple, Rabbi Shlomo Kohen. Rabbi Sorasky's writings were invaluable in the preparation of this work. Also very useful was *Rabboseinu*, whose editor, Rabbi Yosef Avraham Wolf, was founder of the Bais Yaakov Seminary of Bnei Brak and a confidant of the Chazon Ish.

Scattered throughout the book are quotations from a lengthy appreciation of the Chazon Ish by Rabbi Shlomo Kohen, published in the *Digleinu* periodical shortly after the Chazon Ish's death. I am grateful to Rabbi Moshe Kolodny, Director of the Orthodox Jewish Archives of Agudath Israel of America, for having provided copies of this and other articles. Rabbi Nisson Wolpin provided material regarding *Shemittah* published in *The Jewish Observer*. An article on the Chazon Ish by Rabbi Aharon Brafman, also published in *The Jewish Observer*, was very useful. Additional material was provided by Mr. Micha Oppenheim, Senior Cataloguer at the Jewish Theological Seminary Library. A complete bibliography of sources is found at the book's end.

I am deeply indebted to *HaGaon HaRav* Shmaryahu Karelitz, an illustrious nephew of the Chazon Ish, for having given of his time to provide numerous anecdotes and insights, many of which have never before appeared in print. Rabbi Karelitz was close to the Chazon Ish, both in Vilna and in Bnei Brak, and has much to relate regarding the life and outlook of his uncle. His desire that the portrayal herein be accurate has had a marked effect on the book.

HaGaon HaRav Asher Katzman, a *rosh yeshivah* at Mesivta Torah Vodaath, has provided previously unpublished information that he heard from the Chazon Ish's family and other authoritative sources. Rabbi Katzman is well known to the Yiddish-speaking public through his historical essays in *Dos Yiddishe Vort*.

I am grateful to *HaRav* David Cohen, *HaRav* Hillel David, and *HaRav* Hersh Goldwurm for their gracious assistance.

I am indebted to many others, not the least of whom is Howard Shapiro, who skillfully edited the entire manuscript. Moshe D. Yarmish provided photos from his vast archives of *gedolim* photos. The cover portrait is the work of Mrs. Mindy Greenspoon of Spring Valley, N.Y., whose *gedolim* portraits grace many Jewish homes.

My long-time *chaver*, Rabbi Shmuel Geller of Zichron Yaakov, Israel, has provided me with copies of two recently published works: *Dinim U'Minhagim Chazon Ish*, which contains both halachic practices and letters; and *Hisorerus*, which contains excerpts from the Chazon Ish's writings on a host of *hashkafah* themes. In addition Reb Shmuel has provided anecdotes which were related to him by the Chazon Ish's family.

I am indebted, as well, to two other *chaverim*: Rabbi Yitzchok Yarmush, my *chavrusa* in the study of the Chazon Ish's *Emunah U'Vitachon* as a preparation for this project; and Rabbi Yisroel Reisman for having taken the time to read and comment on a significant portion of the manuscript.

I can only echo the many praises already accorded ArtScroll's General Editors, Rabbi Meir Zlotowitz and Rabbi Nosson Scherman. Despite intense pressures, Rabbi Zlotowitz gave this project the necessary attention whenever it was needed. I must extend a particular debt of gratitude to Rabbi Scherman, my mentor in this and other endeavors. That a man so busy can consistently give of his time in so relaxed a manner is a lesson in itself.

It was Reb Akiva Eiger who said that the impact of a *sefer* is greatly enhanced by its aesthetics. The impact of Mesorah/ArtScroll Publications on the English-speaking Torah public bears witness to the superior artistic talents of Reb Sheah Brander. My thanks also to his associate Michael Horen.

Rabbi Avie Gold has served as consultant, coordinator and more throughout this project. I am grateful to him as well as ArtScroll's other resident editor, Rabbi Yehezkel Danziger.

My thanks also to Shmuel Blitz of ArtScroll/Jerusalem, Shimon Golding, Yossi Timinsky, Michael Zivitz, Menachem Mendel Brogna, Sheila Tennenbaum, Lea Freier, Mrs. Esther Feierstein, Mrs.

Faygie Weinbaum, Mrs. Menuchah Silver, Mrs. Surie Maline, Zissi Glatzer, Bassie Goldstein, and Faigie Zlotowitz.

The *Lakewood Cheder School* has played an important role in the dissemination of this and many other ArtScroll publications.

My father and mother, שיחיו, are sources of inspiration to their children and anyone who has the good fortune to know them. May they be blessed with long life together, in good health.

I once again express a debt of gratitude to my wife's parents and grandparents, שיחיו, who are symbols of commitment to authentic Torah values.

As time goes on, I become ever more cognizant of how indispensable my wife, Tova, תחי׳, is to my work. In the words of Rabbi Akiva, what is mine is hers. May she be granted long life, good health and all her heart's desires.

I close with a prayer that this work does justice to the Chazon Ish's awesome stature. May the lessons of his life and teachings become inscribed upon our hearts, inspiring us all to greater service of Hashem.

Shimon Finkelman

II Adar 5749

The Chazon Ish

CHAPTER ONE
For Its Sake Alone

R' Meir said: Whoever engages in Torah study for its sake alone merits many things. Furthermore, the [creation of the] entire world is worthwhile for his sake alone. He is called "Friend, Beloved." He loves Hashem, he loves [His] creatures, he gladdens Hashem, he gladdens [His] creatures. [The Torah] clothes him in humility and fear [of G-d]; it makes him fit to be righteous, devout, fair and faithful. It moves him away from sin and draws him near to merit. From him people enjoy counsel and wisdom, understanding and strength, as it is said: "Mine are counsel and wisdom, I am understanding, Mine is strength." [The Torah] gives him kingship and authority and analytical judgment. The secrets of the Torah are revealed to him; he becomes like a steadily strengthening fountain and like an unceasing river. He becomes modest, patient, and forgiving of insult to himself. [The Torah] makes him great and exalts him above all things (Avos 6:1).

A Youth's Resolve

ON 11 MARCHESHVAN 5652 (1891), a *bar-mitzvah* celebration took place in Kossowa, White Russia. It was an extraordinary celebration — for reasons known to few. It was on that day that young Avraham Yeshayah Karelitz made a solemn resolution to dedicate himself to the study of Torah *lishmah*, out of pure love of Hashem, his sole motive to acquire a knowledge of Hashem's will and to fulfill His commandments. For the next forty years, the Chazon Ish, as he came to be known (after his famous multi-volume work by that name), studied with legendary diligence, devotion and self-sacrifice, as a

virtual unknown, learning alone and in seclusion. And then, when he decided that the time had come, he emerged as a leader of his people. All the world soon came to realize that, indeed, the Chazon Ish studied Torah *lishmah*, for he possessed every wonderful quality enumerated by R' Meir in the above-cited *braisa*.

IT IS NOTEWORTHY that Rabbi Isser Zalman Meltzer and the Ponovezher *Rav*, Rabbi Yosef Shlomo Kahaneman, were but two of the great personalities who made mention of this *braisa* in eulogizing the Chazon Ish. Among the Ponovezher *Rav*'s words were the following:

Rewards of Torah Lishmah

He loves Hashem — We were literally amazed at the depths of his love for Hashem and His *mitzvos*; *He loves His creatures* — Note the use of *creatures* as opposed to *men*; [he loved people simply because] they were Hashem's creations. Anyone who ever came to speak with him felt this love and saw how the Chazon Ish dedicated his every fiber to helping his fellow Jew.

He gladdens Hashem, he gladdens His creatures — When studying in Radin, I observed some of the ways of the *Chofetz Chaim*, of blessed memory, including what is meant by "gladdens His creatures" — how he received everyone with joy, love and pleasantness. I never saw anyone anywhere like this, save for the Chazon Ish.

It [i.e., the Torah] clothes him in humility — Humility cannot be pretended. The Chazon Ish's humility was natural; this he merited through the study of Torah *lishmah. And the man Moshe was exceedingly humble* (Numbers 12:3) only because *I [Hashem] speak with him [Moshe] face to face* (ibid. 12:8). Moshe's intimacy with Hashem caused him to appreciate how minuscule man is and that he has no reason to be haughty.

From him people enjoy counsel and wisdom — From all over the world they streamed to Bnei Brak in search of his counsel. Even among our lowly generation, he was transformed into a holy man of G-d. Awesome stories concerning his wonders are told. All this had its source in his study of Torah *lishmah*.

Understanding — It is known that he was the wisest Jew alive. He studied Torah *lishmah* for sixty years! Ultimately, his wisdom was beyond his own abilities. It flowed directly from Hashem: *Mine are counsel and wisdom*.

It [the Torah] gives him kingship and authority — This man, who was secluded within the four walls of his room, was the unofficial king of world Torah Jewry. All hearkened to and heeded his word.

So said the Ponovezher *Rav*, himself a giant in his time.

THE *BRAISA* IN *AVOS* STATES that for studying Torah *lishmah*, one *merits many things. Furthermore ... he becomes ...* The

"Furthermore ..." wording implies that such a person acquires *many things* that are in addition to those which R' Meir goes on to cite. If the *braisa* does not list these additional qualities, how then are we to know what they are?

Rabbi Chaim Ozer Grodzensky once said that from simply looking at the *Chofetz Chaim* one could readily recognize the *many things* he had merited. Since these merits are beyond description, the *braisa* does not specify them. Rabbi Shmuel Greineman took these words said of the *Chofetz Chaim* and applied them to his brother-in-law, the Chazon Ish. One merely had to gaze at his saintly features, radiating wisdom, purity and kindness, to see that one who studies Torah for Hashem's sake alone possesses qualities that are beyond description.

Of the *Rambam's* classic halachic work, *Mishneh Torah*, the Chazon Ish writes, "It is a work composed with superhuman abilities, granted only to one who has studied Torah *lishmah*" (*Chazon Ish, Yoreh Deah* pg. 182a). This statement could well have been said of the Chazon Ish's own twenty-three-volume classic, in which virtually every Talmudic topic is expounded upon with breathtaking depth, breadth, and clarity. Appropriate as well would be a paraphrasing of *Rashi's* comment as he attempts to unravel the complexities of the Third *Beis HaMikdash* (*Ezekiel* 42:3): "As for me, I had neither teacher nor helper for the [understanding of] this building — only what I was shown by Heaven."

Our Sages teach (*Berachos* 63a), "The Torah's wisdom can only endure in he who kills himself over her," meaning that Torah can become a true *kinyan nefesh*, an integral component of the mind and soul of he who studies it, only if it is studied with genuine *mesiras nefesh* (self-sacrifice).

It is known that the Chazon Ish would not conclude his studies until he had absolutely no strength left to go on. He once told Rabbi Moshe Yehudah Landau of Jerusalem, "Statements found in *sefer Chazon Ish* such as, 'A copy of *Rashba* is presently not at hand,' do not necessarily mean that I did not have a *Rashba* in my possession at the time; rather, it could be that I simply did not have the strength to rise from my chair and go over to my bookcase."

The Forty-eight Qualities

AS ELEVATING AS THE STUDY of Torah *lishmah* with total sacrifice can be, it alone does not suffice to bring one to his full potential as a *ben Torah*. Among the qualities required, as listed in a second *braisa* in *Avos*, are: awe and reverence of Hashem, modesty, joy, purity, limited physical pleasure, slowness to anger, a good heart, faith in the [teachings of the] Sages, acceptance of suffering, being happy with one's lot, being beloved by all, loving Hashem, loving one's fellow man, distancing oneself from honor, sharing the burden of others, and learning in order to teach and practice.

Rabbi Yaakov Yisrael Kanievsky, renowned as the *Steipler Gaon* and successor to his brother-in-law, the Chazon Ish, as a leader of *Klal Yisrael*, once commented, "Shortly before his [the Chazon Ish's] passing, it became obvious to me that he had forgotten none of his learning [despite his advanced age and failing health]. I discussed with him a *sugya* that he had pored over decades earlier and he revealed a wonderful freshness in it, as if he was then studying it!" Someone present then asked, "Perhaps he recalled it so well from having reviewed it many times over?" To this, the Steipler answered, "I know with certainty that it was in the merit of his *tzidkus*, for he studied Torah *lishmah* and possessed the 'forty-eight qualities.' "

Countless anecdotes and statements of the Chazon Ish attest to the truth of the Steipler's words:

✥ Awe and Reverence of Hashem

"The only pleasure for me is to fulfill the will of Hashem. I could suffer no greater hurt than to be ensnared by sin. My teachers taught me that before any move, one must consult the *Shulchan Aruch* . . . That is all I have in this world" (*Kovetz Igros Chazon Ish*, sec. I: §153).

Letter in which the Chazon Ish writes,
"The only pleasure for me is to fulfill the will of Hashem."

◆§ Modesty

He once asked his disciple, Rabbi Shraga Feivel Steinberg, to examine a particular piece of *Gemara*. It was on a Friday night and a kerosene lamp illuminated the room. The Chazon Ish said that in keeping with the *halachah*, he would stand watch so that Rabbi Steinberg would not unthinkingly adjust the lamp's wick while involved in study. Rabbi Steinberg countered that the *halachah* waived this requirement in such cases where "the awe of the teacher is upon the student," since this is sufficient to ensure that the disciple not sin unthinkingly. Completely abashed, the Chazon Ish replied that he did not think himself to be the kind of teacher that *Chazal* had in mind when formulating this *halachah*.

◆§ Joy

"Ever bend your heart towards happiness, for from happiness one can receive an abundance of Heavenly wisdom" (*Igros* II: §9).

◆§ Purity, Limited Physical Pleasure

"Man's main vitality stems from self-control. The righteous are in control of their desires, rather than finding themselves governed by their desires. It is the sweetest of pleasures, the greatest of joys, to rule over one's animal instincts. It means constant happiness, and it restores one's soul" (ibid., I: §13).

He once remarked that he never felt a need for food; he relied on his *rebbetzin* to decide when and what he should eat. On one occasion, he was about to partake of his meal when someone entered to discuss a pressing matter. The Chazon Ish laid the silverware aside and involved himself in the problem. As soon as the visitor left, another man appeared and then still another. When the last person had left, the Chazon Ish said, "It seems to me that all these disruptions indicate that there is no need to eat at this time." And he left the table without having tasted a morsel.

A short while later, it was discovered that among the foods that had been placed before the Chazon Ish was a vegetable from which *terumos* and *ma'aseros* had not been separated (as is required of produce grown in *Eretz Yisrael*). Thus, by not eating, the Chazon Ish was saved from having sinned inadvertently. *Rebbetzin* Kanievsky, who prepared the Chazon Ish's meals from the time that his own *rebbetzin's* health failed, testified that similar incidents occurred many times.

◆§ Slowness to Anger

Rabbi Shmuel *HaLevi* Wosner, *Rav* of Bnei Brak's Zichron Meir section, said of the Chazon Ish, "He responded to every request and never became upset with anyone. He once remarked that he did not know the meaning of impatience or anger."

◆§ A Good Heart

One *Erev Pesach* the Chazon Ish asked a newlywed to conduct the *seder* for a group of girls who had been orphaned during the Holocaust. The young man replied that his wedding had taken place only a few days earlier and he and his bride were looking forward to spending the *Yom Tov* with family. The Chazon Ish responded, "A great *mitzvah* has come your way. One cannot imagine the pain those girls will suffer if they will have to conduct the *seder* by themselves. If you will not join them, then I will!" The young couple heeded the Chazon Ish's request.

◆§ Acceptance of Suffering

Rabbi Yitzchak Hutner, late *Rosh Yeshivah* of Yeshivah Rabbi Chaim Berlin, referred to the Chazon Ish as the "classic master of the covenant of affliction."

He suffered from a variety of ailments all his life. In a letter the Chazon Ish wrote, "All my studying is done with affliction — the physical sufferings that have been with me since my youth."

In another letter, he wrote, "In reality, there can be no depression for one who recognizes the light of lights of truth" (*Igros* I: §36). His body could be weak, racked with pain, but the Torah's words strengthened his soul and brought joy to his heart.

◆§ Being Happy With One's Lot

From the time he arrived in *Eretz Yisrael*, the Chazon Ish survived on the meager income from the sale of his *sefarim*. Never would he accept generous offers of assistance from grateful visitors who benefited from his counsel, concern and blessing. His apartment had the very barest of furnishings: beds, chairs, tables and bookcases. Amazingly, he did not even own a complete set of the Vilna *Shas*. When the need arose he would borrow the missing volumes from others.

He would establish what he felt was a fair price for his *sefarim* and would never accept a penny more. Once, a relative sold some *sefarim* for him while he was out. Later, the relative presented the Chazon Ish with the purchaser's check. The amount was more than the Chazon Ish's asking price, and the check was torn up.

ಆ§ Loving Hashem

There is no better way for a subject to show loyalty to his king than by carefully observing the king's every command. The Chazon Ish's self-sacrifice for *mitzvah* observance was legendary.

During World War I, he found himself in a town where, only two days before the *Succos* holiday, no *esrog* was to be found. The trip to Minsk, where it was said the *arba'ah minim* were still available, was fraught with danger, but this did not stop the Chazon Ish from journeying there alone in search of an *esrog*. His efforts proved successful, and he remained in Minsk for the *Yom Tov*. Upon returning home, someone asked him why he had gone to such lengths when the *halachah* clearly freed him of his responsibility. He replied, "If you found yourself a few days before *Pesach* without matzos, would you resign yourself to not eating on *Yom Tov*?" To him, *mitzvos* were food for the *neshamah*. He could not live without them.

ಆ§ Sharing the Burden of Others

"You are missing the experience of sharing the pain of others," he wrote in one of his many letters. "The way to achieve this is by trying to help others and shelter them from suffering. Your actions will then affect your heart. Also, attempt to pray on behalf of someone else, even though you do not yet fully feel his anguish" (*Igros* II: §123).

A few days before his passing, his close ones attempted to turn away those who came to his door seeking his help. They asked him, "How can one accept visitors under such conditions?" He replied, "How can I not see those who come to me with broken hearts?"

IN ATTEMPTING A PORTRAYAL of the Chazon Ish, it is fitting to quote the words of his nephew, Rabbi Meir Greineman:

Portraying a Giant Our hearts are filled with fright and our faces with shame at the impression that we are worthy of portraying the sun in all its strength, our master of blessed memory, who all his life cleaved with a constant cleaving of love to his Creator and His holy Torah. He illuminated the world and its inhabitants in virtually all *sugyos* of *Shas* with a depth, breadth and clarity in *halachah* fit for those of earlier generations. No area of Torah was beyond him, including those areas in which there is little in the works and commentaries of our Sages, such as the orders of *Zeraim*, *Kodashim* and *Taharos*. For many generations we did not merit such things; through him, a portion of Torah that was virtually forgotten has been transmitted.

Also, he weighed and probed and stood the nation on its watch to make the Torah great everywhere and in our Holy Land in particular; to guard the details of *halachah*, especially with regard to Land-related laws, of which he ground, finely sifted and arranged a code, establishing them and bringing them into practice. All this he did with tremendous toil and wondrous strength — as he himself once expressed with regard to a particular piece that had been printed in one of his *sefarim* years earlier. He said that he had been toiling over his own words in recent days and had been unable to plumb their depths. He concluded that this [i.e., to delve so deeply into Torah] required super-human abilities.

To all this, [we recall his] great humility, saintliness, removal from the physical, love of his fellow men and all those qualities enumerated in the final chapter of *Avos*. How then can we be so brazen as to think thoughts and attempt eludications in that from which we are so far removed?

Rabbi Greineman concludes that one can but cite some of the Chazon Ish's words and ways. These are sufficient to "illuminate with a glorious brilliance his paths for those that seek them."

CHAPTER TWO
The Early Years

"Already in his youth, the Chazon Ish was Kodesh Kodashim [holiest of holies]" (Rabbi Aharon Kotler).

Golden Lineage

"I WAS RAISED IN A HOME that was a living *Mesilas Yesharim*.* Every quality mentioned in that *sefer* was to be found in my parent's house."

So said Reb Itze'le Karelitz, a brother of the Chazon Ish. It was no exaggeration. The home of Rabbi Shmaryahu Yosef Karelitz and his *rebbetzin*, Rasha Leah, was a wellspring of Torah study, *chesed*, and Heavenly fear.

The *Rav* and *Rebbetzin* of Kossowa were descended from distinguished lineage that included Rabbi Zerachiah *HaLevi*, the *Ba'al HaMaor* (tenth century); Rabbi Yehudah Loewy of Prague, the famed *Maharal* (sixteenth century); and Rabbi Aryeh Leib Epstein, the *Ba'al HaPardes* (eighteenth century).

Rebbetzin Rasha Leah Karelitz was a daughter of Rabbi Shaul Katzenelenbogen, who was a fourth-generation direct descendant of the *Ba'al HaPardes* and a towering personality in his own right. Reb Shaul once paid a visit to Rabbi Yitzchak Meir of Ger, the famed *Chiddushei HaRim*, and the two became involved in deep Torah discussion. When the visit ended, the *Chiddushei HaRim* accorded his guest an unusual honor, escorting him in the darkness of night to the courtyard entrance.

In 1858 (5618), the city of Kossowa, at the behest of Rabbi Yitzchak Elchonon Spector, invited Reb Shaul to become its *Rav*.

---

* Classic *mussar* work by Rabbi Moshe Chaim Luzzato (1707-1746).

Rabbi Shmaryahu Yosef Karelitz

Reb Shaul served in that position until 1882 (5642) when he assumed the rabbinate in Kobrin. In his stead, the Jews of Kossowa selected Reb Shaul's thirty-year-old son-in-law, Reb Shmaryahu Yosef Karelitz, to become their new leader.

Reb Shmaryahu gained renown as a *gaon* and corresponded in Torah with Rabbi Meir Simchah of Dvinsk, author of *Or Sameach*, and Rabbi Shlomo Kohen of Vilna, author of *Cheshek Shlomo*. Reb Shmaryahu's eldest son, Meir, married a daughter of the *Cheshek Shlomo*. The *Cheshek Shlomo* once told his son-in-law, "Ah! How well does your father perceive the truth in Torah! How sweet is his lot!"

In 1915, only a year before his death, Reb Shmaryahu published *Beis HaTalmud*, his commentary to *Masechta Chulin*, in which the *Mishnah* is explained according to the *Gemara's* conclusion and the *halachah* as recorded in the *Shulchan Aruch*. Rabbi Chaim Soloveitchik, famed *Rav* of Brisk, and Rabbi Yisrael Meir Kagan, better known as the *Chofetz Chaim*, would often extol the brilliance

Rebbetzin Rasha Leah Karelitz

and exactness of Reb Shmaryahu's *chiddushei Torah*, some of which are scattered throughout *sefer Chazon Ish*.

He was a *tzaddik*, beloved by all, from the simple to the scholarly. His love for every Jew was effervescent and it was through this love that he exercised so great an influence over his community. He cared for everyone as he did for his own children. The people recognized this and appreciated it. Equally discernible was his deep humility, which would often prevent him from offering rebuke face-to-face. Sometimes, when Reb Shmaryahu felt that criticism was warranted but difficult to administer, he would rise early, enter the *beis midrash* before anyone else, and place a copy of *Mesilas Yesharim* inside the appropriate *tallis* bag. The owner understood that this was the work of the *Rav* and that the "surprise" was a message that he mend his ways.

All his life, Reb Shmaryahu strove to conceal the far limits of his piety. A glimmer of his stature can be gained from a memoir found among the Chazon Ish's papers after his death in 1953 (5714). There, the Chazon Ish tells of his being visited in a dream by a man who, decades earlier, had challenged Reb Shmaryahu's position as *Rav* in Kossowa. The man died and for many years his soul found no rest. In the dream, he beseeched the Chazon Ish to come to his rescue. As the Chazon Ish wrote, "He would not let me go until I blessed him. I said to him, 'May you go in peace.' He was not satisfied. I then said, 'May it be His will that this soul be brought to perfection and may its sins be forgiven.' Immediately, he was calmed."

The Chazon Ish's mother was well known for her exceptional modesty, wisdom, and acts of *chesed*. Most outstanding was the spirit of holiness with which she infused her home and which was manifest on the features of her exceptional children.*

She was once asked if she could think of a particular *z'chus* that had brought her such offspring. She replied that perhaps it was due to her having followed the example of Kimchis, the woman whose exceptional zealousness in matters of *tznius* had merited her seven sons, all of whom served as *Kohanim Gedolim* (High Priests) [see *Yoma* 43a].

Reb Shmaryahu Yosef passed away in 5676 (1916), in the midst of the first World War. *Rebbetzin* Rasha Leah outlived her husband by twenty-five years; toward her life's end, she emigrated to *Eretz Yisrael* where she had the pleasure of seeing her second son in his role as the generation's leader.

ON THURSDAY, 11 MARCHESHVAN, 5639 (1878), Avraham Yeshayah Karelitz was born. From birth, he was reared in accordance with exceptional standards of holiness and virtue. From his very first day, a *yarmulke* covered his head as a *segulah* (auspicious omen) for possessing an abundance of Heavenly fear. When he turned thirty days old, his mother began washing his hands according to the alternate system of *negel vasser* to remove the spiritual impurities that descend upon a person's hands while he sleeps. When he attained the most minimal level of understanding, Avraham Yeshayah's parents began to instill in him love of Torah and train him in a most sublime manner of behavior. In addition to being taught kindness, modesty, and the like,

Reared in Holiness

---

* She had four sons and five daughters. The sons, in order of birth, were: Meir, *Rav* of Lekovitch (Poland) and a prominent Torah leader both in Poland and *Eretz Yisrael*, where he lived his last years; the Chazon Ish; Yitzchak Zundel ('Itze'le'), who succeeded his father as *Rav* of Kossowa; and Moshe, a member of Vilna's *Va'ad HaRabbanim* and editor of the highly regarded *Knesses Yisrael* Torah journal. The sons-in-law were: Rabbi Shmuel Eliyahu Kahan, *Rav* of Ortshe; Rabbi Shmuel Greineman, disciple of the *Chofetz Chaim* and confidant of Rabbi Chaim Ozer Grodzensky and the Chazon Ish; Rabbi Abba Swatitski, *Rav* of Kossowa and later Tiktin; Rabbi Nachum Meir Karelitz, *Rav* of Maishegola; and Rabbi Yaakov Yisrael Kanievsky, the Steipler *Gaon*.

he was impressed with the importance of speaking in a refined way and of not even listening to *lashon hara*.*

That he was bright was apparent at an early age. At age three, already a "master" of the *Aleph-Beis*, Avraham Yeshayah approached his father and announced: "I am fluent in all of *Shas*!" Before Reb Shmaryahu Yosef had a chance to ask his little boy how this was so, Avraham Yeshayah explained, "Show me one letter anywhere in *Shas* that I cannot read!"

However, there was more to this child than genius alone. Once, as the family sat around the dinner table, *Rebbetzin* Karelitz noticed that seven-year-old Avraham Yeshayah was not eating. When asked for an explanation, the little boy said softly, "I do not have a fork." Looking down, his mother saw that she had somehow forgotten to give him not only a fork, but a portion as well. Avraham Yeshayah's sensitivity at that early age had caused him to minimize his mother's oversight as much as possible.

A Prodigy's Training

AN AGED SCHOLAR named Reb Moshe Tuvia taught Avraham Yeshayah privately in the child's formative years. Reb Moshe Tuvia was a disciple of Rabbi Yitzchak Volozhiner, son of Rabbi Chaim Volozhiner who, in turn, was the most famous disciple of the *Vilna Gaon*. As a youth, Reb Yitzchak Volozhiner had frequented the *Gaon's* place of study and it was known that the *Gaon* had a special affection for him. Thus, Avraham Yeshayah was already absorbing the *Gaon's* teachings and method of study at a very early age. As he matured, Avraham Yeshayah strove to follow the *Gaon's* teachings in every way possible, be it method of study, *halachah*, or custom. He saw great significance in every letter that flowed from the *Gaon's* pen.

In later years the Chazon Ish wrote,

> We ascribe to the *Gra* (acronym for *Gaon Rav Eliyahu*) a place in the line beginning with Moshe *Rabbeinu* and continuing with Ezra [the Scribe], Rabbi Yehudah *HaNassi*, Rav Ashi, the *Rambam* and then the *Gra*, for the Torah was revealed through him as through a *kadosh* who was destined for this. He illuminated that which was not illuminated until he came along and "took his portion." He is considered as one of the *Rishonim* and therefore contends with them — even the *Rif* and *Rambam* — on numerous occasions ... His level of *Ruach HaKodesh*,

---

* As the *halachah* requires.

piety, wisdom, toil in study and breadth and depth of knowledge in all areas of Torah cannot be depicted (*Igros* I: §32).

Further illustrative of the Chazon Ish's awe of the *Gaon* is his comment on the *Gaon's* understanding of a particular topic in Talmud *Yerushalmi*: "On the day when the *Gra* revealed this comment, it was announced in Heaven, 'Take heed of Eliyahu and his Torah, [he] who revealed this secret to the Children of Israel.'"

❧ ❧ ❧

Rabbi Meir Karelitz once said that all of the Chazon Ish's incredible mental abilities were apparent in his early youth. Nevertheless, he did not rely on his quick comprehension and flawless memory, but toiled and reviewed as he would in his later years.

When Avraham Yeshayah was about ten years old, Reb Moshe Tuvia decided that the boy's advanced range and depth of knowledge demanded a change of teachers. So it was that Reb Shmaryahu Yosef became his son's private and prime teacher of Torah. They studied *Gemara* in depth each day and Reb Shmaryahu Yosef also set aside time for study of *Mesilas Yesharim, Shnei Luchos HaBris* (*Shlah*) and other ethical and philosophical works.

Reb Shmaryahu Yosef's role as *Rav* limited the time that he could allot to his son, so Avraham Yeshayah spend most of his day and much of the night studying alone in a local *beis midrash*. This arrangement was a portent of things to come, as the Chazon Ish would never attend a yeshivah and would spend most of his life studying alone in seclusion. He and his father recognized that *dibuk chaveirim* (association with colleagues) is among the forty-eight qualities needed to acquire Torah wisdom *bishleimusah* [in its entirety] (*Avos* 6:6). In fact, Avraham Yeshayah did forge close friendships with some of the outstanding young scholars in Kossowa. When he later moved to Kweidan, Avraham Yeshayah asked his friend, Rabbi Moshe Ilvitzky (author of *Minchas Kohen*), to come join him there so that they could continue to benefit from each other's abilities. Somehow, though, Avraham Yeshayah and his father understood that his success in Torah would come primarily from studying alone.

"There is no delight in the world as in studying Torah." So wrote the Chazon Ish in his later years. This feeling was already with him in his youth and surely contributed to Reb Shmaryahu's confidence in his son's ability to study in solitude. In her later years, the Chazon Ish's mother related that in the way of young boys, Avraham Yeshayah would lie in bed at night reading by the light of a small lamp that was concealed under his blanket. Invariably, he was "reading" the *sefer* whose words had occupied his mind earlier that day and whose thoughts he could not bear to part with.

He studied intensely and ceaselessly, even at times when his poor constitution made such study incredibly difficult. The concern for others for which he was later known often caused him to hide his suffering from everyone, including his parents. Once, while studying with his father, he began experiencing excruciating abdominal pains. He excused himself, went behind the curtain in the women's section of the *beis midrash* and muffled his groans until the attack passed.

His attachment to Torah study did not prevent him from finding time to help Jews in all sorts of ways. In Kossowa there lived a man whose illness prevented him from performing his bodily functions normally. Someone had to assist him and many of those close to him found the task too repulsive to bear. Avraham Yeshayah, who was squeamish by nature, visited the man a few times a week to be of help.

His kindness extended beyond assisting people. Once, a stray animal fell into a pit and was writhing in pain. Avraham Yeshayah lowered himself down and rescued the creature from its suffering.

Setback and Recovery

AT AGE FOURTEEN, Avraham Yeshayah journeyed to Brisk in the hope of forging a relationship with the city's new *rav* and *gaon* of his day, Rabbi Chaim Soloveitchik. A number of factors, not the least of which was illness, prevented him from realizing his desire. Avraham Yeshayah's intense studying had taken its toll and for a few months his learning was restricted to relatively light material such as *Nach* with *Rashi's* commentary. Years later, he wrote to a student who was upset over his own poor state of health:

> I received your letter. Know, my precious one, that there is no sin or guilt [to be sought as a cause for illness]; rather, it is natural to become fatigued. One should not make light of nature's ways, for that which we call nature is actually the more constant will of the One from Whom all emanates, Blessed is He.
>
> Therefore, it is incumbent upon you to interrupt your learning for two weeks, [during which time] you will eat an abundance of nourishing foods and add to your time for

sleeping, going for walks and other idle activities. Perhaps it would be proper for you to come here for a few days until your strength is renewed.

After recovering from his illness, Avraham Yeshayah resumed his intensive study schedule, which still included a daily session with his father. Reb Shmaryahu transmitted to his son his own method of Talmudic analysis, which was patterned after that of the *Gaon*, and in the course of time he taught Avraham Yeshayah general rules for ascertaining *halachah* and understanding *Kabbalah* which were handed down orally through the generations.

"Ish" from Kossowa

IN THE MEANTIME, Avraham Yeshayah was recording his own *chiddushim*, and had also taken to sending letters to Reb Chaim Soloveitchik in which he wrote his most challenging questions to the *Rambam's* laws on the order of *Kodashim*. In his early twenties, he began submitting his *chiddushim* and comments for publication in such prestigious Torah journals as *HaPeles*, published in Berlin by Rabbi Akiva E. Rabinowitz, and a Vilna-based publication which was overseen by Rabbi Yitzchak Blaser. These letters were always anonymously signed *"Ish* from Kossowa."*

Avraham Yeshayah's writings aroused great interest among the cream of Lithuanian Torah scholarship, both for their style and content. Rumor had it that the anonymous *"Ish* from Kossowa" was the second son of Kossowa's illustrious *rav*. In Vilna, Rabbi Chaim Ozer Grodzensky would often discuss Avraham Yeshayah's *chiddushim* with the learned visitors who frequented his home. Reb Chaim Ozer had lavish praise for the *"Ish"* and made known his desire to meet him.

In 1905, twenty-six-year-old Avraham Yeshayah Karelitz came to Vilna and was introduced to Reb Chaim Ozer. From that first brief encounter, Reb Chaim Ozer ascertained the degree of brilliance, character refinement and potential that his visitor possessed. He saw in Avraham Yeshayah the makings of a Torah giant and from that day on he made a point of inquiring after the young *gaon's* progress and well being.

✿ ✿ ✿

* איש, *Ish*, literally translated as *man*, is an acronym for אברהם ישעי׳, *Avraham Yeshayah*.

Rabbi Chaim Ozer Grodzensky

Those were turbulent times for the Czar's kingdom. Russia and Japan were embroiled in war and the winds of Socialism and revolution were in the air. Scores of young Jews were swept up by the Socialist promises of equal rights and improved living conditions to the point where they embraced the movement totally, including its rejection of Torah living. It was not uncommon for *battei midrash* to be invaded by young Jewish Socialists who sought to engage *b'nei Torah* in ideological debates and win them over to their cause. At the very least, such discussions distracted the Torah students from their learning; at worst, the invaders succeeded in their mission.

Avraham Yeshayah realized full well the dangers of such discussion and he steadfastly refused to have any part of it. In his later years, the Chazon Ish would reflect upon those days and say that his fortitude in ignoring the tumult around him was crucial to his continued development in Torah study and as a Torah Jew.

CHAPTER THREE
Marriage, Authorship, and Uprooting

The Right One

BY THE TIME AVRAHAM YESHAYAH had reached his early twenties, virtually every reputable matchmaker in the region had made his way to the Kossowa *Rav's* home. Rabbinic positions, *rosh yeshivah* posts, lucrative business careers, enormous dowries — Avraham Yeshayah could have had anything he desired. His sole desire, though, was to study Torah *lishmah* and he sought a partner in life who would be a fitting helpmate in realizing his wish.

Some time around 1905 a match was proposed between Avraham Yeshayah and Basya, the daughter of Reb Mordechai Bei, a businessman from distant Kweidan (Constantine). Reb Mordechai was a *talmid chacham* and was known to complete all of *Shas* every year. His home was infused with his own love for Torah and his daughter was willing to accept upon herself any hardship for the sake of a husband who would dedicate his life to its study. Prior to the engagement, it was agreed that Avraham Yeshayah would spend all his days toiling in the study of Torah and would not even enter the rabbinate or assume a position as a *rosh yeshivah*, if he would not wish to. The couple's needs would be provided for by the modest income from a textile shop that Basya would run.

The new couple settled in Kweidan where Basya opened her shop. The years that followed were most tranquil ones for Reb Avraham Yeshayah as he studied alone virtually undisturbed. Basya upheld the pre-marriage agreement in the way of a most exceptional *aishes chayil*. Her income provided for their modest needs all their days in Europe and she took great pains to avoid disrupting her husband's studies.

There were some close to Basya who found it hard to comprehend why a woman would work so hard to support a man who apparently did not aspire to any sort of position in life. Basya could only smile to herself when asked such questions. It was not always easy to make others realize that her husband *did* aspire to a most lofty position: *One thing shall I ask of Hashem, that shall I seek: That I dwell in the house of Hashem all the days of my life ... (Psalms* 27:4). Besides, few people knew what Basya had been told before her engagement: that Reb Avraham Yeshayah was already a scholar of outstanding repute and his potential was limitless.

His future hinged on Basya's dedication to helping him realize his potential. Basya recognized this, appreciated it and came to see herself as much more than a textile dealer. Hers was not a chore but a rare privilege.

It was the will of Providence that their marriage not be blessed with children. Our Sages teach, "Whoever teaches his friend's son Torah is considered as if he had borne him" (*Sanhedrin* 19b). Furthermore, the teacher's status as father is, in some respects, halachically preeminent to that of the natural father (see *Bava Metzia* 33a). The Chazon Ish was truly father to an entire generation and his noble partner in life can justly be called its mother.

GENERALLY SPEAKING, Reb Avraham Yeshayah left the *beis midrash* only to visit his wife in her shop each day after *Shacharis* and wish her a "good morning"; to assist her

Out of View with her bookkeeping at the conclusion of market day; to accompany her when she was forced to travel to outlying areas to collect outstanding payments from her customers; and to journey to Kossowa to fulfill the *mitzvah* of honoring one's parents.

Customers who were present when Reb Avraham Yeshayah would pay his morning visit to his wife's shop took note of the young man's exceptional nature and pure countenance. There were superstitious gentiles who came to believe that his presence when they made their purchases would insure good fortune in their business endeavors. Before long, Basya's shop became overly crowded with gentile customers during the morning hours. Reb Avraham Yeshayah was repulsed by all this, though his wife's business was prospering from it. He therefore took to visiting the shop from a rear entrance where he remained unseen by the customers.

The Jews of Kweidan did not imagine that the quiet, simply attired son-in-law of Reb Mordechai Bei was one of the great Torah geniuses of their day. This suited the young man very well, as he loathed honor and knew that recognition would only interfere with his learning. However, while he remained engrossed in his studies, he took note of the needs of his neighbors and organized a daily *Gemara shiur* for the city's working men, which he attended and often led. The Chazon Ish was also cognizant of the individual in need. One of Kweidan's Jews desired that his son study in one of Lithuania's great yeshivos, but lacked the financial means to accomplish this. Reb Avraham Yeshayah heard of the problem and undertook to solve it. Using a generous donation from his dowry as a start, he raised the funds needed to send the boy on his way. From then on, Reb Avraham Yeshayah would present the father with a monthly sum to help him provide for his family.

One day, R' Avraham Yeshayah approached the city's *Rav*, Rabbi Moshe Rosen (author of *Nezer HaKodesh*), suggesting that they together visit a local Jew whose reputation for dishonesty and underhandedness had caused his own family to virtually disown him. The man had taken seriously ill and no one was caring for him. "This is not *bikur cholim* (a visit to the sick)," Reb Avraham Yeshayah told Rabbi Rosen, "it is *hatzalas nefashos* (the saving of a life)."

Their visit had its intended effect. When the man's family saw that the *Rav* had personally involved himself in their relative's case, they too became involved. The patient was nursed back to health — and he subsequently mended his ways.*

Of all Kweidan's Jews, only Rabbi Rosen recognized Reb Avraham Yeshayah's true worth. How surprised everyone was to see the *Rav* often in attendance at "Reb Avraham Yeshayah's *shiur*"! Rumor had it that Rabbi Rosen was simply showing his appreciation to the young man for having assisted him in the founding of a yeshivah in the city.

On one of Rabbi Rosen's visits to Reb Chaim Ozer, Vilna's famed *Rav* asked after the Chazon Ish, inquiring of his well-being, achievements in study, methodology, habits and relationship with others. When Rabbi Rosen had completed his report, Reb Chaim Ozer exclaimed, "*Baruch Hashem!* Providence is already preparing a light for the next generation."

---

* Told by Rabbi Rosen to Rabbi Asher Katzman.

Title page of first volume of Chazon Ish

IN 1911, WHILE REB AVRAHAM YESHAYAH still resided in Kweidan, the first volume of *sefer Chazon Ish* was published. It contained novellae to topics in *Kodashim*; the *Orach Chaim* section of *Shulchan Aruch*; and the laws of *Niddah*, and was published in Vilna by the Chazon Ish's younger brother, Reb Moshe Karelitz. Like the *chiddushim* that preceded it, the work was published anonymously. After Reb Chaim Soloveitchik examined a copy, he remarked, "There is no need for the author to conceal his identity; he has nothing to be ashamed of."

Years later, when asked why he had not affixed his name to the *sefer*, the Chazon Ish replied jokingly, "I am indolent by nature, so I only wrote as much as I had to!"

The *sefer* made waves in the Torah world. As one of the generation's giants expressed it, "From its style and content alone, one would have thought that this was a manuscript of some eight centuries ago that had recently been uncovered. Only citations from the works of the *Vilna Gaon* and other later commentaries make it clear that such is not the case."

Calm Amid the Storm

THE OUTBREAK OF the First World War brought all tranquility to a turbulent end. Kweidan was near the Russo-German border and by the summer of 1914, Kaiser Wilhelm's forces were bearing down on the city. Most of Kweidan's Jews, among them the Chazon Ish and his wife, took flight. The couple settled in Stuyepitz where they enjoyed but a brief respite, as the city soon came under attack by German forces. Years later, the Chazon Ish pointed to a *chiddush* of his to *Masechta Eruvin* and said to his disciple, Rabbi Shlomo Kohen, "I propounded this *chiddush* in a cellar in Stuyepitz, as bullets whizzed above my head."

It was during his tumultuous stay in Stuyepitz that the Chazon Ish wrote his work on the exceedingly complex *Masechta Keilim*.* One of the volume's chapters is prefaced with the following:

> "With the help of Hashem, Sunday, Tammuz 15, 5675 (a year in which the land is engulfed by war between Germany and Austria on one side, and Russia, England and France on the other. Provinces and cities inhabited by Jews have been ravaged and destroyed; tens of thousands of our people have been exiled with no support of any kind; the young men of Judah have fallen dead on both sides of the front; *battei midrash* in which Torah is studied are few, as there is no one to maintain them and the Jewish nation's upheaval is great), Stuyepitz (which was almost entirely burned down on Monday, 25 Sivan, and all its inhabitants now find themselves in dire straits with no place to live)."

---

* *Chazon Ish* to *Masechta Keilim* is unique in that, unlike other volumes of *Chazon Ish*, it is a commentary to the *Mishnah* rather than a collection of halachic expositions on topics covered in the *masechta*. Rabbi Shmaryahu Greineman, a nephew of the Chazon Ish, related that after the First World War had ended, the Chazon Ish sought to publish an edition of *Masechta Keilim* adorned by his commentary and that of Reb Chaim Ozer and Rabbi Moshe Rosen. Unfortunately, this idea was never realized.

Getzel Reiser, a Stuyepitz resident, would stroll past the Chazon Ish's window in the post-midnight hours. At times, the full moon would allow him to observe the Chazon Ish at study. A *sefer* lay open on a small table while the Chazon Ish, engrossed in his learning, paced back and forth wearing slippers so as not to disturb his slumbering wife. His lips moved, but no sound escaped them. From time to time he would approach the table, dip his pen into ink, and record his thoughts.*

The Treasure Revealed

AS IN KWEIDAN, the Chazon Ish did all he could to avoid attention while he resided in Stuyepitz. His clothing, while immaculate, were as simple as could be, and save for the daily *tefillos* when he joined one of the local *minyanim*, he was rarely seen. His wife managed to revive her textile business and, as related by Rabbi Yehoshua Dov Leiberman (who later served as the city's *Rav*), the Chazon Ish would spend all of market day in Basya's shop, since the swarms of customers made the possibility of error on his wife's part a likely occurrence. The Chazon Ish would personally measure each piece of material to insure that none of the customers, Jewish or not, overpaid a *grush*.

There was but one day a year when the Chazon Ish could not restrain himself from doing that which attracted attention. In the way of the *Arizal*, *Vilna Gaon* and other Jews both great and ordinary,** he would rejoice with the Torah on *Simchas Torah* with all his strength. Observing Reb Avraham Yeshayah as he clutched a *sefer Torah* to his bosom and danced with great fervor was a sight that few in Stuyepitz would ever forget.

Despite his desire to the contrary, a series of occurrences led to the Chazon Ish's gaining renown among a noteworthy segment of Stuyepitz' Jews. Rabbi Meir Leiberman of Richmond, Virginia, served as a *rosh yeshivah* in Stuyepitz during that period and related the following:

One Friday night at the conclusion of *Ma'ariv*, someone who had fallen behind the congregation in his prayers asked the Chazon Ish to recite the chapter of *Vayechulu* (Genesis 2:1-3) along with him. This request was in accordance with the halachic opinion (see *Mishnah Berurah* 268:19) that recitation of *Vayechulu* is a testimony

---

* From *Sefer Zikaron l'Kehillas Stuyepitz*, Tel-Aviv, 5725.

** See *Mishnah Berurah* 669:11.

to Hashem's having created the universe. For testimony to be valid, the *halachah* requires two witnesses. The Chazon Ish, however, disputed this view, as he held that *Vayechulu* in the *Ma'ariv* of Shabbos is not a testimony, but a part of the prayer, the same as any other (see *Chazon Ish, Orach Chaim*: §38). The Chazon Ish held that one who was praying alone should specifically not recite *Vayechulu* with someone else in the way of testimony.

As such, the Chazon Ish could not oblige the man who approached him that particular Friday evening. He smiled and said, "Does the *Ribono shel Olam* need us to testify that He created heaven and earth and that He rested on the seventh day? Why, all of creation bears witness to this ..." And he proceeded to demonstrate at length how the wonders of creation leave no room for doubt as to how the universe came into being.

The listener was spellbound by the pleasant, brilliant and moving words of the usually reserved young man. As the congregation filed out of the *beis midrash*, the man related his encounter with the Chazon Ish to a group of friends. One of them said, "You think that is something unusual? One day this week, I watched as Reb Avraham Yeshayah *davened Minchah* in a room off to the side of the *beis midrash*. He wept so profusely that by the time he was finished, a pool of tears surrounded him. On a regular weekday! He thought no one was looking. In public he contains himself ..."

Another man spoke up to relate yet another incident. It was known that a Stuyepitz Jew had recently experienced a miraculous recovery from illness. What was not widely known was that shortly before his recovery, the man had been visited by Reb Avraham Yeshayah. Tearfully and with intense concentration, he had prayed for the man's recovery. His prayers were answered.

Slowly, word got around. A brilliant young *tzaddik* was dwelling in their midst.

Reluctant Rav

AS THE RUSSIANS STRUGGLED to withstand the German onslaught, they turned to the Jews as likely scapegoats for their troubles. Jews were accused of aiding the enemy; scores were exiled and many died. Most vulnerable were *rabbanim* and community leaders whom the government accused of organizing their followers to commit treason. The *Rav* of Stuyepitz, Rabbi Yoel Sorotzkin (elder brother of the

Rabbi Yosef Eliyahu Henkin

Lutzker *Rav*, Rabbi Zalman Sorotzkin), was ordered by the government to leave the city for the duration of the war. As he prepared to depart, Rabbi Sorotzkin sought a qualified replacement for himself until his return. He saw one individual as especially suited for this. The Chazon Ish was summoned to the *Rav's* home where an interesting episode transpired.

In the anteroom to the *Rav's* study sat Rabbi Yosef Eliyahu Henkin, who would later be renowned as head of *Ezras Torah* in America and one of his generation's foremost *poskim*. Rabbi Henkin, who had been serving as *Rav* of Kulash, had come to Stuyepitz to head a yeshivah for boys that was then being founded. The Chazon Ish, in his simple garb, was easily mistaken by strangers for a common laborer. When he entered the anteroom, he and Rabbi Henkin exchanged greetings, after which the following dialogue occurred:

"And who, may I ask, are you?"

"The son of the *Rav* of Kossowa."

"And what is your profession?"
"I own a shop in the city" (i.e., his wife's shop).
"And when does a Jew find time to learn?"
"Whenever he is free to do so!"
"And what, may I ask, brings one to see the *Rav*?"
"The *Rav* has summoned me."

How shocked Rabbi Henkin was to discover why the "shopkeeper" had been summoned and that he was the anonymous author of *Chazon Ish*! Indeed, this man *did* learn "whenever he [was] free to do so" — that is, virtually every waking moment. From then on, Rabbi Henkin visited the Chazon Ish on a regular basis to discuss matters of *halachah*.

As much as he loathed occupying an official position, the Chazon Ish realized that the chaotic wartime situation did not allow for him to refuse Rabbi Sorotzkin's request. He served as *rav* for almost a full year, during which time he rendered halachic decisions, presided over monetary disputes, stood watch over local *shechitah* and *eruvin* matters, strove to raise funds to renovate the city's *mikveh*, and worked tirelessly for the sake of Stuyepitz' yeshivah and *chadarim*.

It was in the area of Torah education for the young that the Chazon Ish invested extraordinary effort during this time. *Haskalah* in Stuyepitz had become a powerfully destructive force and hundreds of Jewish children were being lost to schools that stressed Judaism based on language and land as opposed to Torah. The Chazon Ish organized the founding of new *chadarim* and initiated a drive to convince parents to enroll their children in these institutions. To this end, he employed the services of *talmidim* from the Mirrer Yeshivah, which had taken up temporary residence in Stuyepitz after its building in Mir was destroyed by arson. Many of the *talmidim*, encouraged by their *Roshei Yeshivah*, Rabbi Elya Baruch Kamai and Rabbi Eliezer Yehudah Finkel, and by their *Mashgiach*, Rabbi Yerucham Levovitz, visited the Chazon Ish to discuss Torah and were quickly awed by him. The Chazon Ish requested that *talmidim* with the necessary abilities take to the city's *shuls* on Shabbos to address the congregations on the need to provide their children with an authentic Torah education. His request was granted and the *talmidim* went about their mission armed with *divrei Torah* related by the Chazon Ish and designed to inspire their listeners.

Minsk

IN SPITE OF his many accomplishments as *Rav*, the Chazon Ish relinquished the post at the earliest opportunity. Rabbi Shlomo Leiberman, one of the city's senior *talmidei chachamim*, succeeded him. When Rabbi Leiberman died two years later, it was the Chazon Ish who saw to it that the late *Rav's* son, Rabbi Yehoshua Dov Leiberman, took over.

Circumstances forced the Chazon Ish to leave Stuyepitz in 1917 and take refuge in nearby Minsk. There, he found lodging in a small apartment occupied by Rabbi Zalman Sorotzkin, then *Rav* of Zhetl, who had been forced to flee his own city. Later, the Chazon Ish would return to Stuyepitz. Uprootings, food shortages, and other hardships did not affect his studying in the least. A relative who was with him in Minsk recalled, "Those were good days for him, for few people knew who he was, and the population in general had no idea as to his true stature."

During this time, he propounded new insights in Torah with his usual clarity of thought. The headings to many pieces in *sefer Chazon Ish* attest to their having been written during this period.

While in Minsk, he was served a draft notice by the Russian Army. It was then that his term as *rav* in Stuyepitz became a source of salvation. Rabbi Zalman Sorotzkin, aside from being one of the foremost Torah luminaries of his time, was a classic *shtadlan* (intercessor) for many a Torah cause, and he journeyed to St. Petersburg in an attempt to obtain deferments for those who could be classified as *rabbanim*. Rabbi Sorotzkin made a very favorable impression upon the Czar's ministers and his mission ended in success. When he returned to Minsk, he happily presented the Chazon Ish with his deferment.

A few days later, the Chazon Ish presented Rabbi Sorotzkin with a token of appreciation: a copy of *Sh'eilos U'Teshuvos Rabbi Akiva Eiger*. Rabbi Sorotzkin was astounded by the front page inscription. It was a poem of thanks, its initial letters forming an acronym that spelled "הרב זלמן סורוצקין, Rabbi Zalman Sorotzkin." More amazing was the poem's content, where the Chazon Ish depicted Rabbi Sorotzkin's mission in detail, describing the dangers, efforts, struggles and success. Everyone had assumed that the Chazon Ish, forever surrounded by his *sefarim*, was totally unaware of anything, save for the fact that he was in danger of being drafted.

Rabbi Nosson Zvi Finkel   *Rabbi Yerucham Levovitz*

WHILE IN MINSK AND STUYEPITZ, the Chazon Ish enjoyed a number of encounters with two great exponents of *Mussar*, Rabbi Nosson Zvi Finkel, better known as the *Alter* of Slobodka, and Rabbi Yerucham Levovitz of Mir. They spent time discussing the system of *mussar* study that then existed in most Lithuanian yeshivos, a system with which the Chazon Ish differed. In no way did this difference of opinion lessen the enormous reverence that these towering personalities felt for each other. In a letter written some twenty years later, the Chazon Ish reflected, "I encountered the *Alter* of Slobodka and the *Alter* of Mir (a reference to Reb Yerucham) many times, and also some of their great *talmidim*, may they live; and the great men of Novaradok. Always, a boundless love existed between us ... never did I refrain from mentioning a sharp critique. They delighted in it and I delighted over them ..." (*Igros*, I:§154).

Among the Giants

Once, the Chazon Ish attended a *shmuess* delivered by the *Alter* of Slobodka before *talmidim*. At the *shmuess'* conclusion, the *Alter* approached his guest listener and said, "What brings my friend to my place? I thought he was opposed to our *mussar* philosophy!"

The Chazon Ish responded, "True, but I am even more opposed to your opponents."

Rabbi Chaim Soloveitchik also found himself in Minsk during

Rabbi Chaim Soloveitchik

the war. So it was that the Chazon Ish finally was granted that which he had been denied in his youth — an opportunity to develop a relationship with the *gaon* from Brisk.

One day, the Chazon Ish entered Reb Chaim's lodging, only to find him concluding a lecture before an assemblage. The Chazon Ish turned to Reb Chaim's son, Reb Yitzchak Zev, and asked if he would repeat for him what his father had said. That discussion marked the beginning of a relationship between two of *Eretz Yisrael's* guiding lights in years to come — the Chazon Ish and the Brisker *Rav*.

CHAPTER FOUR
In Lithuania's Jerusalem

Return

WORLD WAR I ENDED in 1919. For the Jews of Eastern Europe, life would never be the same. Revolution had toppled Czar Nicholas II in 1917, and after a short-lived reprieve under the Kerensky regime, Russian Jews became prisoners of the "liberating" Bolsheviks. It was with great difficulty that the Chazon Ish and his wife succeeded in crossing the border into Poland. They planned to return to their home in Kweidan but soon changed their minds. The city that had been the scene of their tranquil first years of marriage was now a city of the dead. Some Jews, like the Chazon Ish, had managed to flee to safety during the war. The rest — every last one — were no longer alive.

Two illustrious brothers of the Chazon Ish — Reb Meir and Reb Moshe Karelitz — and a brother-in-law, Reb Shmuel Greineman, resided in Vilna, which was under Polish rule between the two world wars. They sent word to the Chazon Ish that he come join them and in the winter of 1920 the Chazon Ish and his wife arrived in Vilna.

Reb Chaim Ozer and the scholars of Vilna who were familiar with the Chazon Ish's writings were elated at his arrival. As for the rest of Vilna's Jewish community, they saw nothing earth-shattering about the coming to town of an obviously poor couple who took up residence in a simple two-room dwelling. As always, the lack of recognition was just what the Chazon Ish wanted and he managed to maintain this low profile throughout his twelve-year stay in Vilna.

Rebbetzin Karelitz opened a textile shop in one of her apartment's two rooms, while the other room served as living quarters and library for the Chazon Ish's modest *sefarim* collection. The business did not prosper. Moreover, thieves broke into the Karelitz apartment one night and stole most of the merchandise, leaving the Chazon Ish and his wife virtually penniless. To further aggravate their financial predicament, a gentile customer accused *Rebbetzin*

Chapter 4: IN LITHUANIA'S JERUSALEM / 43

The Chazon Ish during his days in Vilna

Karelitz of embezzling him, hired false witnesses to support his claim and summoned the poor woman to court. On the eve of the trial, with no apparent hope in sight, the Chazon Ish asked his wife for the customer's name. He then went off to pray. The gentile died before the trial could begin and all charges were dropped.

The din from visiting merchants and would-be customers was sufficient to disturb the Chazon Ish's studies. It was thus that Reb Shmuel Greineman set aside a small room in his own home, complete with a bed, chair, table, lamp, writing materials and some *sefarim*, so that his brother-in-law could study undisturbed. For three consecutive years, from early morning until late into the night, the Chazon Ish remained closeted in that room, pausing in his studies only to pray the *Minchah* and *Ma'ariv* services in a nearby *kloiz*.

It was during this period that Reb Shmuel came to appreciate his brother-in-law's ability to focus his mind on a single Torah topic for incredible lengths of time. For three consecutive months, fifteen hours a day, the Greineman family listened as the Chazon Ish chanted the words of one particular *mishnah*. After a while, the children could recite the *mishnah* verbatim and would playfully run after their uncle as he entered their home, tugging at his *tzitzis* and shouting, "Uncle Avraham Yeshayah! *Shesh ma'alos b'mikvaos ...*"

Rabbi Shmaryahu Karelitz, son of Reb Meir, recalls that from his vantage point as a youngster, the Chazon Ish seemed forever happy during his days in Vilna. He would enjoy playing and joking with his young nieces and nephews, all of whom were extremely fond of him as well. Rabbi Pesach Karelitz, son of Reb Moshe, recalled the Chazon Ish as forever exuding the joy which Torah study inspires.*

---

* Related by Rabbi Asher Katzman, who studied with Reb Pesach in Europe. Reb Pesach also related having heard from his father, "He [the Chazon Ish] is not merely a *gaon*; he is a *gaon* among *gaonim* and is of a type that was to be found two eras ago."

(As a *bachur*, Reb Pesach authored a scholarly work, entitled *Pesach HaChiddush*. He met a martyr's death in the Holocaust.)

The incredible strain with which the Chazon Ish studied demanded that he have some sort of break each day. He found that in comparison to learning alone, studying with a young partner was relaxing. Thus, from his fourth year in Vilna and on, he spent two or three hours each day studying with a *bachur*.

OBTAINING A HIGH-QUALITY SET of *arba'ah minim* was a difficult task in Eastern Europe. One year, the Chazon Ish learned that a certain Vilna Jew had obtained an *esrog* that was confirmed to be *bilti murcav* (non-grafted). The Chazon Ish made his way to the man's home where he used the *esrog* to fulfill the *mitzvah*. Before leaving, he was introduced to the man's son, who was attending a secular high school in the city. Discerning the boy's fine character and scholastic abilities, the Chazon Ish offered to set aside time each day to study Torah privately with him. The boy agreed and thus began a study session that lasted for an hour and a half each day for four consecutive years.

Fateful Encounter

At the end of the fourth year, the boy's parents pressured him into enrolling in a local university. The Chazon Ish feared that his continuing to study with the boy would be misconstrued as condoning his attendance at university and so, with deep regrets, the Chazon Ish terminated their sessions. However, they continued to maintain a close relationship. The boy graduated university still faithful to the Torah way of life.

During World War II, the boy, by then a grown man, suffered through tortures and torment. He survived the war, but only physically. Spiritually he was a broken man. He settled in Russia at war's end and became a loyal Communist. Gone were all vestiges of his Torah past, and he lived the life of a full-fledged secularist. He climbed the ladder in the Communist Party and eventually became a ranking diplomat.

Some time after the formation of the State of Israel, a sleek sedan pulled up at the Chazon Ish's modest apartment in Bnei Brak. Out stepped a well-dressed man who asked to see the Chazon Ish. Recognizing his long-lost *chavrusa* of old, the Chazon Ish fell upon his shoulders and kissed him. The Chazon Ish invited the man into his study, where they spoke for more than an hour and a half. When the man finally appeared in the outer room, his face was stained by tears and he continued to weep as he made his way to the door. After he left, the Chazon Ish related to *Rebbetzin* Miriam Kanievsky what had transpired. "He told me about the life he was now leading — my hair stood on end when hearing of it. He wants desperately to do *teshuvah*. I told him that he must remain here, for there is no hope of repentance if he returns home. But he insisted that it is impossible for him to remain. I reiterated that he must stay, but to no avail. He is broken to the very depths of his soul. He finally said to me, 'I would rather be dead than alive.'"

A few days later, a Soviet airliner crashed, killing those aboard. Among the passengers was this diplomat. When the Chazon Ish was told the news, he said with deep emotion, "He died while contemplating *teshuvah* . . ."

Reb Shlomo Kohen

IN THE SUMMER OF 1923, the Chazon Ish's ill health forced him to seek country air. He and his wife joined Reb Chaim Ozer and many others from Vilna at the summer resort of Volkonik, on the outskirts of Vilna. Among the vacationers was seventeen-year-old Shlomo Kohen, grandson and namesake of the *Cheshek Shlomo*. The Chazon Ish took an immediate liking to the boy when they met at the daily *minyan* in Reb Chaim Ozer's lodging. The Chazon Ish suggested that they begin a daily study session, and thus began a lifelong relationship. Their learning session, which usually lasted some two and one half hours, continued until the very day, ten years later, when the Chazon Ish left for *Eretz Yisrael*. Not long after, Reb Shlomo followed his *rebbi* and made his way to the Holy Land.

Reb Shlomo had many fond recollections of those years in Vilna, much of which he recorded immediately following the Chazon Ish's death in 1953.

Through the course of those ten years, the two studied the orders of *Moed* and *Nashim*, in addition to other *masechtos*, in their entirety. One day, Reb Shlomo entered the *beis midrash* that was their place of study and found the Chazon Ish in an unusually happy mood. To his young *chavrusa's* inquiry, the Chazon Ish responded, "I figured out that we have already studied 400 *blatt* together — is this not cause for joy?"

The Chazon Ish guided Shlomo along the path toward *shleimus* (perfection), showing him the way toward proper Torah study, Heavenly fear, and character refinement. There were occasions when

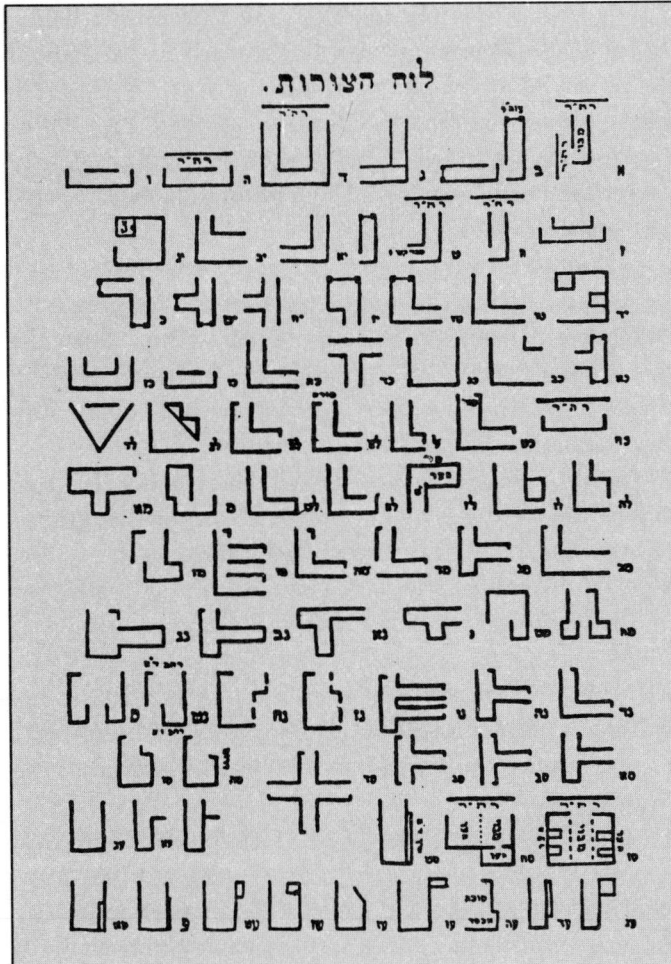

Explanatory diagrams to the Chazon Ish's chiddushim on hilchos eruvin, drawn by Reb Shlomo Kohen in 1929

the Chazon Ish deemed it necessary to criticize his young partner. He did so — but only in writing.

The Chazon Ish would pray the *Shacharis* service with a *minyan vasikin* (reciting the morning *Shemoneh Esrei* at sunrise, the most preferred time). He was always the first one in the *beis midrash* and Reb Shlomo would watch in awe as he would pour out his heart before his Creator with unrestrained emotion — until the door opened and another congregant entered. Immediately, the Chazon Ish's *tefillah* took on a very ordinary form as he strove to appear no different from anyone else. It was because of such behavior that he lived in Vilna for more than twelve years without the common folk ever imagining his true worth.

Chapter 4: IN LITHUANIA'S JERUSALEM / 47

Soon after they began to study together, the Chazon Ish began to learn the laws of *shofar*-blowing with his partner, as he wanted Shlomo to serve as his *ba'al tokeia* the following *Rosh Hashanah*. That year, seventeen-year-old Shlomo Kohen sounded the *shofar* blasts for the Chazon Ish's *minyan*. The Chazon Ish was obviously pleased with the performance: he enlisted Reb Shlomo Kohen for this task for the next thirty years.

One *Rosh Hashanah* in Vilna, the Chazon Ish approached Reb Shlomo after the Torah reading and instructed that the congregation forego the usual break prior to the *shofar*-blowing, skip the customary seven-time recitation of *Lamenatze'ach Livnei Korach* (*Psalm* 47), and proceed with the *shofar*-blowing without delay. Reb Shlomo did not understand, but asked no questions.

Following *Mussaf*, the puzzle was solved. The Chazon Ish had overheard a son pleading with his aged father, "Please eat something now; you have a weak heart . . ." The father had replied, "All my life, I have never eaten before *tekias shofar*." The Chazon Ish feared for the man's health; hence his instructions to Reb Shlomo.

THE CHAZON ISH POSSESSED a keen desire to publish his writings. He once said, "When a *sefer* of mine comes off the press, I experience the joy of one who leads his child to the *chupah*."

Out of the Flames

One afternoon as the Chazon Ish and Reb Shlomo studied, someone entered the *beis midrash* and said that a fire had broken out in the vicinity of the Chazon Ish's apartment. The Chazon Ish "jumped from his place in a frenzy, girded himself with amazing strength and ran toward his home with incredible haste," recalled Reb Shlomo. "Understandably, I hurried after him, but I could not keep up. At that time, I did not understand the reason for his haste. Was he running to salvage his broken furniture or his threadbare clothing?

"As I neared the apartment, I met him returning toward the *beis midrash*. He was walking calmly and peacefully with a heavy bundle under his arm. This bundle contained his unpublished manuscripts, the fruits of his study, his precious treasures, to which he had devoted days and nights of intense toil for many years. How boundless was his joy in having salvaged them from the fire! The joy and emotion of that moment did not allow him to even think of the fate of all his other earthly possessions."

The rest of his belongings, including his modest *sefarim* collection, had been consumed by the flames, but his — and surely his loyal wife's — most priceless possession was tucked safely under his arm.*

In the months that followed, the Chazon Ish wrote his *chiddushim* using little more than a *Shas* for reference. Later, he found that the essence of most of his novellae was to be found in the works of the *Rishonim*. This way of study was not new to him; he would often say that one who studies a topic in depth, using a logical and accepted approach, should be able to deduce the fundamental thoughts of commentators on his own. In fact, he would often encourage *bnei Torah* to examine the questions raised by *Acharonim* and then toil to deduce the answers on their own.

Whenever he would amass enough material for a new volume, the Chazon Ish would turn the manuscript over to his brother-in-law, Reb Shmuel, and brother, Reb Moshe, for publication. During his years in Vilna, three volumes of *Chazon Ish* (*Kuntreis HaMuktzah*, *Eruvin* and *Gittin-Kiddushin*) were published. Each new *sefer* was welcomed with great acclaim by the scholars of Lithuania, especially those in Reb Chaim Ozer's circle.

The Chazon Ish continued to use pseudonyms when signing *chiddushim* he submitted for publication. One piece (published in Reb Moshe Karelitz' *Knesses Yisrael*) contended with certain points in Reb Chaim Ozer's *Achiezer* and was signed *Mipi HaShmuah* ("Overheard"). In the periodical's next issue, Reb Chaim Ozer prefaced his response to these contentions with, "Much graciousness to the man (*Ish*) who disguises himself with the name *Mipi HaShmuah*."

His Wisdom is Sought

IT WAS DURING this period that the Chazon Ish corresponded with Rabbi Elchonon Wasserman regarding the latter's *Divrei Sofrim*. Other Torah giants who already then expressed their awe of the Chazon Ish's scholarship included Rabbi Shimon Shkop, Rabbi

---

* The *Aderes* (an acronym for אליהו דוד רבינוביץ־תאומים), in his *Over Orach* (§334), writes, "Although the *halachah* is that the Written Law takes precedence over the Oral Law, nevertheless, it is possible that when one possesses unpublished manuscripts they are rescued first, since none like them exist. It might also be suggested that this is a question of endangering the life of the one who worked and toiled over them all his days and who could, Heaven forfend, become ill and depressed."

Reb Shimon Shkop with Reb Chaim Ozer

Eliezer Yehudah Finkel, Rabbi Baruch Ber Leibowitz and the Chofetz Chaim.

At Reb Chaim Ozer's invitation, the Chazon Ish was often present at meetings of *roshei yeshivah* in Vilna. At one such meeting, Reb Shimon Shkop implored the Chazon Ish to honor the assemblage with a Torah thought. The request was modestly declined. At that point, Reb Elchonon Wasserman told the Chazon Ish that while it was wrong to pressure a person into doing that which was not his will, this did not apply when one seeks to hear someone else's Torah thoughts. The Chazon Ish relented, but could not bring himself to offer more than a question of his own regarding a statement of *Ran* in *Masechta Nedarim*. Reb Shimon followed with a refutation of the question. The Chazon Ish did not respond, implying that he had been bested. Later, Reb Shimon received a letter in which the Chazon Ish raised his own questions to Reb Shimon's response.*

Reb Chaim Ozer valued not only the Chazon Ish's scope of knowledge, but also his proficiency as a *posek* and his astuteness and pragmatism in *klal*-related matters. They would spend many hours together in Reb Chaim Ozer's apartment discussing halachic questions and pressing issues of the day. In a number of chapters in *Achiezer*, Reb Chaim Ozer makes reference to halachic rulings found in *Chazon Ish*. One chapter is actually a responsum addressed to the Chazon Ish (*Achiezer*, I: §34). It begins, "With all my heart I thank his glorious honor for having obliged to fulfill my request that he peruse and inspect my published monographs and point out that which he discovered with penetrating understanding."

Reb Shlomo Kohen recalled, "While the Chazon Ish was not an official *rav*, he did rule on matters of *halachah*. Our master, Reb Chaim Ozer, would send him halachic queries of enormous complexity. Reb Chaim Ozer implored him to accept a rabbinical post, but such was not his desire and he steadfastly rejected all such proposals."

In one instance, continued Reb Shlomo, Rabbi Ezriel Munk of Berlin sought Reb Chaim Ozer's opinion as to the permissibility of stunning animals after the German government passed edicts against *shechitah*. The question was a complicated one and was pondered by all the *gedolim* of Vilna. "When the question was posed to the Chazon Ish, he offered an irrefutable proof from a *Gemara* in *Masechta Chulin* that amazed all who heard it."

There was one occasion when Reb Chaim Ozer's deep humility brought him to express his admiration for the Chazon Ish. Someone came to Reb Chaim Ozer in search of a blessing that he be saved from dire personal straits. Reb Chaim Ozer replied that he was the wrong

---

* See *Chazon Ish, Orach Chaim* pg. 167.

person to beseech for such a thing. Asked the distraught petitioner, "If Reb Chaim Ozer is not fit to offer blessings, then who is?" Replied Reb Chaim Ozer, "Go to the Chazon Ish and to Reb Naftali Eisenstadt* (another of Vilna's hidden *tzaddikim*)." The man followed this recommendation and soon saw miraculous Divine intervention in his affairs.

REB CHAIM OZER WAS LEADER of the generation and scores of personal and public issues were brought to his door each day. He felt that the Torah community was in need of the Chazon Ish's guidance and he encouraged him to give up his prized anonymity and allow himself to emerge as a leader. The Chazon Ish, however, persistently refused. When Reb Shlomo Kohen asked him why he was not stirred by the needs of the time to take an active role in communal affairs, he replied that the study of Torah was of itself a great benefit for the *Klal*, as the mere presence of someone great in Torah and Heavenly fear has a pronounced effect on his entire surroundings. He then made his point with the following metaphor: When a full jug is emptied into smaller vessels, a point is reached where nothing remains in the jug and so nothing more can be poured into the vessels. However, such is not the case when vessels are placed around a jug which is receiving a constant flow that continues even after the jug overflows. In this case, there is a never-ending flow to the smaller vessels while the jug continues to remain full. The latter represents the influence of one involved in Torah study on those around him.

Communal Involvement

When the Chazon Ish settled in *Eretz Yisrael* any hesitancy on his part became a matter of the past. From then on, he involved himself in every sort of issue and problem, be it public or private. Reb Shlomo Kohen explained, "In Europe, he did not involve himself in these matters on a large scale, for such work was carried on by others, namely, the *gaonim* of the time — the Chofetz Chaim and Reb Chaim Ozer, of blessed memory. They gave their very lives for the strengthening of Torah and *chesed* during that period. In a situation where such men were present, the Chazon Ish did not find it proper to give of his study time, in accordance with the *halachah*. This was not the case in our Holy Land, where he fulfilled the teaching, *In a place where there are no leaders, strive to be a leader (Avos 2:6)."*

---

* His father was the author of *Pischei Teshuvah* to *Shulchan Aruch.*

By no means, though, was the Chazon Ish locked in an ivory tower in Vilna, unaware of the burning issues of that time. He knew well and understood profoundly the many currents and tensions that existed within the Jewish world. *Haskalah* had made powerful inroads into Vilna's Jewish community and its effects, particularly among the youth, deeply pained the Chazon Ish.

One day he noticed a poster announcing the founding of a religious-nationalist school for youth. The Chazon Ish took down the announcement and tore it into shreds. The hyphenating of "religious" with "nationalist" implies that there can exist a concept of nationalism apart from religion, and this idea is contrary to Torah. From then on, the Chazon Ish did all he could to minimize the school's influence. It was in Vilna that the Chazon Ish authored a lengthy essay on Torah education, which stated unequivocally the goals and ideals of a system based purely on Torah. The essay* was circulated among Vilna's religious educators and had a profound impact.

As time went on — especially as he approached the age of fifty, which the Sages call the age of "counsel" — the Chazon Ish became somewhat more involved in communal affairs. The *Va'ad HaYeshivos* and the *Chorev* network of religious schools, Agudath Israel leaders who needed guidance in political planning, and other activists concerned with the needs of the Torah community all beat a path to his door.

Dos Vort, the Orthodox newspaper which followed the directives of Reb Chaim Ozer, opened its columns to the Chazon Ish. Rabbi Yosef Shub, the paper's publisher, had already become the Chazon Ish's confidant and recognized the impact of his literary contributions on communal themes. So it was that the Chazon Ish became a frequent contributor to *Dos Vort*. As always, his writings were unsigned, but those in the know could readily discern from whose pen they flowed. The newspaper became an important conduit for the dissemination of his views.

The Chofetz Chaim

LIVING IN VILNA brought the Chazon Ish in close contact with the Chofetz Chaim. It did not take the sage from Radin long to discern the true essence of the genius from Kossowa. When a Torah student

---

* Cited, in part, in chapter fourteen.

The Chofetz Chaim

asked the Chofetz Chaim if one should better seek to master the Torah's breadth or its depth, he replied, "One must know both how vast the Torah is and how deep it is — a living illustration of this is the Chazon Ish."

Jews the world over revered the Chofetz Chaim as the *tzaddik par excellence* of the generation. The Chazon Ish once remarked that to uproot oneself from Eastern Poland and move to another country outside the Holy Land was akin to leaving *Eretz Yisrael* for the Diaspora, "... for the *yeshivos* are established there, and the *chasid* (pious one), the Chofetz Chaim, resides there ..."

Many in the generation did not realize that, aside from his incomparable piety, the Chofetz Chaim was a veritable *gaon* of his day, as reflected in his classic halachic work, *Mishnah Berurah*. However, the other great minds of that generation, including Reb Shmaryahu Karelitz and his illustrious son, did appreciate this. The Chazon Ish's father once said, "It is inconceivable to me that a *sefer* such as *Mishnah Berurah* could be written without the author being endowed with *Ruach HaKodesh*."

The Chazon Ish would never rule on a halachic matter related to the *Orach Chaim* section of *Shulchan Aruch* without first consulting the *Mishnah Berurah*. In *sefer Chazon Ish*, not one relevant *p'sak* of the *Mishnah Berurah* is omitted, and of the few contemporaries whom the Chazon Ish cites in his work, only the Chofetz Chaim is referred to as *Rabbeinu*.

The Chazon Ish once told the Slabodker *Rosh Yeshivah*, Rabbi Mordechai Shulman, "The Chofetz Chaim's clarity in study and in his halachic conclusions is *Reb Akiva Eiger'dik*."* In a letter he wrote "... In conclusion, the halachic traditions that have been transmitted by our teachers, from whose utterances we live, such as *Maran Beis Yosef*, the *Magen Avraham* and the *Mishnah Berurah*, are unchangeable rulings akin to those of the Sanhedrin in the Chamber of

---

* The writings of Rabbi Akiva Eiger (1759-1837) are renowned for their sharpness, clarity, and irrefutability.

Hewn Stone [during the Commonwealth eras] — there is no room for leniencies" (*Igros*, II: §41).

The Chofetz Chaim and Reb Chaim Ozer, as the two guiding lights of their generation, worked hand-in-hand on matters affecting *Klal Yisrael*. It was not uncommon for an aged Chofetz Chaim to journey to Vilna to discuss a pressing issue with an ailing Reb Chaim Ozer.

It happened once that the Chofetz Chaim visited Reb Chaim Ozer's home where he addressed an assemblage of scholars and communal leaders. Among the crowd was the Chazon Ish. In the course of his talk, the Chofetz Chaim bemoaned the generation's weakened spiritual plight and declared that the hour demanded everyone's casting aside feelings of modesty to offer his contribution to *Klal Yisrael*. "Every *nistar* (hidden personage) among us is obligated to reveal himself!"

Upon hearing these words, Reb Chaim Ozer, who was sitting at the Chofetz Chaim's side, turned himself completely around to face the Chazon Ish and asked, "To whom do these words apply if not you?" The Chofetz Chaim then rested his holy gaze on the Chazon Ish and added, "Is it any wonder that in this way one can become a *gaon*? Even I — do you hear — even I could develop into a *gaon* were I to cast aside the yoke of communal responsibilities and meditate within the four ells of *halachah*!"

The Chofetz Chaim's visit proved to be a turning point. From then on, the Chazon Ish began to take the initiative in shouldering the burden of communal responsibility. His nature, of course, would not change. He worked behind the scenes, shrinking from publicity or adulation and wanting no part of any official position. Many were the initiatives that spilled forth from his brilliant and deeply perceptive mind, but tracing their roots often proved difficult, for all was done behind a curtain of anonymity. He wanted desperately to remain unknown.

IN 1931, RABBI MOSHE BLAU, a leader of the Torah community in *Eretz Yisrael*, was sent to Europe in search of an assistant and eventual successor to Jerusalem's aged *Rav*, Rabbi Yosef Chaim Sonnenfeld. Naturally, his mission brought him to Vilna, where he met Reb Chaim Ozer for the very first time. One morning, Reb Chaim Ozer instructed his attendant, Rabbi Meir Leiberman, to show his guest

Rabbi Moshe Blau

Rabbi Moshe Blau

the "treasures of Vilna." When they returned, Reb Chaim Ozer asked Rabbi Blau's guide, "Tell me, where did you go?"

"The *Gaon's kloiz*, the old cemetery, the Strashun Library..."

"That's fine, but you overlooked Vilna's *living* treasure. Take Rabbi Blau to meet Rabbi Avraham Yeshayah Karelitz."

The two met and became engrossed in a lengthy discussion. It was then that the Chazon Ish revealed to Rabbi Blau his strong desire to emigrate to *Eretz Yisrael*.*

Rabbi Blau was elated by the revelation and promptly offered the Chazon Ish the position he was seeking to fill.

Procuring entrance visas to Palestine was a difficult business in those days. The British had enforced a strict quota on the number of Jews allowed to immigrate, and the Jewish Agency, which was responsible for the distribution of these visas, allotted a pitiful few to Poland's Agudath Israel organization. Rabbi Blau explained that the Chazon Ish's accepting the post of assistant *Rav* would insure his visa application's swift acceptance.

The Chazon Ish replied that he would not assume any position that would demand his rendering halachic rulings, especially in monetary matters.**

When Rabbi Blau related his encounter with the Chazon Ish to Reb Chaim Ozer, the latter said, "Only now have you seen Vilna's exquisite treasure. He is a *gaon* and a *tzaddik*; as for his wisdom — I

---

* In a letter, the Chazon Ish writes, "... That it is a *mitzvah* to settle in *Eretz Yisrael* [even when the *Beis HaMikdash* does not stand] has already been decided by the *Rambam*, *Ramban* and other halachic authorities. It is known how much the Chofetz Chaim, of blessed memory, yearned to ascend to the Land" (*Igros*, I: §175).

** Rabbi Sonnenfeld died the following year. R' Yaakov Rosenheim, President of the World Agudah Organization, corresponded with Reb Chaim Ozer regarding Jerusalem's vacant rabbinate. In one letter, Reb Chaim Ozer wrote, "With regard to the *gaon*, our guide, Rabbi Avraham Yeshayah Karelitz... I asked him once again in a letter. It appears, however, that he is far removed from accepting any judgeship. While he is not among those who are afraid to render halachic rulings, still, because of his extreme piety, he is reluctant to rule in monetary matters."

do not decide on any significant communal matter without first hearing his opinion."

His Dream Realized

CIRCUMSTANCES PREVENTED the Chazon Ish from realizing his dream for another two years. On the day after *Pesach* 5693 (1933), he summoned Reb Shlomo Kohen to his home. The Chazon Ish requested his disciple to ask confidentially of Reb Chaim Ozer to write to Rabbi Blau bidding him to secure entrance visas for both himself and his wife. The Chazon Ish made clear his desire to emigrate as soon as possible.

The Chazon Ish would later reveal that on the previous night, he had dreamt two dreams. In the first, he was told to immerse in a *mikveh* all the pots which he used year-round. In the second dream, he was shown a wagon drawn by a horse adorned with bells.

The following morning, the Chazon Ish learned that the *rav* through whom he had sold his *chametz* to a gentile prior to *Pesach* had erroneously sold the pots (instead of the *chametz* absorbed within the pots' walls), thus requiring their immersion. He understood the second dream as a Heavenly message that he journey to

Reb Chaim Ozer's letter to Reb Moshe Blau on behalf of the Chazon Ish

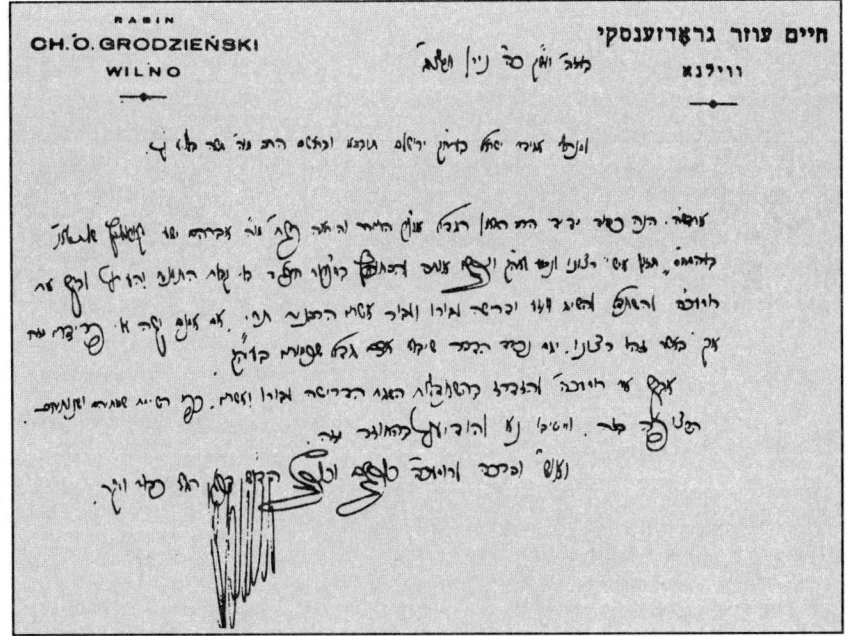

Eretz Yisrael to help bring about a spiritual arousal, signified by the bells.

In his letter to Rabbi Blau, Reb Chaim Ozer wrote, "While his parting is difficult for me, this is his desire. It will be great, indeed, for such a personage to be found in the Holy City."

Rabbi Blau invested great efforts in securing the visas. However, before he could complete the task, the needs of his community forced him to leave *Eretz Yisrael* on an overseas mission. In his absence, Rabbi Moshe Glickman Porush, Secretary of Agudath Israel in Jerusalem, undertook to fulfill Reb Chaim Ozer's request. Rabbi Porush believed that the Chazon Ish could be prevailed upon to succeed Rabbi Sonnenfeld, and he expressed his belief in the cover letter that accompanied the visa application. The application was accepted with amazing swiftness, and only sixteen days later Rabbi Porush was in possession of the visas. He immediately dispatched them to Vilna, and a letter of acknowledgment from Reb Chaim Ozer was soon forthcoming.

Rabbi Porush was disappointed by the reply. Reb Chaim Ozer assured him that, while his intentions had been honorable, his hopes of the Chazon Ish assuming leadership of Jerusalem's Torah community would never materialize. "Because of his great humility and piety, he does not want to assume any official position in the Holy Land."

Rabbi Porush's letter had arrived in Vilna in early Sivan. The Chazon Ish wasted no time in preparing for his move, as he hoped to arrive in *Eretz Yisrael* before the seventeenth of Tamuz, when the mourning period over the destruction of both *Battei Mikdash* commences.

While he and his wife readied themselves for the journey, the Chazon Ish corresponded with the friend of his youth, Rabbi Moshe Ilvitzky (now living in Petach Tikvah), regarding two key issues: the proper tithing of produce grown in *Eretz Yisrael* and the choice of a city in which to make his new home.

At that time, the Karelitz' had made no definite decision as to where they would live, but the Chazon Ish indicated to Rabbi Ilvitzky that their choice would probably not be Jerusalem. Later, he explained, "I yearned to plant Torah in a spiritual desert of the new *yishuv*."*

---

* This was undoubtedly not his only reason, as is evident from the fact that, as related in the next chapter, he rarely even visited Jerusalem.

A Lion Ascends

FINALLY, THE MOMENT arrived for which the Chazon Ish had so long yearned. On *Motzaei Shabbos*, 8 Tammuz, 5693, a small but distinguished crowd gathered at the Vilna railroad station to bid the Chazon Ish and his wife farewell. As Reb Shlomo Kohen put it, "Everyone went home sad and lost in thought, with a feeling that a great *tzaddik* had left our city and that a void had been created that would never be filled. But we were strengthened and encouraged by a feeling that his light would shine ever brighter on the horizons of *Eretz Yisrael*. We were proud of this precious gift that we were sending to Zion, our Holy Land."

The train from Vilna brought the Chazon Ish to Warsaw, from where he made his way to Trieste. There, he boarded a ship which set sail toward Jaffa.

In advent of the Chazon Ish's arrival, Reb Chaim Ozer wrote to Rabbi Avraham Yitzchak Kook, "A lion is ascending from Bavel" (see *Bava Kama* 177a). In another letter, he wrote, "My dear friend, the quintessential *gaon*, is on his way to you ... For us, it is a great loss. *Eretz Yisrael*, however, will reap great benefits from this. I am hopeful that you will reckon with the opinion of the Chazon Ish."

The ship bearing the Chazon Ish and his wife arrived at the port of Jaffa on the 16th of Tammuz. He was met by a delegation from the Agudath Israel leadership, including Rabbi Porush and Rabbi Yaakov Meir Sonnenfeld, son of Reb Yosef Chaim. The Chazon Ish wore the same simple attire that had made him so unobtrusive all his years in Vilna. His way of dress would not change in the years to come.* His days and nights would continue to revolve around his life's delight, the study of Torah. There would, however, be one major change in his life. From now on, he would maintain a keen watch on all that occurred around him, as he strove to lead his adopted community in establishing itself upon the firm foundations of Torah truth.

---

* Some years later, Rabbi Yitzchak Gershtenkorn, Bnei Brak's founder, asked the Chazon Ish to "perform an act of *chesed*" for him; namely, that the Chazon Ish grant permission for a tailor to sew him a new satin frock to wear, which Rabbi Gershtenkorn would pay for. The Chazon Ish replied that he had never worn a satin garment and was not about to wear one now. Rabbi Gershtenkorn asked if he could have a less expensive garment made for the Chazon Ish to wear on Shabbos. The Chazon Ish replied that he still wore the Shabbos garment sewn for him at the time of his marriage; he saw no reason to stop wearing it.

CHAPTER FIVE
Bnei Brak

Why did Moshe Rabbeinu yearn to enter the Land? Did he need to partake of its fruit? This is what Moshe said: "The Jewish Nation was given many mitzvos that can only be fulfilled in Eretz Yisrael. I will enter the Land so that they will be fulfilled through me" (Sotah 14a).

An Immigrant's Concerns

AS THE CHAZON ISH stepped onto the dock on that hot summer day in 1933, he was genuinely taken aback by the sight of his welcoming committee. He blushed as the group gathered around him and each man stepped forward to shake his hand. As soon as the formalities were over, he immediately began to ask about the prevalent procedures regarding the separation of *terumos* and *ma'asros*. His welcomers were dumbstruck. The Chazon Ish had made no arrangements for living quarters and had no idea as to where he and his wife would be spending that night. Yet, this is not what concerned him. It was apparent that Reb Chaim Ozer had been precise in his description of the Chazon Ish as a man of exceptional piety.

Present at the dock was Reb David Potash, a community activist and benefactor who was highly regarded by the Torah leaders of Eastern Europe from the time that he had lived in the Czarist capital of St. Petersburg. The Chofetz Chaim, the Rogatchover *Gaon*, Reb Chaim Ozer and other *gedolim* had been guests of Reb David and often exchanged letters with him. He now invited the Karelitzes to stay at his home in Tel-Aviv, and his invitation was accepted. A few days later the couple moved into a one-room apartment near the shore in Tel-Aviv. There, the Chazon Ish — still a virtual unknown —pored over his *sefarim* amid the same serenity that he had enjoyed in Vilna.

Years later, someone mentioned to the Brisker *Rav* the great merit the Chazon Ish had earned for himself with his efforts on behalf of *Shemittah* observance in the Land. Replied the *Rav*, "It is not only *Shemittah* ... also *terumos, ma'asros* ... were it not for the Chazon Ish we would not know how to tithe properly."

His efforts in these areas began immediately upon his arrival, as he devoted his days and nights to composing a virtual code of law of Land-related laws. He would not satisfy himself with following what had become accepted practice among the observant settlers. As in every area of Torah that he approached, the Chazon Ish now studied the pertinent topics, beginning with the most basic sources, and then applied his findings to the existing situation.

It was only weeks after his coming to Tel-Aviv that the Chazon Ish made known his *chiddush* regarding the setting aside of a special coin known as the *perutah chamurah* for the tithing of *ma'aser sheni* (lit., secondary tithe). His rulings in this and other Land-related areas became the basis for the method of tithing followed by virtually the entire Torah community to this day.

The Chazon Ish could be tolerant of the leniencies of others, so long as they conformed with *halachah*. In his personal life, however, he set the most exacting standards of halachic observance. While he researched and examined the mass of Oral Law pertaining to the fruits of *Eretz Yisrael*, he exercised the most extreme caution with regard to what he and his *rebbetzin* consumed. In a letter to Rabbi Moshe Ilvitzky, he requested that wine for *kiddush* and *havdalah* be sent him from Petach Tikvah, as a *ma'asros*-related question had arisen regarding the grapes being sold in Tel-Aviv.

Though engrossed in his studies as always, the Chazon Ish took note of the goings-on around him. The neighborhood in which he now lived was quite different from his surroundings in Europe: scores of Jewish homes did not have *mezuzos* affixed to their doorposts. Reb Yaakov Halpern, a scholarly, G-d-fearing Viennese businessman who emigrated to *Eretz Yisrael* around the same time as the Chazon Ish, was himself appalled by the situation and gave the Chazon Ish money with which to purchase some two thousand *mezuzos*. Still unacquainted with the land's *sofrim*, the Chazon Ish wrote to Vilna where a local scribe, Rabbi Zalman Kessel, made contact with other *sofrim* in the region. From Slabodka, Grodno, and other cities, *mezuzos* were sent to Vilna until the necessary amount had been procured. When the *mezuzos* arrived in Tel-Aviv, the Chazon Ish sent emissaries from house to house offering the non-religious a "gift" to affix to their doorpost, so that "their days and their children's days be prolonged upon the ground that Hashem swore to their ancestors" (see *Deuteronomy* 11:21).

Historic Invitation

NINE YEARS BEFORE the Chazon Ish arrived in *Eretz Yisrael*, a small group of Polish *Chassidim*, led by Rabbi Yitzchak Gershtenkorn, founded a religious settlement in Bnei Brak, situated between Petach Tikvah and Tel-Aviv. In 1932, one year prior to the Chazon Ish's arrival, a branch of Yeshivah Beis Yosef-Novaradok was founded in Bnei Brak by Rabbi Mattisyahu Zev Shetzigel. Rabbi Shetzigel had invited the Chazon Ish's brother-in-law, Rabbi Yaakov Yisrael Kanievsky, to leave his post in the Novaradok Yeshivah of Pinsk (Poland) to serve as *Rosh Yeshivah* in Bnei Brak. The "Steipler" was having a profound impact on the spiritual growth of his *talmidim* in Pinsk and, largely due to their intervention, some time would elapse before he would finally accept Rabbi Shetzigel's invitation. In the meantime, Rabbi Shetzigel looked for other ways to bolster his fledgling institution.

Only days after the Chazon Ish had come to Tel-Aviv, he was visited by Rabbi Shetzigel. The two knew each other from Rabbi Shetzigel's frequent trips to Vilna. Bnei Brak, Rabbi Shetzigel now said, was a growing settlement with enormous potential for the spreading of Torah study and ideals. He was sure that the Chazon Ish could accomplish much there and he offered the Chazon Ish full financial support to come and study in his yeshivah's *beis midrash*.

The Chazon Ish declined the offer of support, saying that he had decided to make do with whatever money the sale of his *sefarim* would bring. However, the idea of living in Bnei Brak sounded interesting and he promised to visit the settlement after the fast of *Tishah B'Av*.

In typical fashion, the Chazon Ish gave no advance notice of his visit. He and his *rebbetzin* boarded a bus one torrid summer day, were dropped off at a bus depot near the city and made their way on foot up Rechov Rabbi Akiva to a synagogue known today as *Beis*

HaKnesses Eliyahu HaNavi. There the Novaradok Yeshivah was housed and there the Chazon Ish hoped to find Rabbi Shetzigel. However, Rabbi Shetzigel was not there, as an urgent matter had called him out of the city. In his absence, Rabbi Shraga Feivel Steinberg, an outstanding scholar who would one day become a prime disciple of the Chazon Ish, welcomed the visitors.

Soon, the three were heading up Givat HaShalom, a hill from whose peak one could enjoy a panoramic view of the settlement and beyond. There were Tel-Aviv and the Mediterranean Sea to the west, the orchards of Petach Tikvah to the northeast, and the hills of Ramat-Gan to the south. Two chairs were set up and the Chazon Ish and his *rebbetzin* sat down to rest. For a full hour the Chazon Ish sat lost in thought as his gaze rested on the surrounding hills and valleys, the orchards, the houses, the settlers walking to and fro. Finally, he and his *rebbetzin* rose to be directed to the bus station so that they could catch the next bus for Tel-Aviv. They had some packing to do. Rabbi Steinberg promised to find the couple an apartment.

Accommodations and Attitudes

THE CHAZON ISH REMAINED in his first apartment in Bnei Brak for but a few months before moving to a dwelling whose rent was minimal, but whose primitiveness did not even allow for running water. Such inconveniences were of no significance to him and when discussing his situation he made no mention of them. In a letter dated *erev Rosh Hashanah* 5694 (1933), Reb Chaim Ozer wrote to the Chazon Ish, "His honor's precious letter regarding his settling in Bnei Brak has reached me. I rejoiced in hearing that he is well and that the climate there is good for him."

Once, as he and a companion were trekking up a steep incline, the Chazon Ish asked, "Do you know what the difference is between going up a hill and walking along a smooth road?" After a short pause he said, "There is really no difference, save for a measure of tolerance."

As for his *rebbetzin*, she was willing to endure any sacrifice for her husband's sake, as is evident from her remark that "even during wartime [i.e., the First World War], when there was gunfire in the streets, I would run to and from the market so that he would have food for lunch."

Eventually, their living conditions improved. When Mr. Baruch Meyers of Chicago learned of the deplorable state of the Chazon Ish's dwelling, he contacted the Chazon Ish and offered to build him a new home. The offer was firmly refused. Mr. Meyers then wrote to the Chazon Ish's relatives in *Eretz Yisrael* asking their advice. They responded that the only hope was to tell the Chazon Ish that he, Mr. Meyers, wanted to build a home for himself in Bnei Brak but did not plan to move there in the foreseeable future. In the meantime, the Chazon Ish was more than welcome to live there. The Chazon Ish accepted this proposal, on condition that he be permitted to pay rent. Mr. Meyers would not accept rent; however, he reluctantly allowed the Chazon Ish to pay the required property tax and upkeep expenses. The Chazon Ish himself planned the dwelling's layout. In addition to a kitchen, study, bedroom and eating area, the house had a small *beis midrash* where a *minyan* gathered for the daily *tefillos*, and a large porch that was used as a *succah*.*

A Place of Torah

IT WAS NOT UNTIL 1934 that the Steipler, at his brother-in-law's urging, left Pinsk for Bnei Brak to head the Novaradok Yeshivah there. In the meantime, the Chazon Ish acceded to Rabbi Shetzigel's wish that he deliver *shiurim* in the yeshivah. His presence left an indelible imprint on the *talmidim*, some of whom went on to become his prime disciples.

When Rosh Hashanah 5634 (1933) arrived, the Chazon Ish *davened* in the yeshivah. Before the blowing of the *shofar* on the first day, Rabbi Shetzigel asked the Chazon Ish to address the assemblage. The Chazon Ish had never addressed a public gathering and he now attempted to turn down the request. Rabbi Shetzigel, however, was not one to easily give up and he implored the Chazon Ish a second and then a third time to speak. Finally, the Chazon Ish said somewhat bashfully, "I can only relate a single *mishnah*, but not in the *beis midrash*, in a side room." Soon, the assemblage had crowded into a side room.

In a voice filled with emotion the Chazon Ish recited the

---

* After the Chazon Ish died, Mr. Meyers decided to put the house up for sale. He informed the Chazon Ish's family that he would do nothing until a year had passed from the time of the Chazon Ish's death. During that year, the *rebbetzin* was welcome to continue living in the house and the daily *minyan* could continue in the *beis midrash*. On the day preceding the Chazon Ish's first *yahrtzeit*, the Steipler (the Chazon Ish's brother-in-law) was confronted with a problem: The *minyan* wished to *daven* on the *yahrtzeit* in the Chazon Ish's *beis midrash*, but Mr. Meyers had only given permission to use the building for one year! To use it even one extra day — even for a *mitzvah* — without permission was halachically forbidden. The Steipler telegraphed Mr. Meyers, who of course consented.

A group of Bnei Brak residents eventually bought the house and converted it into a boys' *cheder*, which exists to this day.

Rechov Rabbi Akiva, Bnei Brak's main street, during the settlement's early years

following (*Avos* 6:9): *Rabbi Yose ben Kisma said, "Once, I was walking on the road, when a certain man met me. He greeted me and I returned his greeting. He said to me, 'Rabbi, from what place are you?' I said to him, 'I am from a great city of scholars and sages.' He said to me, 'Rabbi, would you be willing to live with us in our place? I would give you thousands upon thousands of golden dinars, precious stones and pearls.' I replied, 'Even if you were to give me all the silver and gold, precious stones and pearls in the world, I would dwell nowhere but in a place of Torah.'"*

With a fervor that caused the entire crowd to be swept with emotion, the Chazon Ish repeated again and again, "I would dwell nowhere but in a place of Torah . . . I would dwell . . ."

He said no more. Those close to him understood his words to mean that he had come to Bnei Brak with the intent of building it into a citadel of Torah. Years later, it would become obvious that the Chazon Ish had in fact accomplished even more, for Bnei Brak developed into a bastion whose concentration of Torah institutions is almost without parallel.

The Chazon Ish fulfilled his desire never to occupy an official position. But the luminescence that shone from his pure and holy countenance, the wisdom that filled his incredible mind and spilled forth from his lips, the fearless and courageous determination to seek

The Chazon Ish with Rabbi Yitzchak Gershtenkorn

no compromises in establishing a strongly committed Torah community — all this had a profound impact on those around him, on his city and on the entire land.

Rabbi Yosef Kahaneman, renowned as the Ponovezher *Rav* and founder of Bnei Brak's famed Ponovezher Yeshivah, was wont to extol Bnei Brak's founder and administrator, Rabbi Yitzchak Gershtenkorn, for having made the Chazon Ish "Master of the City." This was without a doubt the key to Bnei Brak's emergence as the city of Torah that it is to this day.

Keeping Watch

LESS THAN A YEAR AFTER coming to Bnei Brak, the Chazon Ish began inspecting the work of the local *shochet*. It seemed to the Chazon Ish that the fellow was lacking in Heavenly fear. *"Ehr shecht vochadik"* was his comment, meaning that the man slaughtered as one performing a mundane act, not a *mitzvah*. He asked that the man be removed from his post. Sure enough, it was soon discovered that the man was not what people had thought him to be. The Chazon Ish was often heard to say that a lack of Heavenly fear was the worst blemish a *shochet* could possess and he would cite the words of *Rabbeinu Yonah*: "One who has no [Heavenly] fear in his heart will not inspect the slaughtering knife properly" (*Sha'arei Teshuvah* 3:§96).

Finding a qualified *shochet* proved to be no simple task. In the course of his search, the Chazon Ish solicited the help of Rabbi Yosef Zvi Dushinsky, successor to the late Rabbi Sonnenfeld as leader of the *Eidah Chareidis*. In a letter to Rabbi Dushinsky, the Chazon Ish wrote, "The matter is of extreme and pre-eminent importance. I see *shechitah* as absolutely central to Jewish concerns. Establishing standards for *shechitah* which fulfill absolutely the Torah's requirements would be of immeasurable benefit to the entire *yishuv*."

It was his opinion that those meticulous in their *mitzvah* observance ought not carry on Shabbos — even within the parameters of a halachically valid *eruv* — because "in most instances, pitfalls are involved." Nevertheless, he undertook to inspect the *eruv* that encircled Bnei Brak so that those who wished to make use of it could do so. Each Friday afternoon, in the most torridly hot or inclement weather, the Chazon Ish would give of his precious time to trek along the settlement's outskirts, examining wires and poles, climbing up ladders and trees to prevent his neighbors from transgressing. The importance of his work can be judged from the following letter he wrote to the Tchebiner *Rav*, Rabbi Dov Beirish Weidenfeld: "Not once in all the times that I inspected the *eruv* was everything in perfect order. Therefore, if for some reason the *eruv's* components were not inspected on *erev Shabbos* we cannot permit its use by relying on the previous week's examination."

The operations of the city's water supply posed a special challenge. The Chazon Ish discovered that the electric pump used in supplying the water was tended by Jewish workers even on Shabbos. He immediately took steps to have the workers replaced by Arabs.

Once, it became known to him that the pump had been repaired and reset by Jewish workers after the onset of Shabbos. Without a moment's delay, he made his way to Bnei Brak's main synagogue, mounted the podium and — for the first time in his life — addressed the congregation. In decisive terms, he announced: No water may be used on Shabbos, regardless of the purpose. Hands are not to be washed before eating — instead, they should be wrapped throughout the meal.* If the sick require water, then a competent halachic authority should be consulted.

His efforts did not end there. At the conclusion of Shabbos, he prevailed upon someone to donate the necessary sum for technical

---

* See *Orach Chaim* 163:§1.

improvements in the pump, so that its smooth functioning would be assured in the future.

He expended enormous effort in trying to convince the local electric company not to employ the services of Jewish workers on Shabbos. When his efforts ended in failure, he publicized his famous opinion that one should not benefit from electricity produced through the forbidden work of a Jew on Shabbos. It was his contention that, aside from the halachic problems involved with benefiting from such labor, *chilul Hashem* was a critical issue here: "... One who benefits from his [i.e., a Jew's] work, testifies, G-d forbid, that his heart does not ache over the desecration of the Shabbos ..."

It was this opinion that led to what is today a common practice in *Eretz Yisrael*: homes are illuminated on Shabbos either by candlelight or by privately owned generators.

The Milking Controversy

IF THERE WAS ANY DOUBT over what kind of role the Chazon Ish intended to play in the development of Bnei Brak's Torah community, it was dispelled with his involvement in the milking controversy that occurred in the mid-1930's. Milking by a Jew on Shabbos in a normal manner is clearly prohibited by Torah law. As Reb Chaim Ozer wrote to the Chazon Ish, "The Torah observant have a gentile do the milking."* The Chazon Ish concurred with Reb Chaim Ozer that the use of gentiles was the ideal solution to the milking problem. However, in the 1930's, Jewish farmers were very reluctant to hire Arabs as workers, because of the threat they posed to the security of farms and settlements. Thus, religious farmers in various settlements including Bnei Brak fell victim to sin when they took to milking their cows themselves.

The Chazon Ish ruled that, given the situation, it would be permissible for a Jew to milk his cow if the milking would be done directly onto the ground so that the milk would go to waste. Reb Chaim Ozer concurred with this. Armed with Reb Chaim Ozer's support, the Chazon Ish asked Bnei Brak's new *Rav*, Rabbi Yaakov Landau, to publicize his *p'sak*.

The Chazon Ish wrote that one who abided by his ruling would be "observing the Shabbos with self-sacrifice. His milking [in the prescribed manner] will be a form of acceptance of Divine

---

* From a collection of letters by Reb Chaim Ozer to the Chazon Ish, published as an addendum to *Kovetz Igros Chazon Ish*.

sovereignty, a demonstration of faith in the words of the generation's guides. He will create [Heavenly] advocates that will be supportive of his endeavors. He also will be treading a path for others to follow and will be rendering assistance to those who carry the burden of guiding the Nation and preserving its values."

The publicizing of his ruling among the farmers did not have its desired effect. In many areas, including Bnei Brak, farmers continued to milk as they had done. The Chazon Ish met with one Bnei Brak farmer who he thought might possibly be influenced for the better. He sympathized with the man's financial predicament, the struggles and hardships he was enduring for the sake of settling the Land. Gently, he told the farmer to cease his sinful practices and offered to reimburse him for half the loss he would incur from letting the milk go to waste. The Chazon Ish explained that the remaining loss was insignificant in comparison to the eternal reward that the man would receive, for not only would he be observing the Shabbos with sacrifice, but he would also be setting an example for other farmers to follow.

The man remained unmoved. The Chazon Ish was convinced that to tolerate such behavior by those claiming to be observant contradicted the Torah's command to rebuke sinners and endangered the lofty spiritual fiber of Bnei Brak's young and growing settlement. And so, against his nature, he was forced to exchange the fatherly concern of the counselor for the fierce unbending determination of the warrior who would defend the cause of Shabbos, Torah and his Creator.

On another occasion, when pressed to lend his prestige to a matter of communal interest, he had written, "I find it completely impossible to step out of the ranks of the faceless masses to be counted among their mentors and leaders." Now, however, he did that which he had never done before. A fiery proclamation, signed by the Chazon Ish, was disseminated throughout Bnei Brak, calling on the Torah faithful to take the situation in hand:

> As my spirit storms within me, I will speak and be relieved. Our city that stands out with praise and splendor within the new *yishuv** — they call her "Jerusalem" — our city that bears the banner of Torah and is a fortress of authentic Judaism — with

---

* *"Yishuv"* refers to the Jewish settlement in *Eretz Yisrael*. "New *yishuv*" generally refers to those settlements established after 1880 (a large percentage of which were secularist in nature). The old *yishuv* was based primarily in Jerusalem, Safed (Tzfas), Tiberias and Hebron.

> genuine sacrifice did our people safeguard the sanctity of the holy Shabbos, the soul of our nation ... now, suddenly ... men are milking before our eyes ...
>
> ... Those who milk on Shabbos do so not in a spirit of treachery and rebellion; only, they are possessed by their evil inclination and find it difficult to withstand the test and milk onto the ground — which is the permissible method. Their souls plead to us to come to their salvation and rescue them from their inclination which spreads new nets at their feet each day. We will answer their call and come to their aid ...

The Chazon Ish called upon Bnei Brak's citizenry to unite in pressuring the farmers to cease their sinful practices. His call was heeded and the farmers relented. From then on, no farmer in Bnei Brak dared to milk his cows in the forbidden way. The Chazon Ish issued a subsequent proclamation congratulating the community:

> Our brothers in Bnei Brak! We are obligated to inform you that you have merited renown and splendor throughout the land; as the legion of the King in safeguarding Torah and *mitzvos*, who have created a community that has become a tower and fortress for all that is holy to us. Praiseworthy are you for having merited this! May you be blessed with renewed strength to act for the sake of Torah ...
>
> And now ... enwrap yourselves with might for the sake of the holy Shabbos! Calculate the cost of a *mitzvah* against its reward.
>
> May all those who heed our words find their losses replenished, and may they be showered with additional blessing.*

The Inner Circle

OF CENTRAL IMPORTANCE to the Chazon Ish would always be his own Torah learning. As in Europe, his studying in the rarefied atmosphere of *Eretz Yisrael* was performed with superhuman physical and mental exertions. In addition, his literary productivity continued unabated; during 5695-5696 (1935-1936) three new volumes of *Chazon Ish* were published. All the while, he drove his frail body to its limit

---

* Later, when electrical milking machines came into use, the Chazon Ish encouraged the observant agricultural community, in particular *Kibbutz Chofetz Chaim*, to eliminate the problems of milking on Shabbos by finding ways to adjust the machines in accordance with *halachah*.

Rabbi Shmuel Greineman   *The Chazon Ish with Reb Zelig Shapiro*

in pursuing his new goal: the development of Bnei Brak as a genuine Torah center.

An inner circle of learned and G-d-fearing activists formed around the Chazon Ish not long after his coming to Bnei Brak. It was largely through this circle that he was able to accomplish so much for Torah life both in Bnei Brak and throughout the Land.

Rabbi Zelig Shapiro was one such man. One of the original group from Warsaw that founded Bnei Brak's new settlement, he attached himself to the Chazon Ish and was devoted to him with all his heart and soul. Reb Zelig was the classic Torah activist: scholarly, G-d-fearing, resourceful, and a man whose every act was performed for the sake of Heaven.

Rabbi Shmuel Greineman joined his brother-in-law in Bnei Brak in 1935. From then on, he was the Chazon Ish's closest and most relied-upon confidant. Among his many noteworthy accomplishments was the founding, together with other activists, of *Mercaz Chinuch HaTorah*, which established *chadarim* for boys and Bais Yaakov schools for girls in scores of settlements.

Reb Yaakov Halpern dedicated himself and his vast material assets to every holy endeavor, as illustrated in the *"mezuzos* episode" cited above. Of Reb Yaakov, the Chazon Ish once said, "He is a successful businessman — grabbing every *mitzvah* that comes his way."

The Chazon Ish presided over numerous transactions whereby

At a bechinah (examination) of young Torah students in Bnei Brak (l. to r.): Reb Yaakov Halpern, the Chazon Ish, Rabbi Eliyahu E. Dessler

Reb Yaakov sold tracts of land to worthy groups or individuals for the building of Torah institutions. Probably the most noteworthy such transaction was the sale of a hill owned by Reb Yaakov to the Ponovezher *Rav*. The Ponovezher Yeshivah was to become the most famous landmark of Bnei Brak's Zichron Meir neighborhood, an area bursting with yeshivos, *battei midrash, shuls,* and *kollelim.**

Tiferes Tzion

THANKS TO THE ENCOURAGEMENT and active involvement of the Chazon Ish, the new *yishuv's* first preparatory yeshivah, *Tiferes Tzion*, was founded in Bnei Brak in 1935. The yeshivah's stationery bore the words, "Under the supervision of the Chazon Ish." This was true both spiritually and materially. He oversaw the yeshivah's fund-raising activities and turned over to the yeshivah large sums that were given him by petitioners. So linked was the name of the Chazon Ish to *Tiferes Tzion* that virtually all donations sent to the yeshivah were addressed to him.

In a letter calling for support of *Tiferes Tzion*, the Tchebiner *Rav* wrote, "The yeshivah is the praiseworthy product of the

---

* Reb Yaakov sought ways to give material assistance to the Chazon Ish, who, as already mentioned, was determined to support himself from the modest income generated by the sale of his *sefarim*. Reb Yaakov made it known that he would cover the cost of all volumes of *Chazon Ish* purchased by *yeshivos* and *kollelim*. This led to a significant increase in the Chazon Ish's income.

The Tchebiner Rav

gaon hador, the Chazon Ish (of blessed memory), who, with the warmth of his love, was father of the yeshivah. He was concerned with its every need."

The Chazon Ish knew each of the yeshivah's *talmidim* by name and was consulted frequently regarding their individual development. He rejoiced in their successes and was concerned with their failures in the way of a true father.

Often, the Chazon Ish would visit the yeshivah to test the *talmidim* in their studies. Rabbi Yerucham Asher Varhapteg, a Lithuanian *gaon* who settled in Bnei Brak toward the end of his life, sometimes joined the Chazon Ish at these examinations. The following is an excerpt from a letter by Rabbi Varhapteg:

> At the request of the Chazon Ish, I began delivering *shiurim* to the *talmidim* from time to time ... Periodically, they would visit the Chazon Ish and the *gaon* Rabbi Yosef Kahaneman of Ponovezh, to "speak in learning."
>
> ... Participating in the end-of-term *bechinah* (examination) were the Chazon Ish; the *gaon* Rabbi Yaakov Yisrael Kanievsky, author of *Kehillas Yaakov*; myself; and other *rabbanim*. For many hours we tested the students' abilities ... we were quite satisfied with our findings and finally rose to leave, but the boys

were not satisfied and they pleaded with us to ask them more questions. The Chazon Ish smiled at them and asked, "How many more questions should we ask?" "Five!" came the response. The Chazon Ish, in his humble way, acceded to their request and asked that I put forth the five questions. I did, and they responded correctly ... But they were still not satisfied and persisted, "More, more!" Feigning anger, the Chazon Ish said with love, "You are not keeping to your word! ... but, even so, we will grant your request ..."

The Chazon Ish's joy knew no bounds as, with each passing day, more and more children were enrolled in the school. Less than a year after *Tiferes Tzion* opened, plans were begun for the construction of larger quarters. Reb Zelig Shapiro, Reb Yaakov Halpern, and others spared no effort in trying to amass the necessary funds. Their efforts, though, were not enough to cover the entire cost of construction and for a while work on the new building was halted. Then help came from an unexpected source.

In 1936, Rabbi Zalman Sorotzkin, who would later serve as Chairman of the *Moetzes Gedolei HaTorah* of *Eretz Yisrael*, visited *Eretz Yisrael* as part of a rabbinic group representing Agudath Israel of Poland. The Chazon Ish was overjoyed to see the *gaon* who had shown him such kindness during the First World War.

The Chazon Ish insisted that Reb Zalman spend at least one Shabbos with him in Bnei Brak. As his dwelling did not have room for even one additional bed, the Chazon Ish said that R' Zalman would join him for the Shabbos meals and sleep at a neighbor's home. R' Zalman accepted the invitation, but as it was still early in the week, he left Bnei Brak with the intent of returning the following *erev Shabbos*.

When R' Zalman returned to Bnei Brak, he was surprised to see the streets adorned with placards that read: "*Harav* Zalman Sorotzkin, Rav of Lutzk, will deliver an address on Shabbos in the Great Synagogue." That evening, as they enjoyed the *seudas Shabbos* together, the Chazon Ish mentioned almost parenthetically that he was responsible for the announcements. He explained that construction on *Tiferes Tzion's* new building had been halted due to lack of funds. Bnei Brak's community needed to be warmed to the idea of increasing its contribution toward the construction. Someone had to make them understand that a thriving *yeshivah k'tanah* was as vital to their community as bread and water. The Chazon Ish was sure that Reb Zalman Sorotzkin was equal to the task.

A large crowd greeted Reb Zalman that night at the Great Synagogue. The high point of his address was the following:

"When walking through your city, I am reminded of the episode recounted in the *Haggadah shel Pesach*: 'It happened [one *seder* night], that Rabbi Eliezer, Rabbi Yehoshua, Rabbi Elazar ben Azariah, Rabbi Akiva and Rabbi Tarfon were sitting in Bnei Brak ...' Yes, my friends, I find that in the Bnei Brak of today, these great names have once again appeared — your streets bear the names of these sages. However, I caution you, lest people say that you are guilty of practicing the ways of Sodom, whose habits impelled the angels to tell Lot [*Genesis* 19:2], *"No, rather we will spend the night in the street."*

Rabbi Zalman Sorotzkin

"My brethren! Will you allow the spirit of our sages to remain in the street while your facilities for the teaching of their holy words remain inadequate? Will Rabbi Akiva's timeless words be indelibly ingrained upon your sons' hearts, or will his name mean nothing more to them than any other on a signpost? No! Heaven forfend! See that the new building of *Tiferes Tzion* is completed, so that your sons can grow great in the knowledge of Torah."

The Fortress Evolves

THE YEAR 1936 also saw the founding of a *kollel* in the Zichron Meir neighborhood. At that time, the Chazon Ish's nephew Rabbi Shmaryahu Karelitz headed a *kollel* in Tel-Aviv. One day, Reb Shmaryahu mentioned to his uncle that it would be more practical for him to head a *kollel* in Bnei Brak, where he lived. Two weeks later, the Chazon Ish presented his nephew with the sum needed to fund a *kollel* of ten. Thus began *Kollel Avreichim*,* later to be known as *Kollel Chazon Ish*. There, outstanding young married scholars

---

* A word connoting a combination of youth and wisdom (see *Genesis* 41:43).

pursued their Torah studies full-time while their material needs were provided through the support of others. Moreover, they were granted the opportunity to grow great in Torah knowledge under the guidance of the giant of the generation, who generously imparted both his wisdom and his method of study to them.*

As a means of funding this noble project, the Chazon Ish encouraged the arrangement of *Yissachar-Zevulun*** contracts, whereby a married scholar would receive support while his benefactor would receive equal Heavenly reward for the scholar's Torah study (see *Yoreh Deah* 246:1). The Chazon Ish authored a text for such agreements (*Igros*, I:§47) and encouraged both benefactors (ibid. §46) and scholars (ibid. §49) to participate in these very unique endeavors.

Paraphrasing the Scriptural verse that speaks of Jerusalem's spiritual preeminence, many would say, "From Bnei Brak Torah will come forth ..." The Chazon Ish's presence in Bnei Brak and his unofficial leadership of its community motivated scores of great scholars and G-d-fearing, learned laymen to take up permanent residence in the city. Daily *shiurim* were organized, *mikvaos* were built, free-loan funds were established. *Battei Knessios* sprang up in every corner of the settlement, as did *chadarim, yeshivos,* and *kollelim.* Famous European communities and *yeshivos* such as Vizhnitz, Slabodka, Novaradok, and Chachmei Lublin found their legacies reborn in Bnei Brak. Communal institutions, such as *Ohr HaChaim* (where Sephardic girls emigrating from Middle Eastern lands were provided with Torah-true instruction and assistance), and the anti-missionary organization *Magen HaYeled* were founded. The Chazon Ish played a major role in the flowering of them all.

It was during his early years in Bnei Brak that the Chazon Ish narrowly escaped an encounter with death. One night in the pre-dawn hours, he wrapped himself in a white sheet and went out on his porch for some early morning air. As he sat on a bench with his head resting against a wall, totally engrossed in Torah thought, a night patrol watching for Arab marauders noticed what appeared to be an Arab wearing a white *keffieh* (headdress) perched on a porch

---

* The *Kollel* is further discussed in the following chapter.

** Zevulun, son of the Patriarch Yaakov, engaged in commerce and supported his brother Yissachar, who dedicated his days to the study of Torah. It is for this reason that the blessing of Zevulun precedes that of Yissachar, who was the elder of the two (see ArtScroll *Genesis*, pg. 2158).

bench. Again and again the guard called to the man to identify himself. The Chazon Ish, lost in his thoughts, heard nothing. The guard fired. The bullet lodged in the wall above the head of the Chazon Ish. An entire generation, an entire community for generations, had been saved by just inches.

NOT LONG AFTER his arrival, the Chazon Ish's mother joined him in Bnei Brak in an apartment not far from his own. Those who

Reunion participated in the *minyan* that gathered regularly in his home were often treated to a touching scene: The *rebbetzin* would rise early and come to her son's apartment in order to *daven Shacharis* along with the *minyan*. As soon as the Chazon Ish would catch sight of her, he would grab a *shtender* (lectern) and begin dragging it toward her so that she could place her *siddur* atop it. A moment later, the Chazon Ish's *rebbetzin* would appear. Having caught sight of what her husband was doing, and mindful that in his poor state of health he not strain himself, she would take the *shtender* from his grasp and drag it to where her mother-in-law sat.

Eventually, *Rebbetzin* Rasha Leah Karelitz settled in Jerusalem where she lived with her eldest son, Reb Meir. When she passed away in Cheshvan 5701 (1940), multitudes escorted her to her final resting place on the Mount of Olives. She was eulogized by Rabbi Isser Zalman Meltzer and by the Ponovezher *Rav*, both of whom spoke the praises of the woman who had borne such extraordinary children.

INCREDIBLY, WHEN THE CHAZON ISH came to Jerusalem for his mother's funeral, it was only the second time that he had visited

Jerusalem the Holy City since his arrival in *Eretz Yisrael* some eight years earlier. His first visit there was earlier that year, when he had attended the wedding of a nephew. He arrived on an *erev Shabbos*, the wedding day, and remained there through Sunday.

The Chazon Ish entered the Holy City without fanfare, but by the time Shabbos had ended, word of his arrival had spread all across Jerusalem. On *Motzaei Shabbos*, scores streamed to his lodging. The cream of Jerusalem's holy community was there, including the aged *Rav* of Meah Shearim, Rabbi Yosef Gershon Horowitz.

Rabbi Horowitz remarked that his own weakened condition could not prevent him from making the visit, which he described as a demonstration of *k'vod HaTorah*. The Chazon Ish smiled and

Rabbi Ezra Attiah   *Rabbi Isser Zalman Meltzer*

replied, "The *Rav* certainly did not strain himself in vain, for if one intends to fulfill a *mitzvah* and cannot, it is considered as if he did it ..."

The next day, the Chazon Ish prayed at the *Kosel HaMaaravi*. As he entered the Jaffa Gate on his way to the *Kosel*, he rent his garment and recited the verse, "*Zion was a desert, Jerusalem was desolate.*" At the *Kosel*, he wept as he prayed softly, suppressed groans escaping his lips. Surely uppermost in his mind was the plight of the millions of Jews who were then suffering Nazi persecution. As he prayed, the Chazon Ish experienced chest pains. After a brief rest, he continued on his way. Only later did he discover that he had suffered a mild heart attack while praying at the *Kosel*.

On his walk back from the *Kosel*, he visited the Sephardic yeshivah, *Porat Yosef*, where he and the revered *Rosh Yeshivah*, Rabbi Ezra Attiah, discussed Torah; and he entered the cave where the legendary kabbalist, Rabbi Shalom Sharabi, had studied with his disciples. From there he made his way to the city's new quarter, where he visited Yeshivah Torah V'Yirah and the Chevron Yeshivah; Rabbi Yosef Dinkels, author of *Emunas Yosef* to *Talmud Yerushalmi*, whom the Chazon Ish once called a צַדִּיק יְסוֹד עוֹלָם, *tzaddik — foundation of the world*; and Rabbi Isser Zalman Meltzer, famed *Rosh Yeshivah* of Jerusalem's Yeshivah Eitz Chaim and author of *Even Ha'Azel* to *Rambam*.

Reb Isser Zalman greeted his revered guest with genuine awe and love. "Had I known that his honor was going to visit my home, I would have left the city in advance — for his visit has brought me such pleasure, that surely I have used up half the portion awaiting me in *Gan Eden!*"

Why the Chazon Ish waited so long before visiting Jerusalem and why he visited it so infrequently is not known. Remarkable, though, was his clear perception of all the goings-on among the religious factions within the Holy City.

The Talmud relates that when Rabbi Yehudah ben Beseirah, who resided in Netzivin, indirectly brought about the apprehending of a gentile posing as a Jew in the *Beis HaMikdash*, the Sages said, "Peace unto you, Rabbi Yehudah ben Beseirah, for you are in Netzivin but your net is spread as far as Jerusalem" (*Pesachim* 3b). A paraphrase of this could have well been said of the Chazon Ish, who rarely ventured out of Bnei Brak, but whose influence was felt all across the Land.

CHAPTER SIX

The Hidden Leader

Assuming a New Role

MANY WERE THE ISSUES and problems that confronted *Eretz Yisrael's* Torah community in the 1930's. As always, it was the Torah viewpoint, as articulated by the generation's leaders, that guided Torah activists in their holy endeavors. Two whose opinions were sought regularly were Reb Chaim Ozer Grodzensky and Reb Elchonon Wasserman*: Reb Chaim Ozer, for he was the acclaimed *gadol hador*, and Reb Elchonon, for he had emerged as not only a giant in Torah scholarship and piety,** but also as a prime expositor of authentic *da'as Torah*.

Soon after the Chazon Ish's arrival in *Eretz Yisrael*, these two sought to direct queries to him. So, for example, Reb Elchonon penned the following response to the request of one of the Land's foremost activists: "Living in close proximity to you is the *gaon* and *tzaddik*, the author of *Chazon Ish*, whose stature I in no way approach. It is proper for you to seek his counsel and pay it heed, for the *'Ish'* is great in Torah and Heavenly fear and is beholden to no man."

At about the same time, Reb Chaim Ozer advised another activist to seek out the Chazon Ish: "With regard to your main question, it is proper to turn to his honor, my friend, the *gaon* and *tzaddik*, Rabbi Avraham Yeshayah Karelitz, author of *Chazon Ish*, who resides in Bnei Brak. Take heed of his words, for he is close to the situation and with his penetrating understanding and exceptional piety will know how to judge and decide properly."

The actions of these two great men were deliberate, for they felt the Chazon Ish's time had come. So it was that Reb Chaim Ozer

---
* The Chofetz Chaim died in 1933.
** Of Reb Elchonon, the Chazon Ish once said, "Not for a moment does he divert his mind from service of Hashem."

requested the following of a Vilna resident who was soon to emigrate to the Holy Land: "Please inform the Chazon Ish that in *Eretz Yisrael* he will no longer be able to 'hide among the vessels,'* for I have already concerned myself with spreading his fame there."

Yet it was not until the early 1940's, after the death of Reb Chaim Ozer, that the Chazon Ish would attain the world acclaim he so richly deserved. Much of this was due to the Chazon Ish's retiring nature, his lack of any official position

Rabbi Elchonon Wasserman

and his steadfast refusal to participate in virtually all forms of public activity. Nevertheless, the verbal and written praise of the generation's recognized giants, coupled with the Chazon Ish's own decision to assume a leadership — though behind-the-scenes — role in the affairs of *Eretz Yisrael's* Torah community, threw him into the very thick of the *yishuv's* ongoing struggles soon after he settled there.

His communal involvement cost him dearly in terms of his very lifeblood — the study of Torah. There could be no choice, however, for his mind and soul, imbued with fifty years of almost ceaseless, intense Torah study, now told him that this was the will of Hashem. For the next twenty years, he would guide and mold the Torah community in *Eretz Yisrael*. As always, his every move and decision would be dictated solely by Torah.

There was only one known occasion when the Chazon Ish spoke of his role as leader of the generation. Rabbi Eliezer Paltzeyanski, son-in-law of the famed *tzaddik*, Rabbi Aryeh Levin, once spoke with the Chazon Ish regarding the self-imposed exiles of the Vilna Gaon and other *tzaddikim* who disguised themselves as paupers and journeyed from city to city as nameless vagabonds. The Chazon Ish said that the primary difficulty faced by such exiles was not the material discomfort, but the effect such travels had on one's

---

* See *I Samuel* 10:22.

peace of mind. Rabbi Paltzeyanski suggested that a *gadol's* involvement in the needs of *Klal Yisrael* should be considered a form of exile, since the burden of so many problems and requests surely robbed one of some degree of peace of mind. The Chazon Ish nodded in agreement. Asked Rabbi Paltzeyanski, "If *Klal* involvement disturbs one's peace of mind and interferes with his spiritual pursuits, then why must one get involved?" The Chazon Ish responded: "The few leaders whom the *Ribono shel Olam* has planted in each generation have no right to distance themselves from the people and meditate in sanctuaries of pleasure and satisfaction. We are obligated to walk amongst the people and share in their burdens."

The Vilna Connection

BEING SEPARATED BY THOUSANDS of miles did not deter Reb Chaim Ozer and the Chazon Ish from exchanging views on issues of the day, just as they had in Vilna. Their correspondences* covered such topics as a move to relocate the Berlin rabbinical seminary to Tel-Aviv; a proposal by religious Zionists to establish a "Sanhedrin" that would serve as a "supreme halachic body" for world Jewry; the milking controversy discussed above; and the selection of qualified *talmidei chachamim* for rabbinic posts in the new *yishuv*.

Noteworthy is Reb Chaim Ozer's writing to the Chazon Ish regarding a host of issues affecting Jewish communities the world over. Among their correspondences are discussions of anti-*shechitah* legislation in Poland; a move by the Polish government to destroy the old Jewish cemetery in Vilna; an *eruv* controversy in Paris; and the tampering by the American Conservative rabbinate with sacred laws of Jewish marriage and divorce.

In 1935, less than two years after his coming to *Eretz Yisrael*, the Chazon Ish acceded to Reb Chaim Ozer's request that he become involved in the selection of a Chief Rabbi to succeed the late Rabbi Avraham Yitzchak *HaKohen* Kook. The Chazon Ish lent his support to the candidacy of Rabbi Isaac *HaLevi* Herzog. Indeed, his support figured prominently in Rabbi Herzog's being chosen for the post. Earlier, the Chazon Ish had turned his attention to the selection of a new Chief Rabbi of Jerusalem, a city that he had yet to visit, but with whose issues and tensions he was amazingly well acquainted.

---

* See addendum to *Kovetz Igros Chazon Ish*. Additional letters can be found in *Kovetz Igros Achiezer* (Bnei Brak 1970).

Struggle for Survival

AS THE CHAZON ISH arrived on the scene, a fierce ideological struggle was being waged in *Eretz Yisrael*. At stake was the very soul of the new *yishuv*. Would the secularists succeed in their goal of creating a community no different from that of any other nation, or would Torah be the guiding force of the Chosen People who had sacrificed so much to return to the Chosen Land? In letters to Reb Chaim Ozer and Reb Elchonon, the Chazon Ish delineated those requirements that were crucial if the Torah was to prevail in any given settlement:

(1) The presence of a G-d-fearing *rav* to lead the community; (2) a competent and G-d-fearing *shochet*; (3) a *mikveh*; (4) a synagogue; (5) Shabbos observance; and (6) Torah education, especially for the young. The Chazon Ish emphasized that a vibrant, politically active Torah community was vital if all this was to be achieved.

He expended enormous effort in trying to provide communities, even those bent toward secularism, with competent *rabbanim*. He was steadfast in his contention that efforts must be made to bring Torah ideals to every corner of *Eretz Yisrael*, regardless of a particular area's ignorance of or hostility toward religion. Once, when the Chazon Ish spoke of the need to reach out to the residents of a certain settlement, a listener asked, "But isn't that place secularist?" The Chazon Ish became emotional as he retorted, "This Land is ours! The secularists have stolen it from us, and it is up to us to reclaim it."

He would exhort young, married *b'nei Torah* to accept rabbinic positions even if they were not proficient in rendering halachic decisions* — as long as they were learned, G-d-fearing and could guide the community in the right direction. Providing communities with competent *shochtim* was also high on his list of priorities. In a letter, he expressed concern that a young man who served as both *shochet* and Torah instructor not leave his post. "He is devout, G-d-fearing and honest. His livelihood is earned from the slaughter of fowl and from teaching in the local *cheder*. Much hinges on this young man's being retained at his post. I have therefore promised to provide him additional support so that he will not feel forced to leave."

❦ ❦ ❦

The Chazon Ish gave particular attention to the construction of *mikvaos* throughout *Eretz Yisrael*. With his revered and tireless

---

* Since they could consult a competent authority when necessary.

confidant Reb Zelig Shapiro as emissary, he was involved in the establishing of ninety-three *mikvaos* within a period of some twenty years. When asked by benefactors how to apportion their charity, he would advise them to consider the building of *mikvaos* a matter of top priority. Against his nature, he issued a public letter (*Igros*, I:§170) bearing his signature, which called on Jews in the Diaspora to contribute to the cause of family purity in the Holy Land.

Reb Zelig Shapiro recalled:

> Our master's accomplishments in the area of *mikvaos* is well known. All *mikvaos* built recently were erected through his active and material support. It is known that our master was insistent that his name not be associated with any particular project, even when he had high regard for the project and encouraged those involved with it. An exception to this was the building of *mikvaos*, for which he issued a public letter* stating that "it is preferable to contribute to [building] a *mikveh* [as opposed to other causes]." This letter is the prime impetus behind the fund-raising for *mikvaos*.

That each *mikveh* be modern and aesthetically pleasing was of paramount importance to him, "so that Satan will not have an opportunity to interfere" (*Igros*, II:§91). In another letter (II:§21) he writes, "In the northern part of Tel-Aviv we are building *mikvaos* to be a pride and glory. We have already invested huge sums in the buildings, and many of our religious brethren are involved..."

Torah Education

HIS ACCOMPLISHMENTS for the sake of Torah education spanned three critical periods: his first seven years in *Eretz Yisrael*; World War II and the three years following the war's end; and from 1948, when the State of Israel was founded, until his death in 1953.** That he accomplished so much without entering the public arena is truly remarkable. Through his efforts, Torah institutions for boys and girls of all ages, from various groups and backgrounds, sprang up in scores of settlements that without his influence would have remained spiritual wastelands.

In the early 1930's, there were few yeshivos outside Jerusalem and most settlements had little or no organized Torah education for young boys and girls. The Chazon Ish was the driving force behind

---

* Distinct from the public letter cited above.
** This last period is discussed in chapter sixteen.

the founding of *Mercaz Chinuch HaTorah*, an organization that unified and strengthened the existing *chadarim* and helped found new *chadarim* for boys and Bais Yaakov schools for girls. The *Mercaz* was enormously successful in its efforts to spread the study of Torah throughout *Eretz Yisrael*.

In guiding the organization, the Chazon Ish demonstrated wisdom, foresight and self-sacrifice. Once, plans were undertaken to open a school for boys in Netanya. Many wanted to scrap the idea when it was learned that the projected school would have but three students. The Chazon Ish, however, insisted that the school be opened. It was, with a significant monthly budget, of which the Chazon Ish, Reb Yaakov Halpern and Rabbi Shmuel Carlebach* each contributed one-third. Someone asked the Chazon Ish if it might not be wiser to spend the money on a cause that would benefit more than three children. The Chazon Ish replied, "We are not doing this solely for these three children. It is also for the hundreds of other precious souls who will one day attend this *cheder*." The school today has an enrollment numbering in the hundreds.

On another occasion, a *cheder* was on the brink of collapse due to lack of funds. A loan was procured, with the Chazon Ish providing his watch as collateral.

HIS INVOLVEMENT in girls' Torah education is a chapter unto itself. When he was informed that the Bais Yaakov school in Petach Tikvah was on the verge of collapse, he quickly dispatched funds to the friend of his youth, Rabbi Moshe Ilvitzky. Accompanying the money was a letter which included the following: "... All of this world's creatures were made male and female. Would they not complement one another, Creation would be lacking. That young men and women will share a Torah way of life together cannot be assured if they do not strive for this equally ... It is therefore that I have attempted to share the burden with you by sending this ... to help pay the Bais Yaakov's debts, thereby lending you strength ..." (*Igros*, I:§66). At that time, he also dispatched an urgent request to the central Bais Yaakov office in Jerusalem calling on it to assist the school in Petach Tikvah. His call was heeded with alacrity.

For the Daughters of Israel

The Chazon Ish was once visited by a group of girls from *B'nos*

---

* Director of the Ohr HaChaim Institute in Bnei Brak (see further in this chapter).

Agudath Israel* who sought to convene evening educational gatherings but lacked funds for renting a site. A request was soon penned (*Igros*, I:§67) to an acquaintance, asking that the girls be given a meeting room free of charge.

Rabbi Yosef Avraham Wolf, dean of the Bais Yaakov seminary in Bnei Brak, would seek the Chazon Ish's guidance in any important school-related question. Once, Rabbi Wolf confronted the Chazon Ish with the question of whether or not a certain girl's behavior merited her being expelled from school. The case was complex, and the Chazon Ish was therefore inclined to let things be, saying, "A *neshamah* is at stake here. Such cases require a *beis din* of twenty-three..."**

Changing Fronts

THE CHAZON ISH was architect and builder of scores of Torah institutions and their unifying networks. He was also patron of Torah in no small way, funneling huge sums that were sent him from all over the world to help support the study of Torah in *Eretz Yisrael's* rarefied atmosphere. However, his primary relationship to the Land's Torah institutions was — as with Rabbi Wolf's seminary — that of spiritual guide. To his door came problems big and small, some affecting a single school or student while others were ideological questions whose outcome had a bearing on schools all across Israel for generations to come.

One such question involved the use of Hebrew as the spoken language in Torah schools. Well before the Chazon Ish had arrived on the scene, the use of Hebrew had become a central issue in the struggle between the Orthodox and secularist camps in *Eretz Yisrael*. The secularist view was that the Land of Israel and the Hebrew language in themselves guaranteed the survival of the Jewish people, regardless of its ties to Torah. Moreover, it was clear that the secularists' insistence that Hebrew be the spoken language in school was largely a ploy through which they hoped to gain a foothold in Torah institutions. Not surprisingly, then, the Torah leadership of *Eretz Yisrael* had for many years vehemently opposed the adoption of Hebrew as the language of instruction and insisted that yeshivah

---

* Agudath Israel's girls' division.
** According to Torah law, a Jewish court of twenty-three judges is required to judge capital offenses. To expel the girl was to place her spiritual future in jeopardy. Hence, it was a matter of life and death.

Children filing toward the Chazon Ish's home to be tested in their studies

classes be conducted in Yiddish.

Rabbi Yosef Chaim Sonnenfeld, the great guardian of Torah education until his death in 1932, was a staunch opponent of conducting classes in Hebrew. Indeed, during his years as *Rav* of Jerusalem, the strictly Orthodox schools in the Holy City employed Yiddish as their language of instruction. Nevertheless, he ruled that in circumstances where failure to introduce Hebrew would undermine Torah education, the Torah instruction of Jewish children certainly took precedence. Rabbi Sonnenfeld thus approved the use of Hebrew in settlements where the absence of Hebrew would have discouraged parents from enrolling their children in religious schools. In the years following Rabbi Sonnenfeld's death, the use of Hebrew in religious schools became more widespread.

The Chazon Ish was likewise opposed as a matter of principle to the use of Hebrew. Indeed, one of his first projects in Bnei Brak was the founding of a Yiddish-speaking *cheder* under the name *Yeshurun*.* Nevertheless, he was actively involved in the workings of scores of Hebrew-speaking religious schools that flourished in his time. In fact, when *Yeshurun* was founded, the Chazon Ish instructed Reb Shlomo Kohen to enroll his young child in the *cheder*. However,

---

* *Yeshurun* (Jeshurun) is a Torah synonym for the Jewish nation (*Deuteronomy* 33:5). Its root is ישר, *straight, righteous*; the title designates Israel in its ideal state as G-d's upright nation.

Chapter 6: THE HIDDEN LEADER / 87

when Reb Shlomo informed him that the child had already been registered in a Hebrew-speaking *cheder*, the Chazon Ish retracted his instruction, as he feared that a switch would eventually be traced to him and be interpreted as indicative of his opposition to the other school.

When testing students in Hebrew-speaking schools, the Chazon Ish would speak Hebrew and, of course, demonstrate the genuine interest in each child's development for which he was known.

Some of Jerusalem's more zealous element once came to Bnei Brak to ask the Chazon Ish why his support of these schools was so unwavering. He replied with a parable: A certain general once led his country's forces in an extremely successful campaign, culminating in a complete victory. The war ended, years passed and borders changed; old fortresses were abandoned and new ones constructed. Finally, hostilities erupted again. The general, now old, insisted on marshaling his forces on the historic battlefield where he had years before led them to victory, even though the military situation had changed considerably and there were different, more important battles to be fought ... Hebrew, the Chazon Ish explained, is not the battlefield of today. Were opposition to Hebrew to be maintained, there would be a real danger that tens of thousands of students would leave the *yeshivos* and enter secular schools where they would be completely alienated from Torah. This is literally a matter of life and death and one must act in accordance with the demands of such extreme situations. The purpose of opposition to Hebrew was to strengthen Torah, not to weaken it.

Safeguarding Sanctity

HE STOOD WATCH that nothing contrary to the authentic Torah outlook be allowed a place in any Torah institution. A parent of a student attending an Orthodox school once brought the Chazon Ish a book of Hebrew literature from which his son was being taught proper Hebrew — however, the volume's contents were far from proper. The Chazon Ish tore the book to shreds and then summoned the school's principal. A letter to the responsible party followed:

> To ... Peace and much salvation. I wish to point out — an incident occurred where parents, whose children attend a *Talmud Torah* here, brought before me a volume containing a collection of literary "gems" penned by some of our most noted vilifiers. This is what the young are being fed?! Therein, when

asking "Who knows five?"* instead of answering "the five *Chumashim*," five jokes are offered. The parents are shattered. Is this the way to sanctify budding minds? Before their eyes, I ripped the book to shreds. I summoned the principal, who responded that he brought this idolatry into his place upon the advice of experts. I feel obligated to apprise you of this.

One who seeks his honor's peace and well-being, איש (*Ish*)

In contrast to the matter of Hebrew as the spoken language, the Chazon Ish ruled that such literature be banned even at the risk of a school's being shut down. However, he recognized the fact that a lack of proper Hebrew language curriculum would cause many parents to withdraw their children from religious schools. He therefore summoned the same parent who had originally brought the matter to his attention and encouraged him to undertake the herculean task of having a new literature volume published whose contents would be faithful to Torah. The parent, a shoemaker by trade, accepted the task. With constant encouragement and guidance from the Chazon Ish, he engaged the services of competent writers and raised the necessary sums, until his mission was accomplished. In 1940, the first edition of *Yalduseinu* ("Our Youth") was published. Many were quick to deride it as being of inferior literary quality. To counter this, the Chazon Ish issued a letter, which related the chain of events that led to the book's publication, described the self-sacrifice which the shoemaker had borne to accomplish his task and made clear the importance of including the work in the curriculum of Hebrew-speaking religious schools. In the meantime, he said, efforts would be undertaken to improve the work's quality.

The Yaldei Teheran Affair

THE HOLOCAUST BROUGHT FORTH new crises in Torah education as scores of orphaned boys and girls fled the Nazi inferno and found safe haven in the land of their forefathers. Most of these children were of devoutly religious upbringing. Shamefully, these lonely souls often found that in being saved from the fires of the Holocaust, they had exchanged a physical threat for a spiritual one.

In 1943, one thousand children from Eastern and Central Europe miraculously escaped the Nazi dragnet and found their way to

---

* From the lyrical song *Echad Mi Yodei'a, Who Knows One?* sung at the conclusion of the Passover *seder*.

Teheran. Representatives of the Jewish Agency in Teheran wasted no time in seeking to sever their young charges from the rich Torah heritage they had known. The children were indoctrinated with secularist and anti-Torah beliefs and were not even permitted to recite *Kaddish* for their martyred parents. Upon being brought to *Eretz Yisrael*, the children were shipped off to secularist *kibbutzim*.

The Torah community did not stand by idly. A fiery proclamation was issued by the Torah leadership in *Eretz Yisrael*, calling on world Torah Jewry to join forces in saving the children. Strenuous and sometimes dangerous efforts were undertaken to have religious parties gain custody of the children, so that they could be reared in the manner that their parents surely would have wanted.

As he often did, the Chazon Ish preferred to play a very discreet role in the *Yaldei Teheran* (Teheran Children) affair. The above-mentioned proclamation did not bear his signature.* Behind the scenes, however, the Chazon Ish worked tirelessly both to rectify the general situation and to save as many individual children as possible. His involvement with each child's case did not end with the orphan's rescue. The Chazon Ish did whatever he could to mend the child's broken spirit and he took a keen interest in his or her overall development. In a letter, he wrote:

> We have here an eight-year-old boy from the *Yaldei Teheran*. He is staying in a private home as he is broken and bereft from all that he has endured and is in need of motherly care. The woman who is caring for him has an exceptionally kind heart ... However, she has now come to me saying that ... it is hard for her to rear the child properly ... We therefore must bring him to Jerusalem ... It is vital that a compassionate woman come here and spend time with the child until he will consent to return with her, for he now clings to his foster-mother ...

Guardian of Orphans

THE CHAZON ISH was the catalyst behind the founding of two Bnei Brak institutions established primarily for girls orphaned during the Holocaust. When the *Beis Sarah Schneirer* orphanage was conceived of by a group of activists, they immediately turned to the Chazon Ish for guidance and a letter of support. He wrote:

---

* It was signed by the Brisker *Rav*, the Gerrer *Rebbe*, the Ponovezher *Rav*, Rabbi Isser Zalman Meltzer, Rabbi Zalman Sorotzkin, and Rabbi Akiva Sofer.

It has come to my attention that a group has aroused itself toward establishing a faithful home for the rescue of religious girls who have escaped to our land. Until now, these girls have wandered aimlessly in our country after having suffered in ways that one's heart finds difficult to imagine. What a pity that so much time has elapsed before this project was finally undertaken! Praiseworthy are those who lend a hand in building a home for these precious and noble girls, so that they, the splendor of our nation, can lead a life faithful to Torah and *mitzvos*, thereby uplifting their broken hearts ... (*Igros*, II:§48).

The Chazon Ish participated in the dedication ceremony for *Beis Sarah Schneirer*. His interest in each girl's welfare was manifest up to and including her becoming a bride. Some one hundred orphan girls were married with the help of funds that he provided.

The post-war years saw stepped-up activity on the part of Christian missionaries, who found the war-orphans prime candidates for their evil designs. At *Magen HaYeled* in Bnei Brak, scores of girls found a warm place of refuge from those who sought to tear them away from Judaism forever.

To the Chazon Ish, who was consulted by the organization's directors on a daily basis, there could be no turning away any girl in need of *Magen HaYeled's* help. Once, when an administrator tried to explain why circumstances would not allow for a certain girl to be accepted into the institution, the Chazon Ish replied, "Well, then, you might as well cast her into the stormy sea straight away!"

Indeed, it was his sensitivity to the needs of these girls that led to the organization's name. Some among *Magen HaYeled's* founders suggested that it be called "Institution for Those Rescued from Missions." A name so explicit might facilitate fund-raising and general communal support. It was the Chazon Ish's contention, however, that such a name would place an embarrassing stigma upon its enrollees, stamping them as girls who had once been associated with missions; hence the name *Magen HaYeled* ("Protector of the Child").

Sephardic Jewry

ONE YEAR AFTER the founding of the State of Israel, nearly all of Yemenite Jewry left their homes to settle in Israel. Virtually all of them came to *Eretz Yisrael* clinging fiercely to the traditions of their forefathers. As with the *Yaldei Teheran*, a way of life far different from what the

Yemenites were accustomed to was being planned for them by the secularists. The Chazon Ish, like countless other Torah Jews, was pained beyond words as his Yemenite brethren were shipped off to non-religious *kibbutzim* as soon as they arrived.

That these Jews were of Sephardic origin, whose religious practices and customs differed enormously from Jews of Ashkenazic descent, was totally irrelevant to the Chazon Ish. They were Jews and their *neshamos* had to be saved. Indicative of his attitude regarding this is his following comment: "Do you know why it came to be that so many *kollel* men today speak fluent *Ivrit*? No, it is not to facilitate conversing with their wives and children — it is so that they can teach Torah to their Sephardic brethren!"

As always, the Chazon Ish worked for the Yemenite cause tirelessly, but unassumingly. His efforts did not stop with seeing that they be returned to a religious environment. Thus, in *Igros Chazon Ish* (I:§65), we find: "There is a problem regarding ten Yemenite children who are enrolled at Yeshivah _____. It is our desire to bring them under the tutelage of Rabbi _____. A letter must be sent to him in this regard. The situation is urgent; if he is agreeable, he should telegraph us and we will have him brought here immediately. All avenues must be pursued, for their spiritual rescue is in no way assured under current conditions..."

It brought the Chazon Ish great joy, when, in the final year of his life, the *Ohr HaChaim* institute, an educational facility for Sephardic girls, was founded in Bnei Brak.

A Nation of Torah

BEFORE THE CHAZON ISH arrived on the scene, advanced Torah study in the new *yishuv* was in a sorry state. Life was exceedingly difficult and as new immigrants struggled to find a viable means of livelihood, they thought it inconceivable that their sons who were approaching manhood could spend their days and nights learning Torah. Thus, most teenage boys learned a trade and went to work upon completing their required years of schooling.

It was the Chazon Ish who was primarily responsible for spreading the idea that all boys must be granted the opportunity to grow in Torah and develop into *talmidei chachamim*. This, he insisted, was the key to the Torah community's future in *Eretz Yisrael*. As always, the Chazon Ish put theory into action as he guided the founding of a number of *yeshivos*, including those in Rechovot,

Kollel Chazon Ish

Chaderah, Ramat HaSharon (near Herzelia), Yehudeah, Zichron Yaakov and Kfar Saba, where boys could study into and beyond their high school years.

Even more remote from the minds of new *yishuv* settlers was the idea of their young men engaging in full-time Torah study after marriage. The founding in 1936 of what is today called *Kollel Chazon Ish* helped break new ground in this area as one of the first such institutions in the new *yishuv*. Upon the founding of the *kollel*, the Chazon Ish issued a public letter (*Igros*, I:§36):

> As is well known, the wisdom of Torah is unlike any other. While the latter [wisdoms] require study only for a set amount of time in one's younger years, Torah is only acquired by those who toil in it all their days. Once Torah has taken root in a young and understanding heart, it continues to flourish through youthful manhood, middle age, up to and including one's last years, shining forth with the joyous light of its wondrous wisdom. It is therefore imperative that young men of spirit be freed from the yoke of worldly responsibility, so that they can immerse themselves in Torah study even after they have families of their own ...

The letter goes on to cite the statement of *Rambam* (*Hilchos Shemittah V'Yovel* 13:13) that, like the *Kohanim* and *Levi'im* of old, any Jew of uplifted spirit can dedicate his life to the service of Hashem and remove from himself the yoke of worldly responsibility. "... He will then be sanctified as the holy of holies; Hashem will be his portion and lot for all eternity. He will merit having his needs met in this world, as did the *Kohanim* and *Levi'im*. As David *HaMelech* said, '*Hashem is my inheritance and my cup; You guide my fate*' (*Psalms* 16:5)."

After the Holocaust

THE RAVAGES OF WORLD WAR II reduced the great Torah communities of Eastern Europe to smoldering embers. Gone were the great citadels of Torah learning in Poland, Lithuania, Hungary and Slovakia. Of the thousands of yeshivah students studying in Eastern Europe at the war's outbreak, only a fraction survived. Many predicted that advanced Torah learning on the grand scale that had existed before 1939 would be no more. There were few *yeshivos gedolos* in *Eretz Yisrael*, fewer still in America and not many more scattered across Western Europe.

History has proven these predictions wrong. The scores of *yeshivos gedolos* that today thrive in *Eretz Yisrael*, America and elsewhere bear ample witness to the assurance ... *that she* [i.e., the Torah] *will not become forgotten from his children's mouths* (*Deuteronomy* 31:21).

The Chazon Ish found special cause for joy in the flourishing of advanced Torah study in *Eretz Yisrael* during the post-Holocaust years. He saw in this the Torah's arrival at a final destination in a long trek through exile that began in Babylon over two thousand years ago.

In 1949, Rabbi Shabsi Yogel, formerly a *Rosh Yeshivah* in Slonim, Poland, laid plans for the founding of the Slonimer Yeshivah in Ramat-Gan. When Rabbi Yogel's son-in-law, Rabbi Zvi Markowitz, prepared to leave for America on a fund-raising mission for the yeshivah, he took along a letter of recommendation from the Chazon Ish which expressed his feelings about the subject of the Torah's migration:

> In participating in the reestablishment of the Babylonian houses of study on holy soil, his honor has undertaken a task of monumental importance. For centuries now, the yeshivos of Babylon have wandered along a path that would eventually bring them back to the land from which they had been exiled. First, these yeshivos were destroyed in Babylon, only to be rebuilt in the foreign lands of Spain, France and Germany. Their names changed, but their souls did not. This Torah which

experienced ten wanderings* before finding a home in Babylon, and was subsequently exiled from Babylon to the lands of the West, is the very same Torah that is now returning from the desolate plains of the West to the Holy Land — the Land that was given our forefathers as an eternal inheritance and which was the Torah's original home after she was given at Sinai to infuse the Jewish people with her brilliant light ...

As one of the world's largest academies of advanced Torah learning, the Ponovezher Yeshivah symbolizes the Torah renaissance that took place in *Eretz Yisrael* after the Holocaust. As already mentioned, the hill upon which the yeshivah stands became the property of the Ponovezher *Rav* Rabbi Yosef Kahaneman in a transaction between himself and Reb Yaakov Halpern which took place in the presence of the Chazon Ish. How that transaction evolved is a story in itself:

The inspiration to reestablish his yeshivah came to the Ponovezher *Rav* at the height of

The Ponovezher Rav

the war as he lay in Jerusalem stricken with a serious throat ailment. Doctors had given him strict orders not to speak, but news of Nazi atrocities did not allow him to remain silent. The *Rav* forced himself into a sitting position and, in a voice that was faint but conveyed unflagging spiritual strength, said, "The Lithuanian farmer is indolent by nature. One would be amazed, however, to see how invigorated he becomes when harvest season arrives. Even more so, when at the height of harvest season storm clouds are sighted overhead, the thought of his crop being ruined sends a sudden burst of energy through the farmer's bones. One can hardly recognize the lazy farmer of yesterday!"

In a voice charged with emotion, the Ponovezher *Rav* continued, "I will begin immediately the task of reestablishing the Ponovezher

---

* See *Rosh Hashanah* 31a.

The Ponovezher Yeshivah

Yeshivah! In Bnei Brak! There is no time to waste — storm clouds hang overhead — we must act now!"*

Soon after his recovery, circumstances forced the Ponovezher *Rav* to travel out of *Eretz Yisrael* for a short period of time. Before leaving, he went to see the Chazon Ish, who was then recovering from the heart attack he had suffered while in Jerusalem (see chapter 5). In order that the Chazon Ish get sufficient rest, his family had moved him to the home of Reb Shlomo Kohen in Bnei Brak's Zichron Meir neighborhood. At the time of the Ponovezher *Rav*'s visit, Reb Shlomo, Reb Shmaryahu Karelitz and Reb Yaakov Halpern were with the Chazon Ish.

When the Ponovezher *Rav* rose to leave, those present escorted him out. Opposite Reb Shlomo's apartment stood a beautiful hill, owned by Reb Yaakov Halpern. The Ponovezher *Rav* looked at the hill and exclaimed, "What a magnificent site! What a perfect spot upon which to erect a yeshivah!"

Reb Yaakov Halpern named a very reasonable sum for which

---

* Recounted by Moshe Prager in the *Beis Yaakov* periodical.

the *Rav* could purchase the land. The Ponovezher *Rav* immediately accepted the offer. They shook hands and the deal was made — with one condition. Reb Yaakov stipulated that a yeshivah must be functioning on the hill within the year. The Ponovezher *Rav*, master Torah builder that he was, made good on this condition; within a year, a *beis midrash* had already been erected.

To start his yeshivah, the Ponovezher *Rav* went to a settlement near Bnei Brak where the *gaon* Rabbi Shmuel Rosovsky* taught a group of five *talmidim*. Rabbi Rosovsky consented to become the Ponovezher Yeshivah's *Rosh Yeshivah* and his five *talmidim* were its first students. The *rav* of the settlement was upset about Rabbi Rosovsky's departure and he came before the Chazon Ish to plead his case. After hearing the *rav's* position, the Chazon Ish said, "Four years ago we began a *kollel* here in Bnei Brak [i.e., *Kollel Avreichim*] in close proximity to the *kollel* in your own area. Has your *kollel* suffered because of this? No, it has not; you have *talmidim* and so do we. Creating new places of Torah study does not weaken the cause of Torah, it strengthens it. I assure you that your settlement will continue to flourish despite Rabbi Rosovsky's departure. And I assure you that the cause of Torah will only gain from the opening of the Ponovezher's *Rav's* yeshivah."

While he never had an official position at Ponovezh, the Chazon Ish was — in the words of Rabbi Kahaneman — the "soul of the yeshivah,"** for Rabbi Kahaneman adulated the Chazon Ish and regarded his every opinion as irrefutable Torah viewpoint. Rabbi Kahaneman once commented:

"In years past, when I resided in Europe, the Chofetz Chaim, of blessed memory, was my guide. He was my *Shulchan Aruch*. I consulted him in every important matter. From the day that I stepped foot in the Holy Land, I accepted in his stead the Chazon Ish."*** The Ponovezher *Rav* added that the Chazon Ish continued to be a source of guidance even after he had died, for before arriving at any decision, the *Rav* would first ponder what the Chazon Ish might have advised.

It was at the prodding of the Chazon Ish that Rabbi Isaac Sher

---

* A prime disciple of Rabbi Shimon Shkop in Grodno, Lithuania. He came to *Eretz Yisrael* after the outbreak of the Second World War.

** He also assisted in keeping the yeshivah afloat financially, underwriting loans to help rescue the institution in times of crisis.

*** The Ponovezher *Rav* arrived in *Eretz Yisrael* in 1940.

reestablished the Slabodka Yeshivah in Bnei Brak.* The Chazon Ish participated in the cornerstone laying of the Slabodka Yeshivah, delivering a *shiur* in honor of the event. As with Ponovezh, the Chazon Ish was deeply involved in the spiritual development of the Slabodka *talmidim*.

All in all, the Chazon Ish was involved in the founding of a majority of the Torah institutions established in the new *yishuv* during his lifetime. Small wonder, then, that when a philanthropist asked the Chazon Ish which yeshivah he considered to be "his," as the man wanted to present that institution with a generous contribution, the Chazon Ish replied, "All the *yeshivos* are 'mine.'"

Agudath Israel vs. Mizrachi

THE CHAZON ISH was a staunch supporter of the Agudath Israel movement, especially its Jerusalem chapter which espoused the ideals of Jerusalem's saintly *Rav*, Rabbi Yosef Chaim Sonnenfeld. He had high praise for the *chadarim* and *yeshivos* founded and run by the Agudah and frequently visited those in Bnei Brak to test the students' progress. On the other hand, he was a fierce opponent of the Mizrachi and discouraged teachers from having any part of their educational system. His feelings about the two movements were clearly defined well before his coming to *Eretz Yisrael*, as is evident from a conversation he once conducted with Reb Shlomo Kohen:

Among those who frequented the Chazon Ish's home in Vilna was a man whose *mitzvah* observance left something to be desired. Reb Shlomo once commented on this to the Chazon Ish, who replied, "We have not yet merited that all Jews be totally righteous. We dare not distance those who are still on an 'in-between' level." If so, countered Reb Shlomo, why the unforgiving condemnation of the Mizrachi? The Chazon Ish responded that the crucial issue here was whether or not mediocrity in religious observance was a desired end.

---

* Interestingly, an encounter between the Chazon Ish and the Ponovezher *Rav* finalized the determination of the Slabodka Yeshivah's location.

It was during breakfast one morning that Rabbi Kahaneman looked up to see the Chazon Ish coming to speak to him. The Ponovezher *Rav* immediately paused in his meal and rose to greet his guest and ask what had prompted the unusual visit. The Chazon Ish steadfastly refused to discuss anything until the *Rav* had finished his meal. "Otherwise I will leave," he insisted. Later, the Chazon Ish explained that Rabbi Sher was hesitant to open his yeshivah in Bnei Brak, for fear that he might be infringing on the Ponovezher Yeshivah's territory. Replied the Ponovezher *Rav*, "To the contrary — let all the *yeshivos* come to Bnei Brak and transform it into a fortress of Torah!"

"I knew that this would be the *Rav's* response," replied the Chazon Ish.

The typical "in-between" Jew appreciates the sublime ways of the *tzaddik* and he too yearns for the day when all Jews will be perfect *tzaddikim*. It is only that he personally has not yet mustered the spiritual strength to vanquish his evil inclination and sufficiently improve his own behavior. The Mizrachi, however, espouses this "half-way" status as a satisfactory level of observance. Its schools were established according to this philosophy.* The movement is uncomfortable with the true *tzaddik*, as it fails to recognize that he personifies spiritual perfection. The Chazon Ish concluded that the dangers of such beliefs are obvious.**

The secularists came to view the Agudah as their arch-nemesis in the ideological struggles that encompassed the *yishuv*. As a result, a group of Torah activists in Tel-Aviv gave thought to conducting their efforts under a new banner, one that might evoke a less hostile response from the secularists. When the question was posed to the Chazon Ish, his response was unequivocal: The hostility toward the Agudah was precisely the reason to align under its banner. Truth is often not popular among the masses, and an organization based on authentic Torah truth can often be the object of derision and attack. Agudath Israel's open and clear-cut representation of the Torah viewpoint insured that only those faithful to Torah would join its ranks. To form a group under some other name would be inviting membership by those who did not see eye-to-eye with the Agudah and would ultimately destroy the group's ideological fiber.

The Chazon Ish replied that it is better to have only 400 people who honestly and openly identify with the banner of Torah than to have ten times as many whose loyalty is fuzzy and weak. In the long run, he felt, uncommitted followers would weaken rather than strengthen the cause of Torah Judaism.

---

* See excerpt from an essay on this topic by the Chazon Ish in ch. 14.

** Settlers in a fledgling development presented the following question to the Chazon Ish: They wished to open a religious kindergarten, but were short the number of children needed to obtain government funding. Without such funding, the kindergarten would never materialize. The Mizrachi representation in the settlement had the identical problem. Together, the two groups had the required number of children. Was a joint venture with Mizrachi permissible? The Chazon Ish ruled that in this instance it was — on one condition. The walls of the classroom would have to be adorned with pictures of the Chofetz Chaim, Rabbi Yosef Chaim Sonnenfeld and other *tzaddikim*.

The Mizrachi rejected this condition and the plan fell through.

Tainted Activism

THE ACTIVITIES of a certain group of *kana'im* (zealots) evoked both praise and criticism from the Chazon Ish. In a letter, he wrote:

> ... There are some among them who act purely for the sake of Heaven. We have none like them; they are truly deserving of praise. Many are the breaches that have been mended because of them, and many are the fences that they have reinforced against any breach occurring! ...
>
> [Nevertheless] one must judge them in the way that he would judge himself, namely, that if one's actions presently accomplish much good while occasionally being counter-productive, they would accomplish so much more were one to immerse himself in Torah study and refine his character traits. Then, the negative traits of arrogance, anger, degradation of one's fellow man, and the need to triumph over others and to fulfill one's base passions and desires would all evaporate into nothingness. Recognition and appreciation of the Torah's statutes would take root, causing one to constantly ask himself: "Is what I am about to do truly Hashem's will...?"
>
> If now one's haughtiness causes him to think that he is the only one who truly knows and understands, and that the generation's guides are like blades of grass by comparison — how much more could be done were one to recognize his own inadequacies and heed the words of our leaders?

This last point was in reference to an incident where certain *kana'im* cast written and oral aspersions upon one of the generation's acknowledged *gaonim* and *tzaddikim*. In another letter, the Chazon Ish again referred to that incident:

> I am always pained when insults and aspersions are hurled, all the more so when they are directed toward a *talmid chacham*; and not only because of the intrinsic evil of such acts, but also because they do damage to our entire cause. As is well known, our primary weapons against the secularists are our *yeshivos* and *chadarim*. We need to draw the general populace near to us, so that their hearts will be swayed toward entrusting us with their children. It is imperative, then, that our community's behavior evoke positive feelings. Any sort of strife that is not mandated by the Torah is forbidden by the Torah. Lowly conduct is, G-d forbid, in the category of not speaking pleasantly to one's fellow man, of which *Chazal* speak so

disparagingly. We are witness to the damage that such behavior wreaks, as is described in *Yoma* 86a ...*"

The proper approach, as the Chazon Ish wrote in a letter, is that activism for spiritual causes must be conducted with the same careful planning that physical battle requires. Prudence and forethought are a must.

---

* There, the Talmud writes that if one truly loves Hashem, he will not be content to fulfill the commandments himself; rather, he will act in such a way as to inspire others to emulate him:

A Jew should study Scripture and Mishnah, and serve Torah scholars and deal graciously with his fellow creatures. Then, his fellow creatures will say of him, "Praiseworthy is his father who taught him Torah! Praiseworthy is his teacher who taught him Torah! Woe to those who do not study Torah! He who studies Torah — how pleasant is his behavior, how proper are his deeds! To him may the verse be applied: 'And He said to me: You are My servant Israel, in whom I will be glorified' (Isaiah 49:3)."

However, if one studies Scripture and Mishnah and serves Torah scholars, but is not honest in his dealings and does not converse pleasantly with people — what do people say of him? "Woe to he who studies Torah! Woe to his father who taught him Torah! Woe to his teacher who taught him Torah! He who studies Torah — how corrupt are his deeds, how ugly are his ways! To him may the verse be applied: 'In that men said of them: These are Hashem's people but they are departed from His land' (Ezekiel 36:20)."

CHAPTER SEVEN
Master of Halachah

"In every generation, there is particular Providential concern for the few who have been implanted to teach His laws and statutes to the Jewish Nation. When they immerse themselves in the halachah, they are at that moment like angels; a Heavenly spirit rests upon them. Through their word, the halachah is decided in stringent matters such as laws of marriage and divorce, Shabbos, and other areas. Occasionally, a powerful spirit bursts forth from their mouths, manifested in fiery words ... Those who are forever toiling in Torah and whose eyes are cast Heavenward for assistance in properly interpreting the Law — they are the angels produced by toil in Torah. It is their obligation to do as the Torah spirit within them dictates" (from a letter of the Chazon Ish).

WHILE THE WORKS of the Chazon Ish are replete with his halachic opinions, for the most part he refrained from rendering halachic rulings all his years in Europe.* Even after coming to *Eretz Yisrael*, he was not quick to involve himself in an area from which he had always shied away. In a letter to Rabbi Isser Zalman Meltzer, he wrote, "It is difficult for me to become involved in rendering *p'sak halachah* for the masses. I am accustomed to writing [*p'sak halachah*] only through the course of my learning." However, with the passage of time, his sense of responsibility caused him to accept an ever greater role in the area of *p'sak*, until he eventually

The Reluctant Expert

---

* With the exception of his term as *Rav* in Stuyepitz.

became recognized (following Reb Chaim Ozer's death) as the generation's supreme halachic authority.

The range of his rulings runs the gamut of Torah law and includes matters of life and death and thorny cases of *agunos*.* From a variety of responsa works written during his lifetime, it is obvious that his was the final word.

He ruled on questions involving modern-day technology clearly and incisively. When declaring a certain procedure forbidden, he sought to find his own alternative so that the problem could be circumvented. Such was also the case in questions involving modern medicine, an area in which he demonstrated a wondrous familiarity.

To rule authoritatively, one must know definitively when to apply logic, support from a Scriptural verse, or comparisons with other areas in the voluminous body of Oral Law. All this was as clear as day to the Chazon Ish. In fact, he composed a treatise of general rules for the deducing of *p'sak* in the area of *issur v'heter*.**

A renowned authority once expressed his doubts to the Chazon Ish as to whether the generation was truly prepared for *Mashiach's* arrival. Was there anyone proficient enough in the body of law dealing with the Temple and sacrificial services to rule decisively in those areas when the time came? The Chazon Ish replied that he believed himself qualified.

THERE WERE TIMES WHEN he publicized his rulings without being asked, so that the community would cease certain common practices that he held to be contrary to *halachah*. Whether in the laws of Shabbos, *eruvin*, *mikvaos*, separation of *terumos* and *ma'asros*, or halachic standards of weights and measurements, he never hesitated to enter the very thick of halachic debate.

The Chazon Ish's "Shiur"

Particularly insightful is a letter he wrote to Rabbi Avraham Chaim No'eh of Jerusalem, with whose halachic measurements he contended. "My heart tells me and compels me [to rule] that the measurement of an average *agodel* (thumb-width) is 2.5 cm. This is

---

* A responsum by the Chazon Ish in a case of an *agunah* appears in *Sh'eilos U'Teshuvos Heichal Yitzchak* (by Rabbi Isaac *HaLevi* Herzog, who had sought the Chazon Ish's opinion in the case).

** Literally, "forbidden and permitted" — a general term encompassing laws of *Kashrus*, forbidden relationships and other topics covered in the *Yoreh Deah* section of *Shulchan Aruch*.

beyond any doubt. One may rely on this true measurement when needed to permit a woman to remarry or to extract money in *beis din*."

In the world of Torah, the "Chazon Ish's *shiur* (measurement)" is synonymous with *mitzvah* performance in its most exacting form. The *succah, tallis kattan, kiddush* cup and other *mitzvah* artifacts are all of stringent measurement and/or composition when meeting the Chazon Ish's halachic requirements. As will become clear later, the Chazon Ish could be astonishingly lenient in *p'sak* when he felt the situation warranted it and the *halachah* allowed for it. However, his rulings generally leaned toward stringency, and over the years, many *b'nei Torah* have come to accept his stringencies in various areas. Some find a basis for his approach and its acceptance among the Torah community in a passage of *Sh'lah* (I:*Beis Chachmah*, pg. 36). There, the phenomenon of succeeding generations becoming spiritually weaker, yet accepting upon themselves an ever-increasing amount of *chumros* (stringencies), is discussed. According to *Sh'lah*, it is precisely the ever-increasing power of the forces of impurity in the world that demand a strengthening of *mitzvah* observance, so that there will be a proper measure of holiness to counter the impure. "The more the 'foulness of the serpent'* spreads, the more it becomes necessary to erect safeguards . . ."

Land-Related Laws

AS ALREADY MENTIONED, among the Chazon Ish's greatest accomplishments was his inculcating the generation with a practical awareness of the Land-related laws as he understood them. The subject of *mitzvos hat'luyos ba'Aretz* (Land-related commandments) had not been relevant during the centuries of exile when *Eretz Yisrael* was inhabited predominantly by gentiles. From the sixteenth century, when Jews first began returning to the Land, until the mid-1800's, the Jewish population in *Eretz Yisrael* was primarily concentrated in four or five cities with hardly a rural presence at all. Most crops were grown by non-Jews. Thus, involvement in Land-related laws was scarce. However, all this changed in the latter half of the nineteenth century, when various movements to settle and farm the Land emerged and the new *yishuv* began taking root. Knowledge of Land-related laws now became highly relevant, but

---

* A reference to the impurity which came to the world when Adam succumbed to the serpent's enticements and ate from the Tree of Knowledge.

Text of ritual for the separation of terumos and ma'asros as formulated by the Chazon Ish

unfortunately, the general populace remained ignorant of many laws while still other laws remained unclear. It was thus that the Chazon Ish took upon himself the arduous task of researching and clarifying the *halachah*, then publishing and publicizing his findings. The *Ritual in Separation of Terumos and Ma'asros*, a manual composed by the Chazon Ish, has been accepted since its composition as the authoritative guide for these *mitzvos*.

As with the laws of *terumos* and *ma'asros*, the Chazon Ish's works on the laws of *kilayim* (mixed seeds) and *orlah* (forbidden fruit of a tree during its first three years) are basic and all-encompassing. *Kilayim* is an especially complicated subject; to render definitive *p'sak halachah* in it required the diligent, exhaustive study and all-embracing knowledge of the Chazon Ish.

Shemittah Revival

A COMBINATION OF the Chazon Ish's halachic expertise, rising stature in *Eretz Yisrael's* Torah community, assertiveness when the situation warranted it, and practicality resulted in a revival of proper *Shemittah** observance in the Land. It was in advent of *Shemittah* 5698 (1938) that the Chazon Ish rose to the challenge of guiding religious farmers in correct observance of a *mitzvah* which until then had been either ignored or circumvented through questionable methods.

One-half century earlier, in advent of *Shemittah* 5649 (1888-89), the *Chovevei Zion*** movement had decided that ways would have to be found to circumvent *Shemittah* observance if a new *yishuv* based on agriculture was to be developed. Efforts were undertaken to prevent settlers from observing the *mitzvah*. Since it was assumed that the settlers would obey the rabbinic authorities, *rabbanim* were approached with exaggerated reports that there was danger to life if *Shemittah* observance were implemented. In private, however, secular Zionists admitted that there were other motives behind their clamorings. The secretary of *Chovevei Zion*, a secularist, wrote:

> Even if it were necessary to increase [financial support to the settlers] by a few thousand francs because of *Shemittah* observance, that would not have warranted shaking up the world. But, as one of the great *Maskilim* declared, "I look upon this matter from an entirely different point of view. I know the ways of the observant among us ... therefore, if settlers will observe this first *Shemittah* they will, thereby, provide arguments for approaches that are restrictive ... and then it will no longer be possible to relax the *Shemittah* laws. Therefore ... one must avoid, from the outset, giving encouragement to the restrictive ones and must prevent the observance of *Shemittah* altogether."***

Not surprisingly, then, Rabbi Yehoshua Leib Diskin, Rabbi Shmuel Salant and other leading Jerusalem *rabbanim* were adamant

---

* This *mitzvah* requires the Land to lie fallow during the seventh, Sabbatical year of the Torah's agricultural cycle and restricts commerce with the crops of that year.

** A Diaspora-based movement dedicated to strengthening the *yishuv* and promoting further emigration to *Eretz Yisrael*.

*** From *Derech La'avor Golim*, pp. 131-2.

in their efforts to maintain the sanctity of the *Shemittah*. The Torah authorities abroad could only judge the situation in accordance with reports from *Eretz Yisrael*. They deferred to the Rabbinate of Jerusalem, but nonetheless expressed their views in terms of what the *halachah* would permit under extreme circumstances. Most authorities* insisted that whatever the difficulties would be, the laws of *Shemittah* must be strictly observed. There were, however, four authorities** who permitted certain alleviations, *lest the fledgling settlement be totally destroyed, and conditional to the approval of Jerusalem's rabbanim*. They permitted selling the land to a non-Jew provided that the agricultural work, in general, would also be done by non-Jews. The poor among the settlers, who did not have the means to hire non-Jewish workers, might be permitted to do certain types of work — only those that are permitted by the Torah but rabbinically forbidden — but only according to the instructions of the rabbinical court of Jerusalem — *and only for this one Shemittah*.

This halachic dispensation, coupled with the crude economic pressure of settlement officials who threatened to withhold funds from the settlers, resulted in widespread non-compliance with the laws of *Shemittah* in 5649. Only a handful of farmers in Petach Tikvah observed the laws.

In subsequent *Shemittah* years the process continued whereby the land was "sold" to non-Jews. In a letter to Reb Chaim Ozer written on the eve of *Shemittah* 5698, the Chazon Ish described the current situation:

> The problem of the coming *Shemittah* seems to have already been "solved." The Chief Rabbinate has publicized its ruling that the fields can and will be sold. They whisper that even after the sale, it would not be permitted for Jews to engage in labor forbidden by the Torah, yet they know that circumstances prevent [farmers] from hiring non-Jews to perform such work.*** The sale, therefore, is worthless ...

---

* Among them were: Rabbi Naftali Zvi Yehudah Berlin (the *Netziv*), Rabbi Yosef Dov Soloveitchik (the *Beis HaLevi*), Rabbi David Friedman of Karlin, and Rabbi Gershon Henoch of Radzin.

** They were: Rabbi Yitzchak Elchanan Spector (Kovno), Rabbi Yehoshua Trunk (Kutna), Rabbi Shmuel Mohilaver, and Rabbi Shmuel Zanvil Klepfish.

*** Tensions between Arabs and Jews made it dangerous to hire Arabs.

Expression of Faith

ALMOST FROM THE TIME he arrived in the land four years before *Shemittah* 5698, the Chazon Ish was already engaged in his monumental efforts to restore this *mitzvah* to its original glory. He would often say that the renewal of *Shemittah* observance would certainly hasten the coming of *Mashiach* who, the sages relate, is likely to appear in a post-*Shemittah* year (*Sanhedrin* 97a). This tradition can have meaning only if *Shemittah* is properly observed.

He regarded the revival of *Shemittah* observance as particularly crucial for it would "serve as a powerful stimulus to observance of the entire Torah." Moreover, he recognized in the battle against *Shemittah* a denial of the eternal validity and relevance of Torah. In a letter to R' Yaakov Rosenheim, president of the World Agudah Organization, he wrote,

> I yearn with all my soul to wipe away the disgrace wrought by the endless search for leniencies in *Shemittah* observance. This attitude extinguishes those flashes of faith that exist in the hearts of those who have doubts regarding the eternity of Torah.
>
> Our situation today is no worse than that of the Hasmonean era, when poverty forced the Jews to substitute a wooden *menorah* for the golden one that had stood in the *Beis HaMikdash* — yet they entered into a covenant to observe the *Shemittah*. Today, we are not dependent on local food supplies for survival. The issue is one of finances for the farmers. There would be no difficulty at all in observing *Shemittah* were the various factions to approach the matter properly. For example, it could be decided that the year should be set aside for major construction work, or similar projects, and loans could be advanced toward this end ...

The very first volume of *Chazon Ish* to be published in *Eretz Yisrael* deals with the *Shemittah* laws. It appeared in 5697 (1937), the eve of *Shemittah*. In this work, which one of the generation's luminaries called "the *Pri Megadim** of *Hilchos Shemittah*," the Chazon Ish elucidates his firm opposition to the sale of land to non-Jews as a means of circumventing *Shemittah* requirements.** It

---

* An authoritative commentary to *Shulchan Aruch*, the comparison being that the Chazon Ish's work had accomplished for the laws of *Shemittah* what the *Pri Megadim* had accomplished for a lucid understanding of R' Yosef Karo's Code of Law.

** This opinion centered on the following: (1) The sanctity of the Land (upon which the *Shemittah* is predicated) is not compromised through sale of the land to a non-Jew. (2) Sale of property in *Eretz Yisrael* to a non-Jew is actually forbidden. Torah law invalidates forbidden

At a wedding in Eretz Yisrael. (l. to r.): Rabbi Shmuel Wosner, the Chazon Ish, Rabbi Zalman Yankelowitz, R' Yaakov Rosenheim

was his opinion that the sales were themselves void, that even were they to be of any halachic value they would accomplish nothing, and that consequentially, all *Shemittah* prohibitions, whether Scripturally or Rabbinically proscribed, remained binding.

THE CHAZON ISH was not one to rule prohibitively and leave the religious farmer in dire straits. He expended extraordinary effort in seeking to make *Shemittah* observance possible for those who were ready to follow his lead.

Help for the Farmers

In the winter of 5696 (1936), some two years prior to *Shemittah* 5698, the first Agudath Israel *kibbutzim* were founded. Knowing that the *Shemittah* year was not far off, the settlers of *Machaneh Yisrael* in the Jezreel Valley, *No'ar Ha'Agudati* in Kfar Saba, and *Chofetz Chaim* in Gederah turned to the Torah leadership in Jerusalem for guidance. The leadership, in turn, directed

---

acts performed by way of an agent. In this case, the Chief Rabbinate acted as the farmers' agent. The sales, therefore, were invalid. (3) The sales are based on legal fiction, for there is no real intent to relinquish ownership of the land. (In this, the Chazon Ish differentiated between such sales and the sale of *chametz* prior to *Pesach*.) (4) As already mentioned, even if the sales were valid, the problem of who would perform the Torah-proscribed labor still remained.

the request to Reb Chaim Ozer, the acknowledged *gadol hador* at that time. Reb Chaim Ozer, as was his practice in all Land-related issues, referred the question to the relatively unknown Chazon Ish.

The Chazon Ish began his response to Reb Chaim Ozer by delineating his firm case against the sale of land to non-Jews. He then urged the leader of world Jewry to awaken Jewish communities everywhere to offer their financial support to the religious settlers. "With even a modest contribution they will sanctify Hashem's name, by helping to demonstrate to all that it is possible to observe *Shemittah* in accordance with *halachah*. All this talk that its observance will cause endangerment to life comes only from a coldness of heart, a lack of Heavenly fear which is necessary for proper adherence to Torah and *mitzvos* . . ."

The letter went on to suggest possible projects for the farmers to engage in while their fields lay fallow.

That same year, Reb Chaim Ozer promulgated "The Issue of *Shemittah*" proclamation, in which he called on world Jewry to provide material assistance to *Shemittah* observers. In that proclamation, he wrote:

> I join those who have already preceded me in calling on our brethren in the Land and all of the Diaspora: Please take part, my dear brothers, in this great *mitzvah*, with all your strength and resources — each man according to Hashem's blessing upon him — for the sake of those who observe and uphold the *Shemittah*, so that the laws of *Shemittah* will not become forgotten from Israel. Also, assist in finding work for the *Shemittah* observers; this is an extremely significant matter, as the *gaon*, the *Netziv* . . . wrote in his *Kuntreis HaShemittah*, found in his work, *Meishiv Davar*. Among his words, which cleave with shafts of fire, pertaining to the Land's sanctity, he adduces convincingly the urgent need to provide permissible work [for the farmers] so that they not sit idle all year and, G-d forbid, come to the idleness that leads to confusion of the mind.
>
> Praiseworthy are those who assist — either through active involvement or financial support — those who vigilantly observe the Torah. This will be a great source of merit toward the building of the Land and toward the speedy consolation of Zion and Jerusalem . . .

Later, the Chazon Ish asked R' Yaakov Halpern to found the *Keren HaShemittah*, a fund to be amassed from contributions by the *Eretz Yisrael* Torah community. Thus, Reb Chaim Ozer and the

Chazon Ish worked together for the involvement of the Torah community worldwide to support *Shemittah* observers. Such support would go far in minimizing the trials of *Shemittah* for the faithful farmers on the three Agudah settlements.

IN WINTER OF 5697 (1937), as the *Shemittah* preparations were in full swing, the Chazon Ish was afflicted with a painful illness. For

Despite Affliction two months, he was seized with severe abdominal pains. Medications and a diet prescribed by a specialist in Tel-Aviv were of little help. Finally, it was discovered that he was suffering from an inflamed appendix and required immediate surgery.

News of the Chazon Ish's illness aroused grave concern not only in *Eretz Yisrael*, but also in Poland and Lithuania, where his name was becoming ever more prominent. The Vilna weekly, *Dos Vort*, ran a front-page article with an updated report of his condition. The surgery was successful, and reports of possible complications proved to be unfounded.

Despite his weakened and painful state, the Chazon Ish forged ahead in laying the groundwork for the observance of the upcoming *Shemittah*. He aroused farmers on the Agudah *kibbutzim* to make a firm commitment then, in the pre-*Shemittah* year, to faithfully observe the *Shemittah* laws. In *Behar*, where the *mitzvah* of *Shemittah* is detailed, the Torah states (*Leviticus* 25:20-21): *And if you will ask, "What will we eat during the seventh year? Behold, we have not sown, nor have we gathered in our harvest!" [Hashem responds]: "I will bestow My blessing in the sixth year, and it shall produce [enough] for three years..."** If the settlers wished to be the recipients of this assurance, then their unwavering commitment regarding *Shemittah* was needed well in advance of the seventh year.

THE CHAZON ISH'S CALL was heeded. Rabbi Moshe Shoenfeld, a young man in *Kibbutz No'ar Ha'Agudati*, went so far as to publish

Farmers of Faith an announcement in *Kol Yisrael* (Agudath Israel's Jerusalem-based newspaper) that his settlement would be observing *Shemittah* strictly, and that its farmers

---

* The years being the sixth, seventh, and eighth, since time was needed to plant, reap and harvest the crop of the eighth year. As *Rashi* (ibid.) writes, when *Shemittah* is followed by *Yovel* (Jubilee), when the *Shemittah* laws also apply, then the sixth-year blessing will provide a crop that will last for four years.

would be spending the Sabbatical year engaged in the full-time study of Torah.

"We have no intention," he wrote, "of making use of a lenient ruling approved by a few authorities, which others oppose, while still others tolerate it at best. Anyone whose heart throbs with love of Hashem and with a burning passion to give honor to the Torah; anyone who did not emigrate to the Holy Land merely to partake of its fruit, but to live a complete Torah life and to revive the observance of Land-related *mitzvos*, will find himself vexed and embarrassed by this sorrowful solution — or perhaps better said, by the total disregard of one of the basic tenets of Jewish life on holy soil."

Rabbi Shoenfeld concluded with an appeal for the Torah community to join in helping the farmers to observe the *Shemittah*. In this way, all would share in making the seventh year a time for spiritual renewal. *Shemittah* would be to the seven-year cycle what Shabbos is to the week.

At about the same time, Rabbi Moshe Auerbach, spiritual leader of *Kibbutz Chofetz Chaim* in Gederah, informed the Chazon Ish that his settlement was in severe straits and stood to suffer enormous losses were it not given significant outside assistance. Rabbi Auerbach ended his presentation by saying, "What will they eat?"

The Chazon Ish objected, "Does not the Torah ask this question and offer a response?" — a reference to the assurance cited above. Rabbi Auerbach replied that he had asked, "What will *they* eat?" and not, "What will *we* eat?" His question did not derive from lack of faith; he was sure that, inevitably, the settlement would survive the *Shemittah* year. However, he still had a responsibility to be concerned for his fellow settlers and leave no stone unturned in trying to ease their situation as much as possible.

The Chazon Ish smiled and replied that Rabbi Auerbach was correct. Indeed, he would continue to use his every bit of energy and resources in seeking ways to assist the farmers.*

---

* In his work on the *Shemittah* laws, the Chazon Ish writes that the Torah's assurance for abundant sixth-year crops is not an absolute guarantee against suffering extreme deprivation through *Shemittah* observance. The assurance can be rescinded due to sin. Also, it is a communal, not an individual, assurance. A deserving farmer might see his own crops suffer due to Heavenly judgment against his unworthy neighbors.

Ironically, there have been many incidents during the *Shemittah* years of the past half century where observant *kibbutzim* thrived while those which did not observe *Shemittah* suffered. In 1949, a new Agudah *kibbutz*, *Moshav Kommemius*, was founded. Since its founding, the settlement has been in the forefront of proper *Shemittah* observance. The following is from a letter by Rabbi Binyamin Mendelsohn, legendary *Rav* of *Moshav*

Speaking Out

WHEN, ON THE EVE OF *SHEMITTAH*, it became known that the Chazon Ish was waging war against the Rabbinate-sanctioned sale of land, a number of *rabbanim* visited his humble home and attempted to sway his opinion through halachic debate. Though as a rule he never would involve himself in such discussion, he now responded to every argument, so that his position would become better understood and reach an ever-widening circle of settlers.

It was also during this period that a delegation comprised of Chief Rabbinate followers sought the Chazon Ish's signature on a document protesting the proposed partition of Palestine between Jews and Arabs. The Chazon Ish refused, commenting, "They are concerned over half the Land being given away to the Arabs; yet they find nothing wrong with selling the entire Land to Arabs in order to circumvent the *Shemittah* . . ."

One *rav* put forth the suggestion that all farmland be deemed *hefker*, ownerless. By relinquishing their claims to the fields, he argued, the farmers would be permitted to till them. When this was told to the Chazon Ish, he retorted, "The Torah is not *hefker!*"

This outspoken approach, unusual for him, was taken only when the discussion involved practical observance; when issues were purely theoretical, he reverted to his usual reticent way.

A certain *rav* publicized his own opinion regarding a theoretical

---

Kommemius (cited in *The Jewish Observer*, Dec. '79):

In 5717, the Jewish Agency decided to plant orchards in a number of settlements — *Kommemius* included. We agreed, but with one condition: we would keep the laws of *Shemittah* in the *Kommemius* orchard, in accordance with my halachic decisions . . .

For the duration of 5719 [a *Shemittah* year], the orchards were kept in accordance with my guidelines, but the Orchards people insisted that I was endangering the trees because they were not being taken care of properly. Many times I wondered how it would work out, but I found strength in my faith in the *mitzvah* of keeping *Shemittah*, and in the merit of those *poskim* (halachic authorities) whose words guided me in my decisions, especially the merit of the *Rambam* whose stringent decisions I followed in many cases. For sure, G-d would stand by my side to see to it that His name would not be profaned through us.

At the end of 5719, the Supervisor of Orchards came and told me with great emotion that the twelve orchards under his jurisdiction were all worked as usual, except for the one in *Kommemius*, where his words were not followed. The end result was that the *Kommemius* orchard prospered far, far more than all the rest. He asked me to explain the matter to him.

I told him that the first *Ani Ma'amin* (of the *Rambam's* Thirteen Principles of Faith) is that only G-d was, is, and will be responsible for all that happens — and this includes orchards. Because we fulfilled His will in regard to this orchard, He guided our success with it . . . and this has been entered in the registry of the Government Department of Orchards: "The orchard in *Kommemius* was not worked on the entire year of *Shvi'is*, and it prospered."

Rabbi Binyamin Mendelsohn
25 Sivan 5723

aspect of *Shemittah*. It was learned that the Chazon Ish disagreed. The *rav* contacted the Chazon Ish with a suggestion that they debate the matter. The Chazon Ish responded with a letter, "I know well my own poverty in Torah. His honor need not concern himself with my opinion. What difference does it make as to how I hold . . .?"

A Dream Come True

WITH THE START OF *SHEMITTAH* 5698, THE Chazon Ish's dream became a reality. In the Agudah *kibbutzim*, no forbidden work was performed, and among the general Torah community, arrangements were made for distribution of produce that conformed with the restrictions on commerce with *Shemittah* produce.

To further inspire the *Shemittah* observers, in the spring of that year the Chazon Ish published an original piece entitled *HaMetzius* ("The Facts") [*Igros*, II:§69]. It vividly depicts the reflections of a farmer who passed the test of *Shemittah* observance:

> I am a farmer who works hard for his living. As the *Shemittah* year approached, I, as a scion of a stiff-necked people, entertained thoughts of stubbornly observing the *Shemittah* with all its halachic restrictions.
>
> I was bereft and alone, an object of my neighbors' scorn. "Is it possible?" they scoffed. "Behold, he has not sown, nor has he harvested his crops! One cannot wage war against reality!"
>
> However, my stubbornness stood by me. Though any level-headed person "knows" that *Shemittah* observance is impossible, and that the *mitzvah* of *Shemittah* is given only to those who have three years of produce stored in their silos, and that the later generations are not like the generations of old, nevertheless, I persisted.
>
> Now, a half-year has passed, and reality continues to express her love for me. I planted my crops during the sixth year, prior to the start of *Shemittah*. During the seventh year, I have rested, neither planting nor plowing. The crops which I planted in the sixth year and which grew during the seventh year are sanctified as *Shemittah* fruits and I treat them as such, eating them strictly in accordance with the applicable laws.
>
> It is my hope that I will continue to be at peace with reality, or better said, that reality will continue to be at peace with me, in the half-year that is still to come. My neighbors who scoffed at me planted during the seventh year. Reality unleashed its fury against them, destroying their crops with torrential rains.

I offer my apologies to those who permit selling the land for my having ignored their opinion. I would appreciate if they would be so good as to examine the issues once again. Perhaps they will come to the realization that our Torah is eternal, and that the observance of *Shemittah* is dependent solely on our will!

Extenuating Circumstances

KIBBUTZ MACHANEH YISRAEL, in the Jezreel Valley, was experiencing financial difficulties even before the *Shemittah* preparations had begun. As the *Shemittah* progressed the settlement's situation worsened and there was real fear that it might have to close down. When the settlement's leaders wrote to Reb Chaim Ozer, he directed them to the Chazon Ish, writing, "He is close to the situation, permitting him to see and understand all that is involved. I will be in touch with him . . ."

The Chazon Ish's anguish was apparent as two representatives described to him what they and their fellow settlers were enduring. Clearly he was a partner in their suffering. Nevertheless, he firmly refused to allow them to work the fields because of the crippling situation.

Someone suggested that proof for leniency in such a situation might be adduced from an incident in the Talmud (*Sanhedrin* 26). Rome, then in control of *Eretz Yisrael*, levied a tax on the Jews. Realizing that the community did not have the means to meet the government's demands, Rabbi Yanai announced that crops for the purpose of paying the tax could be grown during *Shemittah*. Was this not proof that extenuating circumstances would permit waiving of the *Shemittah* laws?

The Chazon Ish replied that, in fact, this incident proved the very opposite. The Jewish community in *Eretz Yisrael* at that time was pitifully poor, as evident from the fact that they had such difficulty in raising the sums levied against them. Nevertheless, poverty did not give Rabbi Yanai reason to relax the *Shemittah* laws in any way. The tax, however, was an altogether different matter. The Romans were vicious and unforgiving in their treatment of Jews. Failure to pay the tax could have resulted in death. When risk to life was involved, the *Shemittah*, like most other *mitzvos*, had to be waived.

The settlers accepted the Chazon Ish's decision faithfully. However, they returned to him with a new and more ominous problem. Certain laws in effect in Palestine at that time were carry-overs from the days of Ottoman rule. One such law permitted anyone to claim ownership of fallow land simply by sowing and plowing it. Moreover, the law forbade anyone from stopping those who sought to work such land. Now, Arabs were plotting to begin working the land on the *Machaneh Yisrael* settlement so that they could claim it for themselves. The only way this could be stopped was to have the *Machaneh Yisrael* settlers plow the land themselves.

Rabbi Moshe Shoenfeld, who had been chosen to bring the matter before the Chazon Ish, used the opportunity to put forth yet another problem. The settlement's fields were becoming overgrown with weeds. Should the situation become any worse, then planting during the eighth year would not be possible. This would surely cause some settlers to abandon the *kibbutz* and would almost certainly result in Arab takeover of the barren, overgrown land.

The Chazon Ish's face was flushed with emotion. The idea that plowing be permitted during *Shemittah* was no small matter. Here, the Chazon Ish revealed yet another aspect of his greatness as a Torah personality. With the same strength of character with which he forcefully opposed the Rabbinate-sanctioned sales of land to non-Jews, he now issued a *heter* (grant of permission) for *Kibbutz Machaneh Yisrael* to plow during *Shemittah* — under carefully defined conditions. Rabbi Shoenfeld requested that the *heter* and its accompanying conditions be given him in writing, so that the settlement would not be accused of violating *halachah* due to the pressures of the situation. The Chazon Ish's "permit" began:

(1) Fields bordering on lands owned by non-Jews who have already made attempts at encroachment, and where confrontations may result in danger to life, and where such problems could be avoided if the fields were plowed, and where the plowing will not facilitate the sowing of these fields in the eighth year — might well fall under the category of "duress due to government levies" [in the case of Rabbi Yanai; see above].

(2) Given that, unless the weeds will be uprooted, planting in the eighth year will not be possible, which may lead to the abandonment of the entire settlement and the land falling, G-d forbid, into the hands of non-Jews; and since the uprooting of weeds will not facilitate future planting, for the ground will have turned firm by the time planting season has arrived [it is, therefore, permissible to plow, provided that . . .]

The text continued by delineating exactly which method of plowing was to be used and to which depth it would be permitted.

AS SOON AS THE PLOWING began and news of it spread, some jumped to accuse the settlement of having desecrated the *Shemittah*. When Rabbi Shoenfeld encountered one of Jerusalem's foremost *poskim*, the latter demanded an explanation. Rabbi Shoenfeld replied simply that the settlement had acted upon the directives of the Chazon Ish. The *rav* then said, "I was hesitant to issue such a ruling, but the Chazon Ish is different. He has the 'broad shoulders' needed for such a *p'sak* ..."

A Time to be Lenient

The Chazon Ish would explain such rulings by saying, "Better to do like the *halachah* than to transgress the *halachah*." It is for this reason that he permitted certain leniencies (which, while halachically valid, would normally have been rejected) at a time when the *mitzvah* of *Shemittah* was being renewed and first taking root among the settlers of the new *yishuv*. In certain instances, he stated explicitly that a particular *heter* was to be relied upon only during that *Shemittah* year and no other.*

Ironically, some *rabbanim* who were not known for their stringencies in *p'sak* took the Chazon Ish to task for one of his lenient rulings regarding *Shemittah*. There was evidence that this public denunciation was inspired, at least somewhat, by a desire to prove the impossibility of true *Shemittah* observance in our time; that there was no alternative other than to "sell" the fields to non-Jews. Of this approach, the Chazon Ish remarked, "If they would subjugate completely all personal feelings before delving into the halachic aspects of the issue, they would most certainly arrive at a different conclusion."

He used the approach of these *rabbanim* to answer a question on the *viduy* confession text of Rav Nissim *Gaon*,** which reads, "I was lenient in that in which I should have been stringent, and I was stringent in that in which I should have been lenient." It is obvious

---

* From his constant desire to find ways to ease *Shemittah* observance, the Chazon Ish developed a deep and abiding interest in hydroponics. He instructed the Agudah *kibbutzim* to investigate the feasibility of hydroponics in a special laboratory for agricultural research in accordance with Torah. He also initiated the exploration of techniques whereby crops could be planted in the sixth year with their yield being permissively harvested in the sixth and seventh years.

** Recited on *Yom Kippur Kattan*, and by some on *Yom Kippur*.

that one should confess to having been overly lenient; but what is wrong with being overly stringent?

The current situation, said the Chazon Ish, vividly illustrates the need for such a confession. When a *rav* sanctions the sale of land to non-Jews as a way of circumventing *Shemittah*, and at the same time rejects halachically valid leniencies because in the depths of his heart there is a desire to show that proper *Shemittah* observance is a thing of the past — then, he must surely confess and beg atonement for having been lenient instead of stringent and stringent instead of lenient.

Every Fiber of His Being

IN THE *SHEMITTAH* YEARS that followed, the Chazon Ish continued to seek every means for spreading and facilitating observance of this *mitzvah*. During *Shemittah* of 5705 and 5712, it became extremely difficult to procure Arab and foreign-grown produce for consumption. The Chazon Ish conceived and implemented the idea of opening stores in every community that would market *Shemittah*-grown products in a halachically acceptable way. He detailed instructions for the way the stores would operate and wrote the text of a halachic document that was the basis for the stores' functioning within the parameters of the *Shemittah* laws.

The Chazon Ish continued to assume responsibility for the financial stability of the *Shemittah*-observing settlements. Uncharacteristically, he participated in a gathering held at the Ponovezher Yeshivah in 5705 (1945) for the benefit of *Shemittah*-observing farmers. The Ponovezher *Rav* implored the Chazon Ish to inspire the assemblage with an address. Unable to refuse, the Chazon Ish rose and, with deep emotion, uttered three words, כָּל עַצְמוֹתַי תֹּאמַרְנָה, *All my limbs will say* ["*Hashem, who is like You?*"] (*Psalms* 35:10). With every limb and organ, a Jew must sing Hashem's praises. By demonstrating their firm faith and trust that Hashem would not forsake them as their fields lay fallow, the settlers who observed the *Shemittah* surely would be singing Hashem's praises with every fiber of their being.

With the incredible wisdom, planning, direction and energy that he invested in this *mitzvah*, the Chazon Ish, too, sang the praises of his Creator with every fiber of his being.

From *Shemittah* 5698 and on, the settlers of the three Agudah *kibbutzim* would bring all important questions, whether communal or individual, halachic or otherwise, before the Chazon Ish. A deep bond had formed between the settlers and the Chazon Ish. Many of their halachic queries became the basis for some of the more famous rulings found in *sefer Chazon Ish* in topics that include the laws of Shabbos, *eruvin*, *terumos* and *ma'aseros* and *kilayim*.

Most of those rulings were related by the Chazon Ish to settlements' emissaries at his home in Bnei Brak. There were times, though, when the nature of the query made it necessary for the Chazon Ish to examine the facts first-hand. He always utilized such visits to the *kibbutzim* to offer encouragement to the settlers.

Without a doubt, the settlers' personal attachment to the Chazon Ish was a major factor in the acceptance and proliferation of *Shemittah* observance in *Eretz Yisrael*. The Chazon Ish also expended effort to inculcate the general community with an understanding of the *mitzvah*, and with time the Torah communities in the urban areas of *Eretz Yisrael* became infused with a deep-rooted love and appreciation for *Shemittah* observance. The arrival of the *Shemittah* year became the occasion for an uplifting spiritual undertaking for those who live with faith and trust in the Provider of our every need.

CHAPTER EIGHT
The Date-Line Controversy

DURING 1941, HUNDREDS of *b'nei Torah* from Poland and Lithuania miraculously escaped Nazi persecution by making their way from Russian-occupied Lithuania to Kobe, Japan. Later, this group was transferred to Shanghai, China, where they remained for the duration of the war.

Escape to Kobe

Even before these refugees had embarked on their journey from Lithuania, there had been much discussion as to when Shabbos would be observed if and when the group would reach Japan. The question centers around the determination of a date-line as the dividing line between the old and new day. According to international law, which places the date-line in the Pacific Ocean, 180 degrees east and west of Greenwich, England, Japan is six hours ahead of Jerusalem time. However, this is all the result of international agreement, not halachic decision. One could argue that the distance separating these two areas places Japan eighteen hours *behind* Jerusalem time. This would mean that Shabbos would be observed in Japan on Sunday of the secular calendar.*

The question was, of course, not new to the world of Torah scholarship. *Rishonim*, as is evident from a number of their works, grappled with it many centuries ago — but only in theoretical terms. It was not until the twentieth century that the issue became a practical one. During World War I, some one thousand Jewish refugees made their way to Japan. Rabbi Moshe Aharon Kisilav, a respected Lithuanian *rav*, had arrived in Harben (Manchuria) in 1910 and had since that time served as unofficial *rav* for all Jews of the Far

---

* That there must be a halachically accepted date-line is obvious. In the words of *Kuzari* (2:20), "One cannot escape the fact that there must be a point where east begins and west ends." Kobe, Japan, is in the Far East, some 100 degrees east of Jerusalem. However, the Earth's circumference actually allows for a long and short route between any two given lands. Is Kobe to be viewed as 100 degrees east of Jerusalem or should it be seen as 260 degrees west of Jerusalem? The answer to this depends on where the date-line is fixed.

East. He ruled that the day of Shabbos observance around the world and that of Japan was one and the same.

Divergent Views

BEFORE PARTING WITH HIS SONS as they prepared to head for Kobe, Rabbi Isser Yehudah Malin, a prominent *dayan* of Brisk, instructed them to observe Shabbos on the first day of the calendar week. This was based on a ruling that he had personally received from Brisk's previous *rav*, Rabbi Chaim Soloveitchik. Another Brisker *dayan*, Rabbi Simcha Zelig Riger, ruled likewise as is evident from a letter on the matter which he wrote to Reb Chaim's grandson, Rabbi Yosef Dov ("Reb Berel") Soloveitchik, when the latter was preparing to leave for Japan. This ruling was in accordance with the opinion of *Ba'al HaMaor* (*Rosh Hashanah*, ch. 1) and *Kuzari* (ch. 2) that the halachic date-line lies 90 degrees east of Jerusalem. Kobe is some 10 degrees east of the date-line, placing it a full day behind the area just west of the date-line and eighteen hours behind Jerusalem time.

The refugee community in Kobe became engulfed in turmoil as others expressed their opinions and confusion reigned. Rabbi Riger wrote a subsequent letter to Reb Berel which gave instructions for how those who wished to observe both days as Shabbos should conduct themselves.

The bulk of the Kobe refugees were students of the Mirrer Yeshivah. Their *Rosh Yeshivah*, Rabbi Eliezer Yehudah Finkel, had already made his way to *Eretz Yisrael*. The Kobe group was led by Rabbi Yechezkel ("Reb Chatzkel") Levenstein, then the Mirrer *Mashgiach*. Reb Chatzkel had for a time served as *mashgiach* at a yeshivah in Petach Tikvah before returning to Europe to join Mir following the death of Rabbi Yerucham Levovitz. From his days in Petach Tikvah, Reb Chatzkel was well acquainted with the Chazon Ish.*

He now telegraphed the date-line question to Rabbi Finkel in Tel-Aviv, who promptly conveyed the message to the Chazon Ish.

---

* Reb Chatzkel's veneration of the Chazon Ish is apparent from a variety of letters in *Ohr Yechezkel*, a collection of his writings and oral discourses. Among his letters we find, "In my estimation, had I put forth this idea to the Chazon Ish, he would have endorsed it." "I am virtually certain that had I asked the Chazon Ish his opinion, he would have said . . ."

Reb Chatzkel corresponded with the Chazon Ish regarding his decision to sail for America after the war. (He eventually returned to *Eretz Yisrael*.) At the close of one such letter he wrote, "I beseech his glorious honor to mention me in his *tefillos* . . . I appreciate his concern for my welfare . . ."

The Gerrer Rebbe   *Rabbi Yechiel Michel Toketzinsky*

Rabbi Shmaryahu Karelitz was present when the telegram from Reb Chatzkel was brought to the Chazon Ish. The Chazon Ish asked his nephew to open one of the two metal boxes in which his writings were stored and bring him a certain manuscript. Years earlier, in the course of his learning, the Chazon Ish had researched and analyzed the date-line issue in his typical fashion. Thus, he now had before him a thorough and all-encompassing discussion of the problem, concluding — as was the Chazon Ish's way — with the practical *halachah*. The Chazon Ish quickly reviewed his writings to be certain that he still concurred with his original train of thought. He did.

The Chazon Ish saw no room for doubt. To his mind, every *Rishon* who wrote on the subject concurred with *Ba'al HaMaor* and *Kuzari*. Shabbos in Kobe must be observed on Sunday. To observe two days of Shabbos was unnecessary and wrong, one reason being that this would mean not wearing *tefillin* on a weekday.*

Meanwhile, some students from Yeshivah Chachmei Lublin who were in Kobe sent the same question to their spiritual light, the Gerrer *Rebbe*, Rabbi Avraham Mordechai Alter,** who had been safely spirited away from Nazi-occupied Warsaw and was residing in Jerusalem. He presented the question to one of Jerusalem's great

---

* See *Igros*, 2:§162 and *Kuntrus Yud-Ches Sha'os* (found in *Chazon Ish* to *Zeraim*).

** A group of young Gerrer *Chassidim* once asked the Chazon Ish if he knew their *Rebbe*. He replied, "I am unfamiliar with his external appearance, but I *am* familiar with his inner presence!"

scholars and halachic authorities, Rabbi Yechiel Michel Toketzinsky. Rabbi Toketzinsky's ruling did not concur with that of the Chazon Ish. Basing his opinion on the writings of certain *Acharonim* who see the subject as one of debate among the *Rishonim*, he held the halachic date-line to be 180 degrees east and west of Jerusalem. Kobe was six hours ahead of Jerusalem, just as it was according to international agreement.*

That the Gerrer *Rebbe* did not refer the question to the Chazon Ish is not cause for wonder. While the Chazon Ish's efforts during *Shemittah* 5698 (1938) had earned him respect among the broad-based Torah community, most were unaware of his unparalleled command in all areas of Talmudic law — as they were unaware of the depths of his overall greatness. The laws relating to the date-line question are complex and obscure; few *gaonim* of that time considered themselves qualified to render *p'sak halachah* in the matter. Rabbi Toketzinsky, a descendant of Rabbi Shmuel Salant (who served as *Rav* of Jerusalem at the turn of the century), was the compiler of Jerusalem's yearly *luach* (halachic calendar); his expertise in calendrical *halachah* made him the obvious choice to decide the date-line issue.

In the preface to his *HaYomam B'Kadur Ha'Aretz*, Rabbi Toketzinsky wrote, "At the time that I responded to the query, at the request of the *admor* of Ger, I did not know or imagine that in *Eretz Yisrael* there existed a retiring *gaon*, who sat in a hidden corner immersed in the four ells of *halachah* — *halachah* that covered the entire range of Torah law — who was also versed in this particular topic. Had I known this, I would have discussed the matter with him before issuing my response. After I sent my response and was subsequently informed that the author of *Chazon Ish* had responded otherwise, I was very taken aback. An exchange of letters between us followed and as Yom Kippur approached, I visited him and debated the matter face-to-face..."

Reb Chatzkel Acts

THE CHAZON ISH'S RESPONSE arrived in Kobe on a Friday. Reb Chatzkel quickly assembled the Mirrer *talmidim* — many of whom still knew little of the Chazon Ish — and instructed them to observe the Shabbos not on the following day, but on Sunday. It was then

---

* By the following year, the problem no longer existed. The refugees had been transferred to Shanghai, on China's mainland. Shanghai is west of the date-line according to all opinions.

Rabbi Yechezkel Levenstein   The Amshinover Rebbe

that Reb Chatzkel related having heard the following from Reb Chaim Ozer: In every generation, a select few are deemed worthy of a special *siyata dishmaya* in guiding the generation through the rendering of *p'sak halachah*. Reb Chaim Ozer had said that the Chazon Ish was such a person. Reb Chatzkel added that with the death of Reb Chaim Ozer, the Chazon Ish was now the *posek hador*, and his decision had to be obeyed without question.

The next day, as Shabbos was being observed in communities around the world, Reb Chatzkel appeared at *Shacharis* adorned with his *tefillin*, as on any weekday. At the *tefillah's* conclusion, he spoke the praises of a generation that heeds the decisions of its leaders.

However, the *talmidim* of Yeshivah Chachmei Lublin followed the opinion of Rabbi Toketzinsky. A situation thus developed where some *bnei Torah* were engaging in all sorts of weekday activities while others were observing Shabbos in all its halachic stringencies. Many, including Rabbi Kisilov, the *Rav* in that region, voiced concern that the situation would lead to a weakening of Shabbos observance among the resident Far Eastern Jews.

Finally, a prominent Chassidic member of the Kobe refugee community intervened. Rabbi Shimon Kalish, the Amshinover *Rebbe*, was loved and respected by all factions. He prevailed upon everyone to abstain from all Torah-proscribed labor on both

Saturday and Sunday in the interest of general Shabbos observance.*

THE MATTER, HOWEVER, was far from closed. Yom Kippur was approaching, and observing a two-day fast was, for most, out of the question. Telegrams were sent from Kobe to the Chazon Ish, the Gerrer *Rebbe*, the Brisker *Rav* (Rabbi Yitzchak Zev Soloveitchik), and Chief Rabbi Isaac Herzog, requesting that the Torah leadership in *Eretz Yisrael* resolve the matter among themselves.

Yom Kippur Dilemma

As a result, a rabbinic conclave convened by the Chief Rabbinate met in Jerusalem to discuss the matter. However, the vast majority of leading authorities — including the Chazon Ish — did not attend, as they felt that the matter required expertise in a little-known area of *halachah* and was not subject to a majority vote or the like. This rabbinic assembly instructed the Kobe community to fast on Wednesday, when Yom Kippur would be observed around the world.

The Chazon Ish, of course, held that Yom Kippur in Kobe would be on Thursday. He was deeply pained by the rabbinic assembly's decision, as he saw no room for divergent opinions: his view was the unanimous view of the *Rishonim*. It was clear to the Chazon Ish that the apparent peculiarity in the halachic day of the week not coinciding with the internationally accepted day of the week was no small factor in his opinion's unpopularity. In a letter, he wrote, "Though this opinion may seem strange, we must admit that we are distant from being able to discern a proper outlook on the matter. We must not ascribe strangeness to the view of *Rishonim*, who were like Heavenly angels." Another letter reads (*Igros*, 2:§164), "The words of our Sages endure, even if they are difficult for us to comprehend. We are accustomed to 'bending our heads under the soles of their feet' (i.e., total submission). For every question there is an answer. Certainly, we must not veer from their opinion from mere concern that there *may* be a refutation to their view."

It was after the above-mentioned assembly that the Chazon Ish lamented, "*As der Tate shtarbt, tzubrikvin zich de kinder*" (When the father dies, the children squabble). The "father" he made reference to was Reb Chaim Ozer, whose death one year earlier had left a void that was yet to be filled; no one had yet emerged as the

---

* The Amshinover *Rebbe* would spend both days closeted in his room so that no one would know which day he personally held as Shabbos.

undisputed *posek* of the generation in the way that Reb Chaim Ozer had been recognized.

In the Fore, Once Again

AS WITH *SHEMITTAH*, the issue's magnitude now caused the Chazon Ish to abandon his usual approach. He discussed the date-line controversy openly and often, with many of the *talmidei chachamim* who visited his home. He wrote letters on the subject to, among others, the Brisker *Rav*, Rabbi Isser Zalman Meltzer, and his original opponent in the matter, Rabbi Toketzinsky.* In a letter to Reb Isser Zalman, he wrote, "It is difficult for me to become involved with deciding *halachah* for the masses, but the current situation leaves no room for silence."

At one point a "compromise" was suggested, whereby the Kobe community would fast on both Wednesday and Thursday, with the exception of the weak and infirm, who would eat on Thursday the amounts normally permitted on Yom Kippur when endangerment of life is involved.

The Chazon Ish rejected this proposal outright. One of his objections was that by fasting on Wednesday, the refugees would not fulfill the *mitzvah* of eating on *erev* Yom Kippur (*Orach Chaim* 604:1). They were, he insisted, to eat on Wednesday and fast on Thursday.

Aside from the halachic ramifications, the Chazon Ish feared that some who were not physically fit might endanger their health by attempting to fast two consecutive days. In a letter to the Brisker *Rav*, then in Jerusalem, he wrote:

> The situation of our brethren in Japan is extremely grave, due to the doubts concerning *Yom Kippur*. Some among the G-d-fearing are in a life-threatening predicament. Even those who decide that they cannot fast for 48 consecutive hours will still restrict their food intake on the second day, judging periodically whether or not they need to eat and drink.
>
> The responsibility for all this is on us, for we are the ones who have made the issue a matter of doubt. Personally, I have done all I can to resolve the situation, and I am certain that his honor, *shlita*, will do all he can to rescue them from dire straits.

---

* When Rabbi Toketzinsky published his work on the subject, *HaYomam B'Kadur Ha'aretz*, the Chazon Ish wrote a monograph, *Kuntreis Yud-Ches Sha'os*, in response. It was one of the very rare occasions that he took pen in hand to refute the writings of a contemporary.

> It seems to me that one can conduct himself according to our teachers, the *Rishonim*, who were like Heavenly angels and were the Divinely ordained emissaries in transmitting to us the Torah's laws. It is our opinion that according to all *Rishonim*, the calendar day begins at . . .

Crucial Cable

ON THE MORNING of *erev Yom Kippur*, after days of halachic give-and-take, both orally and in writing, with *rabbanim* throughout *Eretz Yisrael*, the Chazon Ish acted. With the Ponovezher *Rav* at his side, he dispatched an emissary to the Brisker *Rav* in Jerusalem, requesting that he and the *Rav* send a joint telegram to Kobe instructing the refugees to eat on Wednesday and fast on Thursday.

Earlier, the Brisker *Rav* had prepared his own telegram to Kobe (which in the end was not sent) in which he refrained from issuing an official *p'sak*, though adding that the Chazon Ish's opinion was that of (at least) seven *Rishonim* and could surely be relied upon. Now, however, the *Rav* would not go along with the Chazon Ish's suggestion. His reason was one for which both he and his father, Reb Chaim, were famous: fear of endangerment to life.* By the time the joint telegram would arrive in Kobe, the sun would quite possibly have set on Tuesday (i.e., *erev Yom Kippur* according to the Chazon Ish's opponents) in Japan. Many of the refugees would probably have begun fasting in observance of Wednesday as Yom Kippur. A telegram signed jointly by the Chazon Ish and the Brisker *Rav* would surely impel many who had planned to fast only on Wednesday to now complete that fast and also fast on Thursday, causing possible endangerment of life. Better not to send any instructions, reasoned the Brisker *Rav*, and let everyone make his own decision as to when to fast. The *Rav* told the emissary that the Brisker *dayan*, Rabbi Simcha Zelig Riger, had also instructed *b'nei Torah* to follow the opinion of *Ba'al HaMaor* and *Kuzari*, and he imagined that the majority of those in Kobe would follow this opinion.

When the emissary returned to Bnei Brak, he found that the Chazon Ish had himself anticipated the problem raised by the Brisker

---

* Both Reb Chaim and his son avoided rendering *p'sak halachah* whenever possible, except when endangerment to life was involved. In fact, it seemed ironic that a family so famous for its halachic stringencies should be more lenient than others in matters of life and death. To this, Reb Chaim once countered, "To the contrary, I am a *machmir* (one who is stringent) in *Vachai bahem!*" (*Vachai beham, And you shall live by them*, is the Torah's admonition that we even transgress a *mitzvah* [except for the three cardinal sins: murder, adultery, and idol worship] when necessary to save a life.)

The Brisker Rav

Rav. The Chazon Ish had therefore dispatched the following telegram to Kobe early that morning, "Dear Brothers: Eat on Wednesday and observe the fast of Yom Kippur on Thursday. Do not worry about a thing!" When the telegram was received, it was still Tuesday in Kobe.

With this *p'sak*, the Chazon Ish demonstrated his confidence in his own knowledge of Torah and the certainty with which he rendered *p'sak halachah*. Moreover, it proved definitively that his stringencies in other areas were not the result of doubts or undue zealousness, but the end product of incomparable fluency in Torah and rare awe of Hashem.

CHAPTER NINE
Wisdom and Approach

No pleasure in this world can equal that of diligent Torah study (Igros Chazon Ish, I:§8).

THOUGH INVOLVED ON MANY FRONTS for the sake of the Torah community, the Chazon Ish remained immersed in Torah study, utilizing the incredibly strenuous diligence for which he was known. He could invest hours of time and energy reviving the observance of *Shemittah* and still grasp pen in hand, committing his *chiddushei Torah* (Torah novellae) to writing. In fact, during *Shemittah* 5698, three new volumes of *Chazon Ish* were published, covering *Masechtos Demai, Ma'asros, Negaim* and *Parah*, with various addenda found at the end of each volume.

Endless Productivity

He told Reb Shlomo Kohen, "All my days, I never ceased to ponder thoughts of Torah, except in extenuating circumstances."

✤ ✤ ✤

The Chazon Ish once remarked that from the day he set foot in *Eretz Yisrael*, its holiness permeated his study, elevating it to even greater heights. For this reason, he relegated to a class of their own those volumes of *Chazon Ish* that were written in *Eretz Yisrael*. His quantitative productivity likewise increased. In all, twenty-three volumes of *Chazon Ish* were published, spanning the gamut of Talmudic law. As his many volumes became part of libraries and *battei midrash* throughout the yeshivah world, the Chazon Ish's reputation as a prince of Torah assumed new meaning.

The radiance of his sublime soul complemented his brilliance. One Shabbos, he discussed a particularly difficult Talmudic concept with his nephew, Rabbi Yehoshua Tanchum Karelitz. When their discussion ended, the Chazon Ish said, "Only on Shabbos, when endowed with a *neshamah yeseirah* (additional soul), can one ascertain the true sweetness of this insight."

Of Another Era

MOST OUTSTANDING about *sefer Chazon Ish* is its scope and the clarity with which every topic, even the most complex, is dealt. The great Torah minds of his day were unanimous in declaring that such breadth and depth in all areas of Torah ranked the Chazon Ish among the Torah geniuses of earlier generations.

No one else in his generation published works to such obscure *masechtos* such as *Keilim, Negaim, Ahalos,* and *Uktzin* that were no less comprehensive, penetrating, and all-embracing than his works to better-known tractates in *Sidrei Nashim* and *Nezikin.* Talmud Yerushalmi and the *Tosefta*, the former particularly in *Zeraim* and the latter particularly in *Taharos*, were also the subject of his exhaustive analyses.

He toiled to arrive at a definitive conclusion in every topic, including those not relevant to his time. There is virtually no halachic topic in all of *Shas* that is not dealt with in *sefer Chazon Ish*.

❧ ❧ ❧

Rabbi Shraga Feivel Steinberg once entered the Chazon Ish's study to find him recording his Torah thoughts. It took some time before the Chazon Ish noticed his disciple's presence. He then said, "The Oral Law has remained just that, though the Sages committed it to writing in Mishnaic and Talmudic times. Even after the completion of the Talmud by Ravina and Rav Ashi, much remained unwritten. In every generation, the *Ribono Shel Olam* 'sits' with Torah sages and together they continue to expound and record." The Chazon Ish seemed to have actually sensed Hashem's presence as he studied.

Every Jew is endowed with an ability to bring to light a portion of the unwritten law that is his alone to reveal. The Chazon Ish strove to reveal his portion in its entirety. Conversely, he would not venture into those areas of Torah in which he deemed himself unfit to expound. His fluency in *Tanach* was incredible, yet he never attempted a commentary to it. In this context, Rabbi Shmuel Wosner once heard him say, "A person's abilities are limited; it is beyond my ability to write such a work."

THOSE WHO WATCHED the Chazon Ish at study found his achievements in Torah little cause for wonder. His mental and physical exertions were, to quote Reb Shlomo Kohen, indescribable. No sound escaped him as he sat, enwrapped and enraptured, with every faculty focused on the matter at hand, to the exclusion of all else. Only on rare occasions, with every fiber strained to its limit, would he rise from his chair to pace the room as he hummed a tune, providing some relief to his inner tensions. Not infrequently, his frail body would collapse from exhaustion onto the iron-framed bed that stood in his room — but not to sleep! As his body relaxed, he recorded *chiddushim* which he had recently propounded, or with his head supported by one arm, he studied from a *sefer* that his free hand clutched.

The Pleasures of Wisdom

Rabbeinu Yonah in his commentary to *Avos* writes that when faced with a Torah topic that he is struggling to master, the dedicated Torah scholar will become distressed "until his heart goes out." Lest one be concerned that such distress may prove physically harmful, *Rabbeinu Yonah* assures us that, "distress in Torah study lengthens one's days, bringing him years of life and tranquility." The Chazon Ish epitomized this teaching.

In Torah study, he found the delight of delights, an experience beyond the comprehension of those who are immersed in earthly passions and whims. As R' Chaim ben Ittar says in *Ohr HaChaim*, "Were people to realize the sweetness and pleasure in Torah study, they would pursue it with a madness." The Chazon Ish often attempted to convey this feeling to others.

In a letter (*Igros*, I:§9), he writes:

> Sweet experiences can impart a sense of pleasure to a person's body and to all his limbs in a limited way; but this pleasure can never compete with the noble pleasures of toiling for wisdom, in which the soul of man is lifted above, where it absorbs pleasure from the glow of elevated wisdom.

IN A LETTER WRITTEN to Reb Shlomo Kohen when the latter was a youth, the Chazon Ish discussed the fundamental role of *ameilus*, diligent toil, in Torah study. It is inconceivable, he wrote, that the vast world of Torah knowledge should be the province of only those with superior intellect. "The Torah was not given only to

The Primary Component

ba'alei kishron (those with superior ability)." Rather, *ameilus* is the primary tool through which one's soul acquires Torah knowledge, is united with it and becomes sublimated through it. *Ameilus* breaks one's soul free of his evil inclination, causing it to spurn earthly desires and strive for the spiritual.

In another letter (*Igros*, I:§1), he writes:

> Diligent toil is the most desired ingredient [in study]; it is this which our Sages had in mind when speaking of the many sublime benefits of Torah study. It (i.e., diligent study) transforms the corporeal into the spiritual, the body into a soul. It permeates all the body's limbs and organs, purifying and refining them towards a pure Torah life ...

His Trademark

AMEILUS WAS THE TRADEMARK of his learning from early youth until death. His natural frailty would have deterred a lesser man from any overexertions. Of himself, the Chazon Ish wrote, "Because of my fragile condition and the physical afflictions which have accompanied me from my youth until this day, all my in-depth learning must be accomplished through perseverance over suffering."

Rabbi Mordechai Shulman, *Rosh Yeshivah* of the Slabodka Yeshivah, boarded with the Chazon Ish during his stay in Minsk (see chapter 3). He recalled, "I observed how he toiled in Torah study to the very limits of his strength, literally. At times, he would pace back and forth lost in thought, after many hours of studying by heart and in-depth. Suddenly, he would be overcome by weakness, to a degree where he could not move a single step. He would then ask for his cane. Leaning on it, he made his way to bed."

❁ ❁ ❁

The Chazon Ish wrote that it was not his habit to commit his *chiddushim* to writing without having thought the matter through to completion.

Someone once read to him a passage from *Aliyos Eliyahu* (on the *Gaon* of Vilna), which told of the *Gaon* having pondered a certain *mishnah* for as long as it would have taken him to review half of *Shas*. Upon hearing this, the Chazon Ish opened a volume of his own work to *Masechta Shevi'is (Shemittah)*, pointed to a particular passage and said that he had worked on that concept as long as it would have taken the *Gaon* to review half of *Shas*. He added, "And how long would it have taken the *Gaon* to review half of *Shas*? About two weeks."

Rabbi Shmuel Wosner heard the Chazon Ish say that he never published a *chiddush* without having first "sifted it through [his] thought process with thirteen sieves."*

His Work

THE STRUCTURE OF *sefer Chazon Ish* is not one that lends itself to easy perusal. As the Chazon Ish said many times, his work is written in the form of notes recorded for the author's personal use. The structure follows his mental association of texts and reasonings as he probed and analyzed the subject at hand.**

The language of the work is highly succinct. Every word is counted and laden with depth. Grasping the essence of a thought demands effort, but is within reach of the scholar who is prepared to knot his forehead in added concentration and refer to the pertinent source material. It is for such scholars that the work was intended.*** The Chazon Ish explained that the difficult style of his work often reflects the difficulty of the ideas and concepts expressed therein, ideas so deep that they are almost beyond the scope of the written word to convey.

His Approach to Torah Study

INVARIABLY, IT WAS the practical halachic application derived from theoretical discussion which the Chazon Ish relentlessly pursued. He strongly disapproved of those whose studies took a very different course, a "superficial analysis of the laws" with little or no intent to arrive at a correct halachic conclusion. The Chazon Ish was adamant in his conviction that Torah study which does not lead to knowledge of precise Torah law is not the study through which man fulfills his ultimate purpose in this world.

In *Pirkei Avos*, the *Mishnah* (4:6) makes clear that Torah study should ultimately lead to proper performance of *mitzvos*. *Rabbeinu Yonah* (*ibid.*) comments, "... in studying Torah, one's intent must be

---

* See *Mishnah Menachos* 6:7.

** After the Chazon Ish's death, the sons of Rabbi Shmuel Greineman published a new edition of their uncle's work. The twenty-three-volume series was reprinted in eight thick volumes, with the material roughly rearranged according to subject matter.

*** When necessary the Chazon Ish's literary style could be utterly simple. Thus, for the *bar-mitzvah drashah* of a nephew, he selected a thought from his writings on *Masechta Horios*, and distilled it into language that a thirteen-year-old could comprehend and relate.

Chapter 9: WISDOM AND APPROACH / 133

to theorize in order to arrive at the truth. He must be willing to toil for days, or even years, in order to attain a single elusive truth, so that he can conduct himself in accordance with it. This should be his primary goal."

The above summarizes well the Chazon's Ish's approach to Torah study.

Master of 'P'shat'

THE BASIC MEANING (*pashtus*) of the primary text(s) was always the center-point around which the Chazon Ish's *chiddushim* developed. Never would he embark on a halachic analysis without having first elucidated the give-and-take of all relevant Talmudic passages. As he strove to discern a *halachah*, clarify a concept, summarize the opinions of *Rishonim*, or compile his wondrous arrangements of halachic applications derived from his analyses,* he strove to clarify ever more the source's *p'shat*.

He would say, "*Hapashtus tamid ha'emes*, the simple meaning is always the true meaning." To the Chazon Ish's mind, the apparent meaning of a text needs no proofs from far-flung areas in *Shas* for support. That it is the simple *p'shat* is reason enough to accept an interpretation's legitimacy. However, given the Chazon Ish's stress on *ameilus*, one cannot claim to have arrived at the definitive *p'shat* without having undertaken a strenuous study of the text, straining one's mind to the utmost. To understand the *p'shat* was always his final goal on the road to determining a given *halachah*.

In contrast to the common concept of *chiddush* — a train of thought linked by successive questions and answers — the majority of the Chazon Ish's *chiddushim* focus on the core of the matter, casting new light on and penetrating deeper into the *p'shat* of a *mishnah*, Talmudic passage, opinion of *Rambam* or other *Rishon*.

Rabbi Meir Simchah of Dvinsk, author of *Ohr Same'ach*, is said to have remarked: "My range of knowledge is, I believe, equal to that of the [author of] *Ketzos HaChoshen*.** I, too, am fluent in the works of many *Rishonim*. The difference between us is that the *Rashba* with which I am familiar is not the same *Rashba* with which the *Ketzos* was familiar."

---

* As is found at the conclusion of each chapter of his work.

** Classic nineteenth-century work to *Choshen Mishpat* renowned for its penetrating Talmudic analysis.

Rabbi Aharon Kotler

The Chazon Ish's disciples applied this assessment of the *Ketzos* to their teacher, who through his amazing exertions uncovered concepts and interpretations in the Talmud and *Rishonim* which no one else had fathomed.

IN HIS EULOGY OF THE Chazon Ish,* Rabbi Aharon Kotler dwelled on the Chazon Ish's style of *chiddush*:

Reb Aharon's Assessment The Torah is called a "wellspring of flowing waters"; the "Song of the Well" (*Numbers* 21) is an allusion to the Torah [and those who toil in it]. Just as a wellspring constantly gushes forth with fresh waters, so it is with regard to the capacity for *chiddush* inherent in Torah, for all that any conscientious student of Torah will ever propound was already given to Moshe *Rabbeinu* at Sinai. One must plumb the well's depths in order to draw out the waters

---

* Published in *Mishnas Rabbi Aharon (Ma'amarim U'Sichos Mussar)*, volume III.

Chapter 9: WISDOM AND APPROACH / 135

that lie deep within it.

As each succeeding generation grows weaker [in Torah knowledge] than the one before it, it becomes necessary to clarify and explain through diligent study that which had previously been obvious. This is the meaning of *chiddushei Torah*. As Rabbi Chaim Volozhiner, of blessed memory, wrote (*Keser Rosh*, §56):

> When through one's study the matter becomes clearer and better perceived in his mind — that is called chiddushei Torah. "As long as one handles them [i.e., the Torah's words], he finds them enlightening [i.e., he forever gains additional clarity and insight]" (Eruvin 54b). The more one reviews, the clearer become those reasonings and interpretations that have been propounded. This is chiddushei Torah, regardless of whether he or someone else is ultimately the mechadesh [one who propounds], so long as the matter comes to light.

He [i.e., the Chazon Ish] enriched the generation with his Torah and *chiddushim*, for he merited to draw, reveal and propound in all areas of Torah, literally. His being was entirely sanctified for diligent toil in Torah, without any personal inclinations or obligations... Because of this he merited a place among the great princes and benefactors who bring to the surface the flowing waters of the Torah's wellspring, until those waters form a deluge, cascading to us all...

Chazal tell us that the Torah does not reveal the reward of each *mitzvah* so that we will involve ourselves with fulfilling all of them [rather than select only those of prime reward] (*Midrash Tanchuma, Parshas Eikev* §2). With regard to the Torah itself, it is certainly the will of *HaKadosh Baruch Hu* that we involve ourselves in its entirety, in its myriad branches and particulars. Now, there are many scholars who when propounding and authoring Torah works do so only in deep *sugyos* and topics which are particularly conducive for *chiddush* — while other subjects in Torah are not studied with ample depth. In those factual areas relevant to Torah and *mitzvah* observance, such as measurements and computations, they do not involve themselves at all. To our teacher, the *gaon* [Chazon Ish] of blessed memory, all areas of Torah were the same, for all his toil in Torah was simply to know it *l'amitah* (in its quintessential truth). He therefore was not drawn after the pleasure that is derived from [propounding] dazzling *chiddushim*. When toiling in any area of Torah, he plumbed the matter to the full extent of his capabilities.

❧ ❧ ❧

In the Chazon Ish's writings, we find a strong aversion to unbridled originality. In one piece, he demands, "What gives us the right to offer such an explanation, when there is entirely no need for it?" In another piece, he states, "By nature, I shy away from that which is innovative." Nevertheless, the Chazon Ish could be highly original — when he deemed it absolutely necessary. However, never would he contend with a halachic ruling of the *Rishonim*; in this regard he stated unequivocally, "We have nothing, save for the [opinions of the] *Rishonim*."

Recollections of a Study Partner

AS ALREADY MENTIONED (see chapter 4), the Chazon Ish and a youthful Shlomo Kohen studied together a few hours each day for twelve consecutive years. After the Chazon Ish's death, Reb Shlomo wrote of those delightful sessions:

The following was our system of study: We would learn a page of *gemara* with nothing more than the commentaries of *Rashi* and *Tosafos*. We examined every passage painstakingly, questioning and answering, refuting and resolving. Then, we would turn to other standard commentaries, and the works of many *Rishonim*. The Chazon Ish would say that

At a gathering in Eretz Yisrael. Reb Shlomo Kohen speaking; seated (l. to r.): Rabbi Binyamin Zilber, Rabbi Eliezer Menachem Shach, Rabbi Chaim Shmuelevitz

one who studies in depth should be able to propound on his own the questions and explanations of the basic commentators. To his mind, this was the optimal method of study.

Every day, I would review before him by heart the essence of the previous day's session. Upon completing a *perek* (chapter of a Talmudic tractate), I would recite the essence of the *perek's* subject matter, according to the order in which it appeared. I recall a time when he was overcome by exhaustion and was forced to lie down. We had only recently completed *Masechta Shabbos*, so he had me review before him the essence of the entire tractate while he rested. Understandably, there were a number of times when I was at a loss to continue. Each such time, he continued from where I had stopped, after which I went on. To my recollection, we did not have to open a *gemara* even once.

Whatever he propounded as we studied was noted in the margins of his *gemara*. Always we would examine *chiddushim* that he had recorded when studying the tractate previously. We studied these *chiddushim* solely in relation to the topic at hand. It happened many times that he was at a loss to understand fully that which he had written previously. He would declare himself unable to plumb the depths of his words, saying that they were not fully understandable to him. However, he would not amend them in any way, for he was certain that when they had been written, he had been more immersed in the topic than he was at the present.

Teaching How to Learn

RABBI AVRAHAM OF SOCHOCHOW, in his preface to *Eglei Tal*, writes that ever since the Oral Law was committed to writing, the primary focus in teaching Torah is the transmitting of a correct method of study to the next generation. The Chazon Ish believed likewise. To this end, he wrote scores of letters to *b'nei Torah* who sought his guidance in their studies.

In one letter he stresses the need for fluency in one's studies:

> One must be fluent in a *sugya's* (Talmudic topic's) sequence of questions and answers; in its original hypothesis as opposed to its conclusion; in the definitive *halachos* that can be derived from it, as opposed to those which require further analyses ...
>
> One should review a portion of *gemara* with *Rashi* and *Tosafos* many times, at the same study session, even without

propounding a single *chiddush*. He should pause to make note of items from which the mind initially derives no pleasure and even finds cumbersome. Such is the way of true *ameilus baTorah*, of which so many wonderful benefits are spoken. The result of such toil is the opening of one's intellect to new gateways of light in which the delight is limitless. One should abstain from devoting an abundance of time to propounding new reasonings. Rather, one should concentrate on delving into the *p'shat* and in clarifying the *sugya's* conclusion ...

In a letter to another *ben Torah* he writes that *chiddushei Torah* need not be *pilpulim*, and goes on to cite Reb Chaim Volozhiner's teaching that whatever becomes revealed through study is a *chiddush*. The Chazon Ish concludes, "The more one attains the attributes by which Torah is acquired, the more lucid does his knowledge of Torah become" (*Igros*, I:§4).

As the end result of his learning was the *halachah*, the Chazon Ish developed a fluency in such works as *Tur* with its *Beis Yosef* commentary, which show the derivation of practical law from the Talmudic discussion. In his younger years, he reviewed these works time and again and, as he would later relate to Rabbi Shmuel Wosner, many of his peers scoffed at this practice. "With such practices you will develop into a *melamed* (teacher of children), not a *lamdan* (erudite Torah scholar)!" they warned. The Chazon Ish, however, would not be dissuaded from his contention that *Tur* and *Beis Yosef* served as basic Talmudic commentaries.

Needless to say, he reviewed all the *masechtos* of *Shas* many times over, developing the flawless fluency which Reb Shlomo Kohen observed during their sessions in Vilna. The Chazon Ish, who could pore over a single *mishnah* for three consecutive months (see chapter four), had the ability to review an entire *masechta* in a single day!*

The Language of Chazal

"ONE'S INSTINCTIVE FEEL for the Talmud's methodology and idiom is fundamental to Torah study geared to deciphering the *halachah*." The Chazon Ish, writer of the above, mastered this foundation and strove to convey its essence to students of Torah. In fact, letters written to individuals concerning this point found their

---

* See the Steipler's appreciation of the Chazon Ish in chapter fifteen.

way into various volumes of *Chazon Ish*.

One such letter was written to the Ponovezher *Rosh Yeshivah*, Rabbi Eliezer Menachem Shach:

> One should not suggest *chiddushim* that do not lie in the *Gemara's* words. The transcribers of the Oral Law used the depths of their terminology and the wisdom of their style to convey their true intent to future generations ... it is inconceivable that a basic concept which deserves lengthy discussion should have no mention in the *Gemara*. Therefore, one who originates such *chiddushim* is in the category of a *talmid* who airs Torah concepts which he did not receive from his *rebbi** ...

In another letter to Rabbi Shach,** the Chazon Ish explains further:

> Just as the authors of the Talmud were meticulous in transcribing the laws and their theories, so too, were they meticulous in terminology and style, for the sake of future generations. Such is the way of wisdom. It is simply not possible that their words conceal a nuance that is inaccessible to us, and most certainly it is impossible that their language should mislead us. True, their words sometimes must be understood in a deeper, more subtle light. This is natural in the writings of the wise — but such interpretations should be clear to the careful reader. With regard to this sort of interpretation, care must be taken. If we will be excessive in reading allusions into their words, we will be left with nothing of substance.

So tenaciously did he hold to this creed, that he would reject *chiddushim* of renowned Torah personalities if he could find no basis for their thoughts in relevant passages of the Oral Laws. In a gloss to a famous work of a great contemporary, the Chazon Ish writes, "[If so,] why was this not explained in the *Gemara*? In similar instances, the *Gemara* offers lengthy explanations, as this is something which is impossible to deduce simply from examining the text."

His belief in the power of language to communicate its intent extended to the words of the *Rishonim*, about whose greatness he

---

*See *Berachos* 27b.

** Published in Rabbi Shach's *Avi Ezri* to *Hilchos Korbanos*.

wrote, "Even that which results from their own discretion is Torah truth, and is studied in the Heavenly Academy."

Consequently, he rejected the opinion of a certain correspondent, saying, "Were this to be true, its essence would be fluent in the mouths of all the *Rishonim*, elucidators of the *Mishnah*. Their first obligation would have been to clarify it and adduce proofs to it ... to my mind, their silence in this matter is the best refutation of all. Thus, we are to understand the passage according to the simple *p'shat*."

The Chazon Ish, who considered the *Vilna Gaon* "like one of the *Rishonim*," wrote of the *Gaon's* commentary to *Shulchan Aruch*:

> It is not his way to be ambivalent about the source from which the *Shulchan Aruch* drew the *halachah*; rather, he establishes the foundations upon which the *halachah* is predicated and always makes known his own opinion when it is at odds with that of the *Shulchan Aruch*. The *Gaon's* words are crystal clear and their power sears ... in conclusion, according to the *Gaon's* way, it is inconceivable for him to contend with the *Shulchan Aruch* while giving the impression that he is simply ascribing a source for the *Shulchan Aruch's* words. He would have revealed his opinion clearly.

When a piece in the *Gaon's* commentary to *Mishnah* ascribed to the Sages a dispute which is not apparent from the *Mishnah's* words, the Chazon Ish had this to say: "It is extremely difficult to believe that the *Gaon* actually wrote these words — not one other such comment is found anywhere in his commentary to *Mishnah*. [Nowhere does he say] that a halachic dispute is concealed within hints and allusions that are impossible to ascertain."

Other Advice

THE CHAZON ISH had other advice for aspiring scholars. "Development in knowledge of Torah is dependent on understanding opposing views and then weighing the merits of each opinion to determine which is more accurate," he wrote to a budding *talmid chacham*.

His own learning was guided by this principle. One of his letters begins with, "I give precedence to the opinion of someone else." Ten paragraphs follow, in which his correspondent's view is detailed and analyzed. He then continues, "However, another view is possible ..."

Of the need for *hasmadah* (diligent study for long uninterrupted intervals), he wrote, "Of paramount importance is to study regularly, without interruption... learning for a time and pausing for an equal amount of time amounts to very little, while in uninterrupted study lies the essence of holiness."

Everything in Torah

THE CHAZON ISH'S halachic writings reveal his expertise in the sciences and other areas of knowledge. In his monograph concerning the date-line (see previous chapter), the master astronomer and geographer is revealed. His writings on the laws of *kiddush hachodesh* (determining the new lunar month), with their accompanying charts, and his

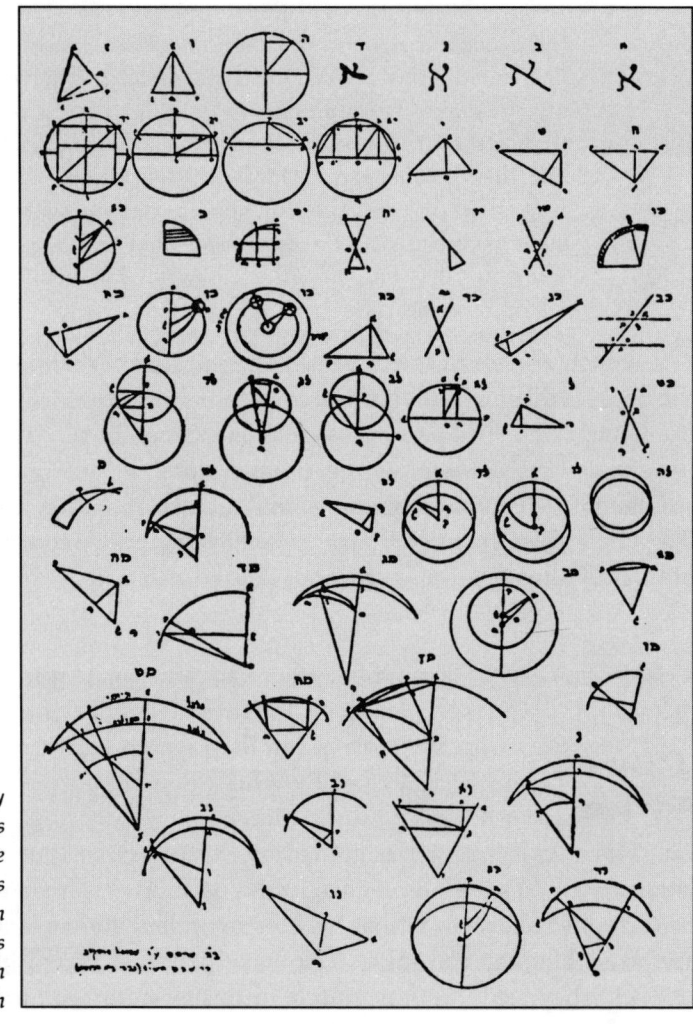

Explanatory diagrams to the Chazon Ish's chiddushim on hilchos kiddush hachodesh

discussions regarding *eruvin* demonstrate a thorough understanding of advanced mathematics.* In *hilchos kilayim* (forbidden mixings of seeds), we find complex geometrical calculations. In another section of his work, the Chazon Ish offers his own proof of the Pythagorean theorem (without citing that name).

A presentation of economic theory, relating to both ancient and modern times, is detailed in the Chazon Ish's discussions of *ribis* (interest). Currency trading and international monetary relationships are also examined. His discussions regarding the Second Temple era and of the transmission of Torah through the generations of *Tana'im* and *Amoraim* display a fluency in the fine points of our nation's history.

The Chazon Ish would stress that these wisdoms were known to *Chazal* not from secular sources, but by way of the Divine Spirit with which they were infused. He strongly condemned a certain work's contention that an astronomic theory stated in the Talmud was adopted from teachings of the ancient secular world. "... Such false assumptions are embraced by one's evil inclination, as in the way of idolatry. While the author is among the G-d-fearing, he erred in thinking it permissible to make such a statement."

In Conclusion

IN ATTEMPTING TO DESCRIBE the Chazon Ish's genius and his approach to Torah study, it is fitting to quote Rabbi Yechiel Yaakov Weinberg, author of *Seridei Eish*:

> The greatness of the *gaon* and *chasid*, the Chazon Ish, [was] his sound and clear logic, a power of analysis that was penetratingly deep, and a love of *p'shat*. He distanced himself from scintillating *pilpul* when it had no basis in the relevant text. Most of all, he sat in solitude for decades, studying all of *Shas*, *Rishonim* and *Poskim*, with consistent, in-depth examination until every law was clear to him. His great level of

---

* Toward the end of his life, the Chazon Ish devoted much of his time to the study of *hilchos kiddush hachodesh*. For two years, he immersed himself in various calculations and studies. At one point, urgent *klal* matters forced him to ask Reb Zelig Shapiro to compute certain figures related to his studies, as he could not find the time for it. Reb Zelig fulfilled his charge, returning to the Chazon Ish with a sum numbering in the millions. The Chazon Ish mulled over the figure for a few moments, declared it incorrect, and offered what he thought to be the total. He was correct.

Reb Isser Zalman Meltzer once remarked, "It was known that the second son of the Kossowa *Rav* was someone very special, but who would have dreamt that he would attain unparalleled heights? It is difficult to fathom even the simple meaning of the *Rambam's* laws to *kiddush hachodesh* and he has authored an amazing treatise to those laws!"

piety did not allow for him to dispute the opinions of the *Rishonim*. Rather, he labored to adduce proofs to their words. Never did such labor cause him to use crooked logic or distort the written word. The Torah of truth was forever on his lips. His approach to the works of the *Rishonim* flowed from his firm belief that *Ruach HaKodesh* rested on them ...

Without a doubt, he was the *gadol hador* in the area of *halachah*. His piety lent him an additional aura of holiness. From the days of the *Vilna Gaon* and on, there was none like him ...

CHAPTER TEN
Emunah and Bitachon

" 'And a tzaddik lives by his faith' [Habakuk 2:4]. Our master's strength and power was rooted in his pure faith. This man was weak and afflicted with serious illnesses and conditions — whence did he draw such powerful determination and decisiveness? From where did he acquire the broad shoulders needed to bear the burden of thousands of communal and personal matters, to involve himself with all sorts of dilemmas, as if the responsibility for the entire generation rested upon him alone? Not once did he seek to remove himself from a problem or ease his load; never did he ask, 'Is it I who has carried this nation; is it I who has given birth to them?' [Numbers 11:12].

"Without a doubt, it was his pure emunah (faith) that permitted him to attain what he did. It was this that uplifted him to his sublime level of service to Hashem. His Heavenly fear preceded his Torah and good deeds."

(Rabbi Shlomo Kohen)

IT WAS THE HEIGHT of World War I. The German war machine was rolling relentlessly onward and the Russian Army was in desperate need of reinforcements. The streets of Minsk were swarming with army officers who were stopping every able-bodied man in sight. Whoever could not produce proof of deferment was promptly hauled away for immediate induction.

Fearless

One man walked calmly through the streets, seemingly oblivious to what was transpiring around him. As the Chazon Ish related to his brother-in-law, the Steipler *Gaon*:

> I was walking from my home to the *beis midrash* ... the authorities were searching the streets [and I was not yet in possession of the necessary papers] ... I walked along without the least bit of fear. I turned to my right and saw swarms of officers conducting searches and identification checks ... I turned toward my left and saw more of the same. I was positive that no harm would come to me ... Soldiers were now on my every side — still, I walked without fear.
>
> Miraculously, they simply did not see me. No one so much as turned toward me.
>
> Earlier that day, I had been studying *Masechta Eruvin*. I had studied in great depth, to the limits of my abilities. It was therefore impossible, I assured myself, that on this day anything could happen ...

Emunah, faith in Hashem, was deeply ingrained in the Chazon Ish's soul from his earliest years. He wrote that already in his youth, he evaluated the circumstances of his life through the looking-glass of the thirteen principles of faith. "I believe that the Creator ... creates and guides all things ... is unique and there is no uniqueness like His ... is the first and the very last ... that all the words of the prophets are true ... that Moshe was the father of all prophets ... that this Torah will not be exchanged ... that the Creator knows all the deeds of human beings and their thoughts ... that He rewards all those who observe His commandments ... I believe with complete faith in the coming of *Mashiach* ... that there will be *techias hameisim* ..."

The Chazon Ish maintained that his constant awareness of these principles infused him with a boundless love of Torah.

A Revealing Work

DURING THE YEAR which followed the Chazon Ish's death, his brother-in-law, Rabbi Shmuel Greineman, published a slim, wondrous volume which the Chazon Ish had authored but, for reasons that he did not reveal, had refrained from publishing during his lifetime. Entitled *Chazon Ish: Emunah U'Vitachon* (*Chazon Ish: Faith and Trust**), it is a veritable gem in the literature of Torah thoughts and

---

* While this title appears on the work's cover, its title page makes clear that *emunah* and *bitachon* are only two of a number of subjects discussed therein. Other topics include: What is expected of man in his pursuit of spiritual perfection; the way to acquire proper *midos* (character traits); the relationship between Torah study and *midos*; and the way to exactness in *mitzvah* performance. (His writings in some of these areas are touched upon in chapter twelve.)

ethics. When reading it, one is left awestruck by the obviously exalted nature of the author. It may be this realization which impelled the Chazon Ish not to publish the work during his lifetime.*

With the publication of this work, a hitherto unknown side of the Chazon Ish was exposed. He became revealed as a classic expositor of Torah philosophy and ethics, whose subtle insights into the depth, breadth, beauty and spirituality of Torah were refreshingly new but at the same time absolutely essential for a true understanding of Judaism.

HOW DOES MAN COME to believe or, better still, feel and experience true faith? The first chapter of *Emunah U'Vitachon* is devoted to resolving this question. The Chazon Ish finds the answer in the words of *Iyov* (*Job* 19:26): *... from my own flesh do I behold Hashem*, and the prophet Yeshayahu who proclaimed: *Lift up your eyes on high and see who created all these!* (*Isaiah* 40:26). Man and the wonders of the world around him are prime vehicles for recognizing the Creator of it all. A refined soul such as the Chazon Ish, free of base desires and uninhibited by faulty character traits, has only to look around him to recognize this fact. As the Chazon Ish once told his disciple, Rabbi Avraham Yaakov Weiner, "Occasionally, a tiny flower may cause me to cease my activity. My soul exults at the wonders of Hashem's creations!"

The Miracles of Nature

In a piece that is more poetry than prose, the Chazon Ish enumerates the marvels of the human body, marvels which one tends to take for granted.**

> How wondrous is the makeup of man! The Architect knew that it would not be possible for man to be crowned with the crown that he bears under the sun, without his having a detailed awareness of the inanimate, plants and minerals that are found in this world. Without such knowledge, man could not survive.

---

* His collected letters, too, which Rabbi Greineman published in two slim volumes in the years 5715-5716 (1955-1956), [today they are published as a single volume] are a treasury of the Chazon Ish's outlooks and opinions. There are personal letters dealing with contemporary issues and correspondences with scores of individuals regarding their personal affairs. Many letters contain words of encouragement to yeshivah students who saw the Chazon Ish as their guide and mentor (see chapter fourteen). In all of them, written as they were in a private sphere, the sublime being of their author lies revealed.

** Unless indicated otherwise, quotations in this chapter are selections from *Emunah U'Vitachon*.

The Architect therefore created a device to which, with the intermediary of light, all that exists upon the face of the earth can appear according to their respective hues and colors. He endowed man with two of these devices, one on the left side of his face and one on the right. We are accustomed to calling this device "the eye."

How much wisdom there is in the human eye! ... In every succeeding generation, men of knowledge learn more of the treasures that lay hidden in the eye. Yet they have not probed its essence ...

... Among the pleasures of wisdom is the relationship between living creatures and the world's atmosphere, with its storehouse of oxygen and carbon. The lungs, with their seven compartments, are the intermediary between man and air. They have the ability to inhale oxygen in order to "water" the field and garden of the living, namely, his flesh and blood, bones and sinews. Indeed, the lungs have a very notable place among the legion which wages man's battle for life ...

... Also among the unfathomable, astounding one's heart, is the forming of man within his mother's womb, his residing there for nine months, enjoying an orderly, sweet existence, steadily growing and developing. When his time comes to leave, he breaks through the opening and exits. All this is arranged within the secret of creation, with forces that complement one another. The many wheels turn according to their respective assignments, each one manning its post and diligently performing its function with astounding speed, until they produce a living baby, new and sparkling — last in deed but first in thought* in the heart of the Creator of all creation.

When leaving the womb, his sustenance comes from the milk of his mother's bosom. Also, the Creator commanded that a wondrous drive within the mother's heart — we call it motherly love — impels her to care for her child without growing weary of her task ...

When a person's mind merits perceiving the truth of Hashem's existence, he is filled with an exhilaration that knows no bounds ... all earthly pleasures disappear and his noble soul becomes enwrapped in holiness, as if it had separated from his corporal self to soar in the upper Heavens.

As one becomes uplifted through such holy assessments, a whole new world becomes revealed before him, for it is possible

---

* Man, the crown of creation, was created last.

for a person in this world to experience moments when he is like an angel, and to bask in the splendor of His holiness. All the pleasures of this world are worthless in comparison with the pleasure derived from man's cleaving to his Creator, Blessed is He.

Everything a Miracle

THE CHAZON ISH once discussed the order of blessings in the weekday *Shemoneh Esrei*. What connection is there between the spiritual requests for wisdom, forgiveness and redemption and the comparatively mundane requests for health and prosperity?

He explained that a Jew's prayer for health and prosperity is a powerful expression of his *emunah*, for he is in effect stating that, while he seeks physical remedies for his ailments and he works to support his family, he still recognizes that it is Hashem Who is the true source of his every provision and the One through Whose benevolence he lives.

Someone once sought the Chazon Ish's counsel in a difficult matter. Expressing his reservations for success in his endeavor, the man borrowed a Talmudic expression, "*Lav bechal yoma esrachesh nisa*, miracles do not occur every day" (*Pesachim* 50a). Retorted the Chazon Ish: "*Lav! Bechol yoma esrachesh nisa*! No! Miracles occur every day!" To the Chazon Ish, the natural and the miraculous were one.

Defining Bitachon

A WOMAN LAY NEAR DEATH in Jerusalem. She had previously bought a plot of land in another city for burial. Would it be permissible to remove her body from the Holy City after death in order to bury her in the place of her desire? When the question was brought before the Chazon Ish, he was not quick to respond. He was quick, though, with a request of his own: "Please tell me her name and her mother's name." It was never too late to pray. *Bitachon*, trust in Hashem, did not allow for despair.

Where does *emunah* end and *bitachon* begin? The Chazon Ish writes:

> *Emunah* and *bitachon* are a single entity, except that *emunah* involves the general world view of a person while *bitachon* involves his perspective on himself. *Emunah* is theoretical, while *bitachon* is practical. It is simple to have *bitachon* when *bitachon*

is *not* truly demanded — but it is not easy to have *bitachon* when it *is* truly demanded!

Only through the following can one prove whether his heart and lips are in tandem with regard to *bitachon*, or if his tongue is merely trained to mouth, *"Bitachon, bitachon!"* while his heart has not acquired [this trait]:

When he meets a situation that demands *bitachon*, a situation where it is *bitachon* that must guide, restore and heal him, will he, at this difficult hour, turn toward *bitachon* and trust in Hashem? Or will he turn not to Hashem, but instead, to the arrogant and those who stray after falsehood,* to disdainful methods and worthless schemes?

Does *bitachon* require us to believe that, whatever the situation, everything will turn out as we desire it to be? The Chazon Ish explains:

> An age-old mistake resides in the hearts of many with regard to *bitachon* ... that when man is confronted by any situation and his future is uncertain — with two possible paths, one good and the other not, before him — then he is required to rest assured that it will be good. [They claim that] if he will be doubtful and plan for the opposite, then he is lacking in *bitachon*.
>
> This is incorrect, for unless the future has been clarified by prophecy, the future is not definite, for who can know Hashem's judgment or His deeds? Rather, *bitachon* involves the belief that there is no coincidence in the world and that every occurrence under the sun is by Hashem's proclamation.
>
> When confronted with an occurrence in which, according to the way of the world, danger lies ahead, it is natural to become frightened. Melancholy causes one to forget that occurrences have no mastery over us, for nothing can restrain Hashem from sending salvation and from setting in motion causes which will overturn the apparent conclusion. Forbearance in such difficult moments in instilling in oneself the known truth that no harmful occurrence is left to chance, for everything is from Hashem, whether good or the opposite; when the essence of one's *emunah* drives away all fear and gives one the strength to believe that rescue is a possibility — this is *bitachon*.

---

* An expression borrowed from *Psalms* 40:5: *Praises to the man who made Hashem his trust, and turned not to the arrogant and to strayers after falsehood.*

EMUNAH AND *BITACHON* are the gateways to a serene and happy life. In his correspondences, the Chazon Ish wrote of the effects which happiness has on a person. Joy, according to the Chazon Ish, is the conduit through which Heavenly wisdom flows. As for worry? "Worrying is the greatest sin of all." Of despair: "Do not turn to despair — the cruel destroyer."

Gateways to Serenity

A confidant was despondent over his apartment having been broken into and ransacked. Noticing the man's gloom, the Chazon Ish asked incredulously, "To be depressed over loss of money — is this the Torah's way? All is by Divine Providence; all is for the good."

Those close to the Chazon Ish bore witness that his own meager livelihood was never any cause for worry. He subsisted on the income from the sale of his *sefarim* and firmly refused the many gifts offered him by those whom he helped. He would even discourage individuals from purchasing his *sefarim* if he felt that the person would not make use of the *sefer*. "I want buyers who are *b'nei Torah*, not benefactors who seek roundabout ways [to support me]. This is not the proper way."

BITACHON DOES NOT PRECLUDE *hishtadlus*, effort on one's part to bring about a desired result. In most instances, *hishtadlus* is required, as one may not rely on miracles. However, *bitachon* does preclude those forms of *hishtadlus* that run counter to trust in Hashem.

The Role of Hishtadlus

The Chazon Ish illustrates this point with an explanation of the dream episode involving Yosef *HaTzaddik* (*Genesis* ch. 40).

Yosef, son of the Patriarch Yaakov, languished in an Egyptian prison after having been slandered by Potiphar's wife. Sharing the prison pit with him were Pharaoh's chief cupbearer and baker. Both dreamt dreams, which Yosef interpreted accurately. The cupbearer, Yosef said, would soon be returned to his post; and so it was. When interpreting his dream, Yosef asked the cupbearer to intercede on his behalf when he would gain release from prison. This did not happen. *And the chamberlain of the cupbearers did not remember Yosef, and he forgot him* (ibid., v. 23).

The *Midrash* tells us that for placing his trust in the cupbearer, Yosef was condemned to remain in prison for an additional two years. Paradoxically, the very same *Midrash* refers to Yosef as one who places his trust in Hashem: *"Praises to the man who* made Hashem his trust," this refers to Yosef, "and turned not to the arrogant" (Psalms 40:5) — because he said to the Chamberlain of the Cupbearers, "Remember me and mention me [to Pharaoh], two years were added to his [term in prison]' (Bereishis Rabbah 89:3).

Why was Yosef punished for his request to the cupbearer? Ostensibly, it seemed a logical and even required method of *hishtadlus*. The Chazon Ish explains:

> Yosef knew that his rescue was not dependent on *hishtadlus*, for all is from Hashem. Only, since a person is obligated to act and not to rely on miracles, Yosef obligated himself to utilize this opportunity and make his request of the cupbearer. However, since the arrogant by nature do not remember others to do them good, this act [of requesting the cupbearer's help] is only fit for one who has despaired, for such a person makes every possible effort, even that which is distant from achieving any results. The *bote'ach* (one possessing *bitachon*), though, does not do such things, and such efforts are not obligated. To the contrary, engaging in them is like throwing dust upon the radiance of one's *emunah* and *bitachon*. Once such an act is not deemed obligatory, it becomes forbidden.
>
> The intent of *Chazal* is [to criticize] the act [of requesting the cupbearer's help], not, Heaven forfend, Yosef's level of *bitachon*. Yosef knew that salvation was dependent on Hashem and not on any man. However, his obligating himself to request the cupbearer's help was, in the opinion of *Chazal*, an incorrect judgment. He should not have turned to the arrogant.

Thus, Yosef epitomized the classic *bote'ach*; however, he erred in this single instance.

Ends of the Spectrum

AT THE OTHER EXTREME, says the Chazon Ish, is the false *bote'ach*, one whose trust in Hashem is only skin deep. In such cases, the result is often *chilul Hashem*.

Reuven is a man of *mussar* and the song of *bitachon* is forever on his lips. He looks disdainfully at abundant *hishtadlus* and is repulsed by those who are in constant pursuit of income. Actually, Reuven is himself a successful man. His store is never lacking customers and he is not in need of much *hishtadlus*. He loves *bitachon*, for does not *bitachon* smile back at him?

Suddenly, we are amazed to see Reuven, the man of *bitachon*, whispering with his friends and men of counsel, over how to thwart the plans of his neighbor who intends to open a store like his own. Reuven is upset. While at first this remains concealed in his heart (for he is ashamed to reveal it, lest he be disgraced in the eyes of those who know him), eventually his shame is lost. He begins engaging in overt efforts to destroy his neighbor's plans ... in deeds that are lowly and shameful in the eyes of all. The dispute between him and his neighbor becomes widely known and is the topic of the day. He knows no shame and contrives all sorts of baseless explanations as justification for his behavior. He even thinks of original reasonings to show that his attack on his friend is actually for the sake of Heaven ... and convinces himself to believe so ...

When his shame is revealed and his despicable schemes against his neighbor become known, then people say, "He who studied ethical works of Torah — how disgraceful are his deeds, how disgusting are his schemes!"

Bitachon, then, must be an acquisition of the heart. It is the nature of the *bote'ach* to conceal his true worth and not to make known that he is among the *botchim*. In fact, he inwardly groans over the shortcomings of his *bitachon* and over his not having perfected this trait. In practice, though, *bitachon* accompanies him. He is not worried about his neighbor opening a store. On the contrary, he seeks to help his neighbor, to advise him well, to assist him, to diligently seek his benefit.

How much holiness is added to the world when a man performs kindness for someone who is destined to become his competitor! He brings praise to those who fear Hashem. Praiseworthy is he, praiseworthy is his generation.*

---

* In the third chapter of *Emunah U'Vitachon*, the Chazon Ish writes that one must always be certain that a given method of *hishtadlus* is halachically valid. For example, a tradesman is allowed to prevent a potential competitor from moving into his city and causing him a loss. This may seem contradictory to genuine *bitachon*, for, if all is in Hashem's hands and one's yearly earnings are decreed in Heaven on *Rosh Hashanah*, then what bearing could competition have on one's livelihood? Nevertheless, the *halachah* views the protection of the businessman from foreign competition as a legitimate expression of self-interest; invoking the Torah prohibition against threatening incursion (*Deuteronomy* 19:14) does not contradict true *bitachon*. However, there are cases where the *halachah* forbids such interference. For example, no action can be taken against a "foreign" *melamed* who wishes to teach Torah in a city, since competition enhances the quality of Torah education. *Bitachon* demands that the native *melamdim* place their trust in Hashem, the Sustainer of all creation, and not take action. If a *melamed* will, after experiencing a loss of income, lay the blame on the "intruder,"

Emunah and *bitachon* can be acquired at various levels. The Chazon Ish once told Reb Shlomo Kohen, "Some see Hashem's hand at work uncertainly, tentatively, as through a murky cloud; others experience His presence with astounding clarity, almost tangibly." In a letter, he writes, "Vast is the difference between those who know of Hashem's providence with absolute clarity and those who waver in that belief. More than being classified as different types of people, they are almost as from variant species; they share no common ground."

His Own Bitachon

THE PROVIDENCE WITH WHICH Hashem watches over an individual is commensurate with his level of *bitachon* (*Chazon Ish, Yoreh Deah* pg. 151). We can gain insight into the Chazon Ish's own level of *bitachon* from the following:

> There is something else relating to *bitachon*, namely, that upon a *bote'ach* rests a spirit of holiness, and a spirit of strength accompanies him which tells him that Hashem will come to his aid. As *David HaMelech* said, "*Though an army would besiege me, I would not fear, though war would rise against me, in this I trust...*" (Psalms 27:3). This is dependent upon the *bote'ach's* personal attributes and holiness.*

An insight into his practical application of *emunah* vis-a-vis *hishtadlus* can be gleaned from a letter written during the *Yaldei* (Children of) *Teheran* affair (see chapter six). The Chazon Ish was consulted with regard to which methods should be employed to gain custody of the children. His response included the following: "Just as with acquiring money and possessions, where *hishtadlus* is but an obligation and Heaven forfend that we think 'it is by the might and

---

then he will have fallen short of the standards expected of a true *bote'ach*: "To the G-d-fearing, it is axiomatic that no creature in the world can harm anyone in any way without Heaven having decreed that this occur." (The case of the *melamdim* is further discussed in chapter twelve.)

* Chassidic literature takes this a step further: One who trusts totally and unreservedly in Hashem's goodness will, in that merit alone, be subject to that goodness. As *David HaMelech* expressed it, "*My G-d, in You I trust, let me not be shamed*" (Psalms 25:2). Our Sages explained this verse with a parable: A stranger approached a city at night and slept outside the city walls. The sentries found him and began to beat him. "Stop!" he shouted, "I belong to the king's household!" They waited until morning and brought him before the king, who immediately declared that the man did not belong to the royal household. The man said, "It is true that I am not a member of your household, but I trusted in your kindness." The king said, "Let him be, for he trusted in me."

power of my hand,' so too is the rescue of a soul but a *mitzvah*. We must bear in mind that, ultimately, the power to effect rescue lies not with us. Yet through our deeds we arouse the Gates of Mercy so that our deeds will accomplish the desired end. One who prays and offers up bountiful entreaties for the sake of rescue accomplishes more than one who engages in *hishtadlus*.

"... in a situation where the possibility for rescue exists [and one stands by idly], he transgresses the prohibition *Do not stand by the blood of your brother* (*Leviticus* 19:16). One who sees a man drowning in a river, and has the ability to rescue him but chooses instead to pray for his rescue, is a murderer. However, if he cannot rescue him, but does not pray that he be rescued, then he is like one who refrains from rescuing [when the possibility exists] ..."

Infusing Others with Faith

IN HIS INVOLVEMENT with Holocaust survivors, the Chazon Ish did his best to mend their broken spirits and hearts, lending them spiritual strength by infusing them with his own unshakable faith.

Shortly after the war's end, the Chazon Ish was asked if one could assume that the Holocaust was the climax of the sufferings which *Chazal* speak of as a prelude to the arrival of *Mashiach*. He replied: A traveler can map out his journey before he embarks on it and mark off how far he has to go as his journey progresses. Such is *not* the case, however, with *Klal Yisrael's* journey through *galus*. Certainly, every travail brings the final redemption that much closer, but what still must transpire is not known to us.

To a broken Holocaust survivor who questioned the workings of Providence, the Chazon Ish had this to say: To an ignorant observer, a man cutting up a piece of beautiful fabric is a destroyer of good merchandise. However, if the cutter happens to be a tailor who is preparing to make a garment out of the fabric, then he is anything but a destroyer ...

In attempting to unravel the workings of the Master Craftsman, we are but ignorant observers. What we do know is that הַצּוּר תָּמִים פָּעֳלוֹ ..., *The Rock (Hashem)! — perfect is His work, for all His paths are just; a G-d of faith, without iniquity, righteous and fair is He* (*Deuteronomy* 32:4).

On another occasion, the Chazon Ish said, "For those with proper *emunah* there are no questions; for those without proper *emunah* there are no answers."

THE CHAZON ISH'S *EMUNAH* and *bitachon* found powerful expression in his *tefillah*. In a letter he writes, "In times when mishaps occur, I grasp firmly to the belief that nothing is left to chance; rather, all is from Hashem. I pray intently that the decree be rescinded ..." (*Igros*, II:§132).

Before Hashem

Rabbi Shmuel Wosner recalled, "Fluent on his lips was the strength of his *bitachon* and his faith that only through *tefillah* could any decree or travail be stopped. In such instances, he would usually say, 'Nu, HaKadosh Baruch Hu wants us to be *mispallel*.'"

"An exalted aspect of *tefillah* is the vivid picturing of how Hashem hears our lips' utterances and takes heed of our heart's meditations" (*Igros*, I:§23). Those who watched the Chazon Ish pray saw a living illustration of this concept. Rabbi Meir Greineman wrote, "He would recite every *berachah*, the *Sh'ma*, *Shemoneh Esrei*, and *Bircas HaMazon* with intense concentration and powerful *dveikus*, slowly and with eyes closed. He recited the *Sh'ma* with awe and trembling, word by word, each one clearly enunciated. Particular concentration was evident at the mention of the redemption from Egypt.* *Pesukei D'Zimra* was said in a sweet tone, with intense feeling. Praiseworthy are the eyes that saw all this!"

Of his *Shemoneh Esrei*, a confidant, Rabbi Baruch Karlenstein, wrote, "He would cling to a wall-pillar, grasping the pillar with his hands the entire time. Sometimes he would place only his fingers on it ... he would pray at great length, silently ... for approximately fifteen minutes."

In 1946, members of the Irgun attacked a British office in Ramat-Gan. A chase ensued, with the assailants heading in the direction of Bnei Brak.

Meanwhile, the daily *minyan* was gathering in the Chazon Ish's home. As the silent *Shemoneh Esrei* was being recited, the sounds of approaching gunfire were heard. The chase headed past the Chazon Ish's apartment and the stench of gunpowder filled the air. Sounds of

---

* It is a positive commandment to mention the Egyptian redemption every day and night.

battle mingled with screams of fright from the neighborhood residents. Everyone in the *minyan* was shaken — except for the Chazon Ish, whose hands calmly rested on his pillar as he continued *davening* with perfect serenity. As someone present put it, the Chazon Ish was in conversation with his Maker and nothing in the world could disturb his concentration.

His letters are replete with encouragement to others to strengthen their manner of *tefillah*. "How wondrous it is that a person has the ability to speak his concerns before the Master of the Universe, Blessed is His Name, as when one person speaks to another — and Hashem refers to the Jew as *a delightful child!** *Tefillah* in times of trouble, regarding which we are commanded, is an enduring help and remedy, gladdening one's heart and illuminating one's eyes" (*Igros*, II:§2).

"Every human being has the ability to attain through *tefillah* that which is good. Hashem craves, as it were, the *tefillos* of *tzaddikim*. *Tefillah* is a staff of strength in the hand of man ..." (I:§1).

"... any *nusach* (version) is acceptable, so long as it flows from the heart ..." (I:§20).

Over the years, the Chazon Ish granted thousands of requests that he pray for the sick. During the blessing of *Refaeinu*, he would mention the sick by name, and tears would flow freely as he beseeched the Heavens for the sake of his suffering brethren.

In one letter, he wrote, "Please inform me of your [Hebrew] name and that of your mother. If this is not possible, then [send me the name of] yourself, your father and his mother. If this too is not possible, then you will be included in [my prayers for] all of Israel."

Torah and Tefillah

REB SHLOMO KOHEN RECALLED, "As was his study of Torah, so was his prayer. His *tefillos* pierced the Heavens. The strength and intensity with which he prayed was superhuman."

Much of that strength and intensity was directed toward his life's primary purpose and delight: Torah study. Already in his youth, the Chazon Ish was shedding tears at those places in the daily *tefillah* where we ask to perceive the wonders of Torah. In a conversation with Rabbi Shraga Feivel Steinberg, the Chazon Ish compared the strain with which he

---

* *Jeremiah* 31:19.

prayed for success in his studies to the strain he exerted when studying the most complex areas in *Shas*.

Rabbi Avraham Yaakov Quint studied with the Chazon Ish and his elder brother, Reb Meir, when the three were in their mid-teens. They would study *Gemara* in depth for six hours at a time. Whenever their learning would reach an impasse, the three would go off to separate corners of the *beis midrash*, each with a *Tehillim* in hand. Submissively, they would implore Hashem to help them discover the truth which they sought. Then, they would return to their seats and forge on together until their eyes would be illuminated with Torah wisdom.

To the Chazon Ish, success in Torah was firmly dependent on one's efforts in *tefillah*. "Man's acquiring attributes of the soul is like his acquiring material wealth and possessions: one must beseech the One to Whom all wealth belongs.

"... All is in the hands of Heaven, including success in Torah study. The more a person places his trust in Hashem, the more he will ascend and achieve and be shielded from that which can impede Torah study at its very best."

The relationship between Torah and *tefillah* is double-edged.

"Torah study and *tefillah* are bound to one another: Toil in study brings to illuminating *tefillah*, while *tefillah* aids one in his learning. *Tefillah* without feeling distances one from true study, while indolent study impedes one's *tefillah*" (*Igros*, I:§2).

He would list the following *tefillos* as those most auspicious for success in Torah study: the morning blessing of the Torah in which we ask, *... sweeten the words of Torah in our mouths ... may we and our offspring ... know Your Torah ...*; the second blessing preceding the *Sh'ma*, in which it is said, *Our Father, merciful Father, Who acts mercifully, have mercy upon us, instill understanding in our hearts to understand and elucidate, to listen, learn, teach, safeguard, perform, and fulfill all the words of Your Torah's teachings with love. Enlighten our eyes in Your Torah ...*; the fourth blessing of the *Shemoneh Esrei*, in which we request wisdom, knowledge and insight; the *B'rich Sh'mei* prayer, recited when the Torah scroll is removed from the Ark on days of public Torah reading, in which one asks, *'May it be Your will that You open my heart to the Torah'*; and the beginning of *Uva L'Tzion*, where a verse which speaks of the Torah never departing from Israel is followed by a declaration of Hashem's supreme holiness. The Chazon Ish would instruct *b'nei Torah* to add their own personal supplications for success in Torah at the conclusion of *Shemoneh Esrei*.

A Parent's Prayer

THE CHAZON ISH ONCE told a man whose child was seriously ill that the prayers of parents on behalf of their children are particularly potent. It was thus that the Chazon Ish composed a prayer* to be recited by mothers, in which they ask that their sons be diligent and successful in their study of Torah and be infused with love and awe of Hashem:

יְהִי רָצוֹן מִלְפָנֶיךָ ה׳ אֱלֹקֵינוּ וֵאלֹקֵי אֲבוֹתֵינוּ, שֶׁתְּרַחֵם עַל־בְּנִי (שֵׁם הַבֵּן) בֶּן (שֵׁם הָאֵם) וְתַהֲפוֹךְ אֶת־לְבָבוֹ לְאַהֲבָה וּלְיִרְאָה שְׁמֶךָ וְלִשְׁקוֹד בְּתוֹרָתְךָ הַקְּדוֹשָׁה וְתָסִיר מִלְּפָנָיו כָּל־הַסִּבּוֹת הַמּוֹנְעוֹת אוֹתוֹ מִשְּׁקִידַת תּוֹרָתְךָ הַקְּדוֹשָׁה, וְתָכִין אֶת כָּל־הַסִּבּוֹת הַמְּבִיאוֹת לְתוֹרָתְךָ הַקְּדוֹשָׁה.

May it be Your will, Hashem our G-d, the G-d of our forefathers, that You have mercy on my son [son's Hebrew name] son of [mother's Hebrew name], and direct

---
* This prayer may be recited in the *Shemoneh Esrei* blessing of *Sh'ma Koleinu*, before the words ... כִּי אַתָּה שׁוֹמֵעַ תְּפִלַּת, or at the conclusion of *Shemoneh Esrei* at the close of אֱלֹקַי נְצֹר.

> his heart to love and fear Your Name, and to be diligent in the study of Your holy Torah. May You remove from before him all circumstances that can deter him from diligent studying of Your holy Torah and may You establish all the conditions that will bring him [closer] to Your holy Torah (Igros, I:§74).

One can only wonder what sort of *tefillos* and how many tears and good deeds *Rebbetzin* Rasha Leah Karelitz sent Heavenward to merit having a son like the Chazon Ish.

CHAPTER ELEVEN
Servant of Hashem

A Sublime Soul

AS LONG AS the Chazon Ish was alive, few people knew that his awesome greatness in Torah knowledge was equaled by his devoted service to Hashem. He served his Maker perfectly, with awe, love and joy, and in thought, word and deed. Here was a man enthralled by what his soul perceived as life's sweetest joy — "There is no bliss that is sweeter and more delightful than that which is earned by subjugating one's base instincts."

Both verbally and in writing he would make reference to the need for acquiring *kedushah* (holiness) and a *ruach taharah* (spirit of purity).

Upon leaving the home of the Brisker *Rav* on one of his infrequent visits to Jerusalem, the Chazon Ish exclaimed, "What *kedushah* permeates this dwelling!" When this remark was repeated to the Brisker *Rav*, he responded with self-deprecation, "*Kedushah, kedushah* ... it accompanied the Chazon Ish into the house."*

Laboring in Torah was to him the prime means for acquiring *kedushah*. "In diligent Torah study lies the secret of *kedushah* ... The more one toils in it, the more he unravels the bonds of his evil inclination. He becomes repulsed by earthly indulgences and his soul begins to crave sensations of *kedushah*, the delight of wisdom, the sweetness of purity ..."

---

* While they met on few occasions, the Chazon Ish and the Brisker *Rav* enjoyed a special relationship from a distance, corresponding numerous times. The Chazon Ish composed a soul-stirring poem in honor of the marriage of the *Rav's* illustrious son, Reb Yosef Dov (*Igros*, II:§94).

Following the War of Independence in 1948, an ailing Brisker *Rav* left Jerusalem for Bnei Brak for an extended stay. On *Simchas Torah*, as the Chazon Ish was being escorted home following *hakafos* at the Ponovezher Yeshivah, he suddenly exclaimed, "Let us go and bring joy to the *Rav* of Brisk!" His entourage followed as the Chazon Ish made his way to the *Rav's* lodging. Upon entering, the Chazon Ish broke out with a lively *nigun* and dance in front of the *Rav*. Amazed at the Chazon Ish's uncharacteristic liveliness, everyone else quickly followed suit.

In a letter to a Torah student, he writes, "Your words are infused with the *kedushah* that comes from immersing oneself in Torah study."

He ate little, slept little and denied himself what most would consider basic necessities. He steadfastly avoided anything that might have tainted the *kedushah* in which his sublime way of life had enveloped him. He was unusually careful in his manner of speech, using only the most refined way of expression. When, in his presence, someone said, "That's a lie!" the Chazon Ish said, "Please don't say 'lie'; better to say 'untruth.' "

His stress on sanctity found expression in unusual ways. As the Chazon Ish sat learning one night, he developed a terrible toothache. The pain made full concentration impossible, so he took pen in hand to record some *chiddushim* that had already been reviewed and perfected. When this became too difficult, he laid pen aside and meditated to whatever degree possible. Finally, the pain became unbearable; the Chazon Ish called for a neighbor to come and massage his gums with alcohol.

When the man arrived, the Chazon Ish directed him to a wash basin and asked that he wash *negel vasser* in his presence — four times alternately, in accordance with the opinion of the *Vilna Gaon*. (This opinion, while not the common one, was that followed by the Chazon Ish.) Only after the man had complied did the Chazon Ish allow him to massage his gums. After the treatment, the Chazon Ish explained his request with a story:

When Reb Eiz'l Charif* became engaged, his bride's father undertook to support the new couple for a number of years, so that his brilliant son-in-law could fully devote himself to the study of Torah. After some years had elapsed and Reb Eiz'l's wife had borne him a number of children, his father-in-law declared that his commitment had already been honored; the time had come for Reb Eiz'l to support his family. Reb Eiz'l, however, disagreed, insisting that his father-in-law was still obligated to provide for his material needs. The two decided to have their disagreement resolved by the local *rav*.

At the *din Torah*, the father-in-law delineated a number of points: the years of support already provided, the size of his daughter's family, his other financial obligations, etc. In conclusion, he offered one last argument: "At least if I would know with certainty that my

---

* *Rav* of Slonim, Poland, during the latter half of the nineteenth century.

son-in-law studies Torah *lishmah*, then perhaps..."

To this, Reb Eiz'l responded, "Whether I indeed study Torah *lishmah*, I cannot say. But I do know one thing: *it is my desire to study Torah lishmah...*"

The Chazon Ish's face reddened with emotion as he told his neighbor, "I, too, desire to study Torah *lishmah*; therefore I am extremely careful as to what enters my mouth."

His *sh'miras ha'einayim* — protection against his gaze beholding that which is contrary to sanctity — was also unusual. Rabbi Shmaryahu Karelitz relates that as young children in Vilna, he and a cousin would go for a walk every Shabbos with their uncle, the Chazon Ish (whose poor health necessitated such walks). Each week the same routine was repeated: the Chazon Ish would take each nephew by the hand and say, "Now, let us make believe that I cannot see. I will walk with my eyes closed and you will be my guides. Warn me each time we approach a street-corner." So they would walk, the Chazon Ish with his eyes shut and his young guides at his sides. Every so often, the Chazon Ish would stop abruptly to make certain that the children were doing their job properly. The boys would laugh, thinking it was all a game. It was years before they realized that this was the Chazon Ish's way of following doctor's orders without compromising the standards of *kedushah* by which he conducted himself.

The Chazon Ish was once shown a photograph of himself. He smiled and said, "Reb Meir!" — thinking that the face was that of his older brother, whose features somewhat resembled his own. Apparently, the Chazon Ish had never looked into a mirror and was unfamiliar with his own countenance.

He actually derived satisfaction from the physical afflictions and other travails which constantly plagued him. He viewed difficulties as "Heavenly emissaries" which strengthened the bond between man and Hashem and uplifted him to a level of existence that was permeated by a spiritual light and devoid of all physical wants.

IN HIS *EMUNAH U'VITACHON*, the Chazon Ish delineates the necessary requirements for one to be worthy of the title "*talmid chacham*." After discussing the minimum level of scholarship that a *talmid chacham* must possess, he writes, "The praises of the scholar cannot be sung if his wisdom is not preceded by fear of Hashem. The Torah's wisdom

Fear of Hashem

cannot come to rest in a heart that is closed ... To be truly wise in the knowledge of Torah, a synthesizing of intellectual analysis and dread of sin is necessary ... One who has not achieved wholesomeness in fear of Hashem will never achieve wholesomeness in knowledge of Torah, even if endowed with superlative mental abilities. The paths of his studies will be crooked and perverse; he will not arrive at the *halachic* truth."

Conversely, the study of Torah enhances one's *yiras shamayim* (Heavenly fear). Accordingly, the Chazon Ish explained why, in the blessing of the New Month, we ask twice for a life imbued with *yiras shamayim*. The second request is preceded by a request for a life filled with love of Torah. With love of Torah, one can achieve greater heights in fear of Heaven.

The Chazon Ish told Rabbi Moshe Yehoshua Landau of Jerusalem that when reading correspondence containing *chiddushei Torah*, he could, at times, easily discern the writer's level of *yiras shamayim*, though they had never met.*

"He would say that success in Torah study is dependent [primarily] on one's level of *yiras shamayim* and overall service to Hashem," related Rabbi Shlomo Kohen. "He said it was impossible for one to be a repository of *da'as Torah* (Torah opinion) without possessing an abundance of *yiras shamayim*."

Like from a Fire

IN PORTRAYING the Chazon Ish's dread of sin, Reb Shlomo related the following story: Reb Chaim Ozer and the Chazon Ish were once riding in a wagon on their way to inspect recent modifications in the city *mikveh*. Suddenly, the Chazon Ish jumped off the wagon — the possibility of the wagon's seats containing *sha'atnez* had come to mind, though to avoid sitting on a seat of *sha'atnez* is actually a *chumrah*.** He continued the rest of the way on foot.

It is no exaggeration to say that he dreaded sin as another would

---

* Someone once told the Chazon Ish that Rabbi Moshe Feinstein was blessed with an incredible memory, as evident by his reputation for amazing clarity in all areas of Torah. The Chazon Ish, who never met Reb Moshe, disagreed; he maintained that this was the result of Reb Moshe's ceaseless, fast-paced review of all areas of Torah. "*Ehr gedeinkt viel ehr hat es yetzt gelernt!*" ("He remembers because he has just now learned it!") Whether this assertion was based on the Chazon Ish's perusal of *Dibros Moshe* (the first volume of which was published in 1947), or from his hearing of Reb Moshe, is not known (related by Rabbi Shmaryahu Karelitz).

** *Kitzur Shulchan Aruch* 176:8 and *Aruch HaShulchan Yoreh Deah* 301:9.

fear physical danger — even when the sin was not his own. It happened once that a group of Israeli soldiers were engaging in target practice near his home on Shabbos. An officer knocked on the Chazon Ish's door to assure him that this was only a training session and that there was nothing to fear. Said the Chazon Ish, "I am more afraid of your desecration of Shabbos than I am of Arab grenades during the weekdays!"

He adhered strictly to the Talmudic ruling (cited in *Kitzur Shulchan Aruch* 3:8) that a man not pass between two women and that a woman not pass between two men. When a woman told him that she found it difficult to abide by this restriction, he replied with amazement, "Would you find it difficult to avoid a fire?"

A disciple related how the Chazon Ish educated him toward an approach to life founded on earnest *yiras shamayim*. The disciple once mentioned to the Chazon Ish that he had walked from Bnei Brak to Tel-Aviv on Shabbos in order to attend a *shiur*. Appearing shaken by these words, the Chazon Ish asked, "Since when is it permitted to walk beyond the *techum** on Shabbos?"

"I did not think that it was beyond the *techum*."

"Did you measure it?"

"No, but it's probably within the *techum*. Many other people walked as well."

The Chazon Ish was unrelenting. "In years past, when the area between the two cities was desolate, it was surely forbidden to undertake such a walk on Shabbos. The previous status should still be assumed without definitive proof to the contrary.

"After such an episode," he continued, "I am hesitant to pour wine in your presence . . . [as with a Shabbos desecrator]."

Only after being certain that his disciple had taken the reproof to heart did the Chazon Ish console the young man — with a glass of wine.

The Chazon Ish had high praise for *Beis HaLevi's* explanation of the commandment against coveting that which is someone else's (*Exodus* 20:14). How, one may ask, can we be expected to curb our desires for that which we naturally want? *Beis HaLevi* explains that when confronted with danger, all physical desires vanish. One should view sin as he would a fire or some other danger. Then, the

---

* A distance of 2000 *amos* beyond a city's limits. Generally speaking, one cannot walk from one city to another unless the area between the cities is populated.

Torah's command will of itself be sufficient to quash any wrongful want.*

Mitzvah Performance

THE CHAZON ISH'S own *yiras shamayim* was manifest in the exactness with which he performed every *mitzvah*, down to its finest stringency. The Ponovezher *Rav* saw in his *mitzvah* performance still another attribute: "We were literally astonished by his intense love of Hashem; we saw this great love in the way he fulfilled each *mitzvah*."

His *mitzvah* observance was of a kind that was rarely seen even in earlier generations. Throughout his life, no *halachah*, custom, or any other act deemed praiseworthy in any of the classical sources escaped him. Nothing was too insignificant to merit his attention and total commitment.

"With regard to his meticulous observance of *mitzvos*, there is much to relate," wrote Reb Shlomo Kohen. "He would concern himself with procuring the *arba'ah minim* well in advance of the Succos holiday. I recall when, back in Vilna, it became known to him during the summer that in some far-off town, a gentile had successfully grown *hadasim* — a rarity in that part of the world. He immediately journeyed there. After inspecting the *hadasim* and finding them *halachically* fit, he procured the rights to the branches in exchange for a handsome sum. His joy was boundless.

"He would not use Passover *matzos* from the bakery in Vilna, as certain aspects of the baking process did not meet his high standards. Instead, his *matzos* were baked in his own apartment. His relatives, among them men great in Torah, baked their *matzos* there as well. The oven was very small; only two or three *matzos* were baked at a time. The baking lasted for about four hours, ending after midnight. It left him drained and exhausted. Many days would pass before his full strength was renewed."

Among his letters is a request to Rabbi Moshe Ilvitzky to oversee

---

* *Ibn Ezra* explains the commandment's rationale with the parable of a peasant and a princess. Though the princess may possess every attribute imaginable, the peasant, if he is a sane man, will not feel any desire for her. He realizes that it is a woman of a similar background whom he must seek to marry; poverty and royalty simply do not mix. He may admire the princess for her qualities, but he will not covet her for his own.

This is how the *Ribono shel Olam* expects us to regard that which He has allotted to someone else, whether it his home, his money, or anything else. Since Divine Providence has allotted it to another, it is by definition undesirable to us.

As a sandak at a bris

the baking of his *matzos* (*Igros*, I:§185). The request was followed by nineteen instructions concerning virtually every aspect of the baking process. The Chazon Ish cautioned, "Do not economize with regard to the *matzos*; money is not an issue at all." This admonition came from a man who survived on the bare minimum.

A letter to the Brisker *Rav* discussed his efforts regarding the *mitzvah* of *tefillin*:

"I am happy to inform you that I succeeded in finding someone who is willing to let me process the skins for the *tefillin* straps according to our wishes. I myself placed the leather in the first solution and said, '*leshem retzuos shel tefillin*' . . ." The letter continues with a detailed description of the entire process (*Igros*, II:§134).

When being called to the Torah, the Chazon Ish had the unusual custom of removing his glasses, so that there should be no interposition between his eyes and the letters of the sacred scroll. This stringency was apparently based on spiritual sensitivity, not *halachah*.

When his eyes set their gaze on a *mezuzah*, the Chazon Ish

appeared to tremble slightly. He was undoubtedly then engaged in what the *Rambam* writes should be done by every Jew who enters a *mezuzah*-adorned doorway: "Whenever one enters and exits, he comes upon the unification of the Name of Hashem; he should then be mindful of his love [for Hashem], and awaken from the slumber and iniquities brought about by the futilities of life. He should be mindful that nothing remains forever, save for the knowledge of the Rock of the universe . . ." (*Hilchos Mezuzah* 6:13). Indeed, the Chazon Ish lived by what he learned.

HE EXPENDED GREAT EFFORT to bring about a proper appreciation for the sanctity of *Chol HaMoed*. Someone once came to

Imparting His Outlook

him on *Chol HaMoed* to repay a debt. The Chazon Ish told the man that he did not engage in monetary transactions on *Chol HaMoed*. The man replied in honesty that if he would be allowed to retain the money, he might feel forced to spend it and the loan might never be paid. Under the circumstances the Chazon Ish agreed to accept the money for safekeeping until after *Yom Tov* when it would be given to him again as payment.

Rabbi Tuvia Shechter of Bnei Brak once came to the Chazon Ish with the following dilemma: He wanted his factory to be closed during *Chol HaMoed*, but his workers were unwilling to forfeit their pay for those days. This seemed to constitute a *davar ha'avud*, an irretrievable monetary loss which would permit the factory's operation during the *Yom Tov's* intermediate days.

The Chazon Ish said that from a *halachic* standpoint, it was certainly permissible to keep the factory open. Nevertheless, he exhorted Rabbi Shechter to reach some sort of compromise with the workers and close the factory. To do so, especially under such circumstances, would constitute a *kiddush Hashem*. All would see and learn from one man's appreciation of a *mitzvah* that was too often ignored. The gain would surely offset the financial loss.

HIS UNQUESTIONING SUBMISSION to the teachings of *Chazal* was legendary. His sister, Rebbetzin Miriam Kanievsky, attended to

Total Submission

his needs in his later years and related the following to her son, Rabbi Chaim Kanievsky of Bnei Brak:

The Chazon Ish would not wear freshly laundered clothing until eight days had passed following their being washed (unless there was no alternative) — though the reason for this Talmudic dictum, as understood by *Rashi* (*Pesachim* 112b), is not applicable in modern times. In a similar vein, he would never drink any liquid that had stood uncovered (and unwatched) for any length of time. Even when a pot of liquid was placed on a stove to cook, he would insist that it be covered until it began to boil. In Talmudic times, there was a real danger of snakes depositing venom in uncovered liquids, but already in the times of the *Rishonim* this fear was virtually non-existent and they permitted one to be lenient in this regard. The Chazon Ish, however, conducted himself in such matters according to the *Vilna Gaon*, who held that "with regard to all that *Chazal* forbade, or any ordinance which they established, even when the apparent reasoning is not applicable, the prohibition or ordinance remains intact. For they revealed only one of many, many reasons for what they saw fit to decree" (*Ma'aseh Rav*, ch. 97).

His confidants once considered it imperative that for the sake of an important *Klal* matter, he read a certain article in a secular newspaper — something which he never did. The Chazon Ish agreed to read the article, but stipulated that the newspaper be opened before him to the appropriate page so that he would not have to grasp it. Were he to hold it, he reasoned, he would not be allowed to return the newspaper. To his mind, it was forbidden to read newspapers, which are generally filled with slander, distortions and other items that contradict the high moral standards expected of a Jew. To hand someone an object of sin is a transgression of *lifnei iver* (*Leviticus* 19:14), which prohibits a Jew from abetting another Jew to sin.

Personal Standards

IN HIS HOUSEHOLD, food was not eaten if it had been kept under a bed while someone slept, because the impurity which sleep brings upon a person descends upon the food underneath him. However, the Chazon Ish would have such food distributed among poor people whose custom it was to each such food.*

If food was brought to him on Shabbos from outside his house by way of the *eruv* that surrounded his city, he would not partake of it. This was because of his personal refusal to rely on any *eruv*. Nevertheless, he took upon himself to inspect the local *eruv* every

---

* See *Pischei Teshuvah* to *Yoreh Deah* 116:4.

Rabbi Meir Karelitz

Friday during his first years in Bnei Brak (see chapter five). Once, he visited another city, and on a stroll along its perimeters, noticed a flaw in the *eruv's* construction. He apprised the city's *rav* of the situation and the *rav* promised to correct the problem. A few days later, the Chazon Ish noticed that in a second spot, an entire section of the *eruv* had been built incorrectly; reconstructing it properly would take hours. Fearing that to point out yet another error would offend the *rav* (and perhaps place him on the defensive), the Chazon Ish, assisted by a disciple, rectified the matter himself.

Among the *halachic* obligations of a man to his wife is that of eating the Friday night meal together with her (*Even HaEzer* 70:2). The Chazon Ish fulfilled this obligation even when illness or other circumstances should have dictated otherwise. He would conduct the *Shalosh Seudos* and *Melaveh Malkah* meals even on *Yom Tov* (which did not fall out on Shabbos), though the *Shulchan Aruch* limits these meals to Shabbos. In this, he conducted himself according to the *Rambam* (as cited in *Tur, Orach Chaim* 529).

The *halachah* requires that one honor his eldest brother (*Yoreh Deah* 240:22).* The Chazon Ish's eldest brother, Reb Meir, was a *gaon* and Torah leader in his own right, and the two discussed *Klal* matters frequently. Reb Meir took care during their discussions never to voice his opinion in an authoritative way, for he knew that should he do so, the Chazon Ish would feel halachically obligated to adopt his brother's opinion against his own.

---

* Whether or not the *halachah* requires that one honor all brothers older than himself is a matter of debate among the commentators.

Stringency with Soundness

IT WOULD BE DIFFICULT to find someone whose zealousness in *kashrus* observance equaled that of the Chazon Ish. Before partaking of a food, he first scrupulously examined it to be sure that it was insect-free. For this reason, he never ate in the dark. He would not drink orange or lemon juice unless it was first strained through a cloth, for fear that small black dots sometimes found on those fruits might be insect eggs.

Such behavior was not a product of a nervous attitude which reflected itself in unwarranted fret and worry. Everything the Chazon Ish did was based on *halachic* considerations, and once those considerations were satisfied, he went no further. Illustrative of this is the testimony of Rabbi Serayah Dovlitsky: "The Chazon Ish was not one who on Rosh Hashanah would insist that the *ba'al tokei'a* sound the shofar blasts again and again, until each blast was perfect. It was sufficient for him that the blast was halachically valid. Most years, not a single blast had to be repeated at his *minyan*."

One year, doctors warned him not to fast on Yom Kippur because of a heart condition. He consulted a religious doctor whose opinion he trusted, saying, "If they are correct, I shall not fast."

The Chazon Ish once attempted to convince an ill acquaintance not to fast on Yom Kippur. He told the man, "There were times when an intestinal illness made it halachically forbidden for me to don *tallis* and *tefillin*. I cried out to the *Ribono Shel Olam*: 'Father in Heaven! It is You Who has commanded us to enwrap ourselves in *tallis* and *tefillin*. I have always heeded these commandments. Now, You are commanding me *not* to wear *tallis* and *tefillin* — in this, too, I shall heed Your command.' "

Throughout his years in *Eretz Yisrael*, the Chazon Ish ate no meat other than chicken which had been slaughtered by a G-d-fearing *shochet* whom he knew personally. Initially, he would insist on inspecting the slaughtering knife prior to *shechitah*. Realizing, however, that the *shochet's* feelings were hurt by this ostensible lack of trust, the Chazon Ish decided to rely on the *shochet's* inspection, while cautioning him to check that the knife conformed with certain unusual stringencies which the Chazon Ish observed. Even while being incredibly zealous in the observance of *halachah*, the Chazon Ish never lost sight of one's obligations toward his fellow Jew.

With such extreme care in *kashrus*-related matters, it is little wonder that the Chazon Ish was granted special *siyata dishmaya* in avoiding the intake of non-kosher foods. One evening, Rebbetzin Kanievsky brought in his evening meal, which included an egg. He partook of everything, save for the egg which was still in its shell. He picked up the egg and turned it slowly between his fingers as he examined it carefully. Finally, he put it down and had it returned to the kitchen. Later, Rebbetzin Kanievsky opened the egg and was amazed to find that it had a blood-spot!

At the *seudas Shabbos* one week, the Chazon Ish was served a bowl of chicken soup along with a plate of chicken that had been cooked with the soup. When he lifted his spoon to partake of the soup, he noticed some dirt on the spoon. Reb Shmaryahu Karelitz, who had joined him for the meal, went into the kitchen to wash the spoon. While Reb Shmaryahu was tending to his chore, the Chazon Ish noticed an abnormality on the chicken lying next to the soup. Examining it more closely, he ascertained that the abnormality presented a *kashrus* problem, rendering the chicken, and hence the soup in which it had been cooked, unfit for consumption. Had the spoon not been dirty, he would have eaten the soup, unaware of the problem.

When Reb Shmaryahu returned to the table, his uncle showed him his discovery. Aware of how others would view the incident, the Chazon Ish tried to make light of it. "There," he jokingly told his nephew, "you've got yourself a מוֹפֵת (wondrous occurrence)!"

RABBI YITZCHAK HALBERSTADT was present when the Chazon Ish was asked if a particular labor related to food preparation was permissible on *Yom Tov*. He replied, "I have no definitive proof, but I do know that my mother, of blessed memory, refrained from doing this on *Yom Tov*. Most probably, this was at my father's behest."

Adhering to Tradition

Someone once asked the Steipler *Gaon* why the Chazon Ish, while following virtually every ruling and custom of the *Vilna Gaon*, did not do so with regard to candle-lighting time on Chanukah. Said the Steipler, "It is possible that, in this, he followed the tradition of his ancestors."

Listen, my son, to the instruction of your father and do not abandon the teachings of your mother (Mishlei 1:8). To the Chazon Ish, the ways and customs of his ancestors were all a part of *mesorah*, Torah tradition, to be observed even if their reasons were not known.

His faith in the supremacy of earlier generations over his own and in the accuracy of their teachings demanded this type of rigid adherence. He would not countenance a disregard for time-honored custom and tradition.

The Chazon Ish was even more vehement concerning the disregard of any Talmudic teaching.

In a letter, he writes:

> It is soul-shattering — as when hearing blasphemy against the Holy Name — to hear anyone express doubt over a teaching of *Chazal*, whether in *Halachah* or *Aggadah* ... One who denies [the veracity of] a teaching of *Chazal* is unfit to serve as a witness [in a Jewish court of law], his *shechitah* is invalid, etc. (*Igros*, I:§15).

Proper Reverence

IN HIS DISCUSSIONS with *b'nei Torah*, the Chazon Ish would speak of the need for proper reverence when referring to Torah teachers and their writings, including those of recent generations. "It is incumbent upon us to exercise caution when being critical of our teachers' opinions ... it is always possible to express oneself in an honorable and refined manner ... when attempting to refute, one should be exceedingly careful to derive satisfaction only from the propounding of Torah thought and not from that which one must not take pleasure in [i.e., 'besting' a renowned commentator] ..."

He was dismayed to read a thesis which suggested that a certain comment of *Magen Avraham* was lacking substance. "*Chas V'shalom* (Heaven forfend)!" the Chazon Ish wrote. "The *Magen Avraham's* words are clear and forthright. Moreover, when attempting to refute, one must use the language of a disciple speaking before his teacher ... the *Magen Avraham* is our teacher, and we are all his disciples — praiseworthy are those who truly merit being counted among his disciples."

The Holocaust Fast

AFTER THE HOLOCAUST, a number of *rabbanim* in the Holy Land wanted to establish a new day of fasting and mourning for the horrors of World War II. The Chazon Ish employed various means in ensuring that this did not come about. He was especially concerned that no bonafide Torah leader endorse the idea. The Chazon Ish explained his opposition to Rabbi Binyamin Mendelsohn, *Rav* of

Rabbi Binyamin Mendelsohn

Moshav Kommemius: "The sufferings which our people have recently endured was above the plane of nature. There are those whose understanding tells them to establish a fast. This is wrong. Only the prophets had the ability to proclaim fast days; we do not ..."

When Rabbi Mendelsohn replied that the *Taz* had established the 20th of Sivan as a fast day, in commemoration of the Cossack uprisings of 1648-49, even though their destructiveness did not compare with that of the Nazi persecutions, the Chazon Ish was ready with a refutation: "Firstly, this was not an ordinance to be observed for all generations: there is no mention of it in the commentary of the *Taz*. Secondly, our spiritual level is not that of the *Taz*. For all we know, succeeding generations may be superior to our own — who are we to establish new ordinances for them?"

In a letter, he reiterated his opposition to the proposal:

> Establishing a fast for all generations is in the category of a rabbinic ordinance (*mitzvah d'Rabbanan*) — all existing fasts are from the times of the prophets. Dare we, a generation that had best be silent, be so brazen as to even think of establishing something for all generations? Such a proposal bears witness to a denial of our sins and lowly state at a time when we are mired in sin, impoverished and bereft of Torah and *mitzvos*.
>
> Let us not seek that which is beyond us. Instead, let us ponder our paths and repent. This is our obligation.

The weight of the Chazon Ish's opinion put an end to the proposal.

The Zebu Affair

IN 1950, THE GOVERNMENT of Israel sought to import inexpensive meat from the island of Madagascar (in the Indian Ocean, off the southeast coast of Africa). The meat was that of the "zebu," a mammal resembling the ox with a prominent hump on its back and a large dewlap. The government asked the Chief Rabbinate to arrange for the proper slaughtering and koshering of the meat.

While the zebu seems to have the characteristics of kosher animals (*Leviticus*, chapter 11), there is no tradition as to its *halachic* status. When consulted by Chief Rabbi Herzog on the matter, the Chazon Ish responded that the sages of earlier generations had already forbade the eating of any species regarding which there is no tradition. "Since the days of the *Shach*, we have a rigid custom against partaking of any hereto unknown species as a safeguard against eating forbidden foods. This safeguard has spread purity among *Klal Yisrael* and we dare not breach it."

The Chazon Ish stood by his ruling even after being informed that Iraqi emigrants originally from India claimed to have eaten of the zebu upon the ruling and tradition of the Torah authorities in their native land. He wrote, "We are not to alter our ways here because of traditions somewhere else. Also, testimony in such matters can only be accepted from a renowned personage."

Some had the audacity to insinuate that his political leanings had influenced the Chazon Ish's decision. When learning of the accusation, the Chazon Ish wrote to one *rav*:

> I do not, G-d forbid, bear any ill will toward those who have spoken against me. Still, I must declare that I am among those who are accused baselessly. I had no predelictions toward a negative ruling. However, my heart is pained that some are prepared to permit this. One breach can only lead to yet another ...
>
> ... I reiterate that I bear no ill will toward those who suspect me. I felt obligated to relate the above, for I recognize his honor's sublime spirit and love of truth. I am confident that he will reconsider the matter after reading this letter, and rule it forbidden to eat of this animal's meat — not because there is doubt over its characteristics, but because of the rigid custom invoked by the luminaries of old.
>
> In conclusion: in our days, when the desire for reform is strong, it is wrong to do anything which appears to permit that which until now has been considered forbidden. I witnessed this as being the opinion of the Torah masters of the past generation. It is unfitting, therefore, to suspect us of ulterior motives, or to hope that we abandon this feeling, Heaven forfend. This feeling is a lofty one. It stems from love of Torah and awe of Hashem.

CHAPTER TWELVE
An Angel Among Mortals

"I must take you to task for I see that you are not evaluating yourself properly, and without thought you are becoming irreverent toward the goal of knowing Torah. Take note of the person who has the good fortune to absorb knowledge of Torah, that is, his intellect takes root in his being — akin to a seed planted in soil — uniting the man and his wisdom. He may walk among men and appear to be a mere person. But in truth he is an angel that lives among mortals. And he lives a life of nobility above and beyond all blessings and praises..."

(*Igros Chazon Ish*, I:§13).

The Road to Wisdom

IN THE SECULAR WORLD, intellect and behavior are independent of each other. One can be acclaimed as a genius in his realm of knowledge, while his personal life is totally immoral, his interaction with others devoid of any concern for his fellow man.

This is not the way of Torah. In *Emunah U'Vitachon*, the Chazon Ish writes:

> Any deficiency in the nobility of one's soul, specifically with regard to *midos* (character traits), will result in a deficiency in his acquiring wisdom [i.e., Torah] which has its roots in refined character and pleasant disposition...
>
> ... One who is bound by the ropes of earthly desire ... pursuing the "sweet things" of life, hungry for pleasures, forever angry, full of arrogance — even if his soul is endowed with superior intellectual abilities, even if he has been granted a double portion of insight and understanding, he will never find

true success in Torah study. Contemptible *midos* dull a person's mind and desensitize his heart. They close before him the doors to wisdom and the gates to understanding.

A wise man, the Chazon Ish continues, will prepare for himself the necessary channels through which wisdom can flow. For success in Torah, one must possess a joyful spirit, a deeply rooted sense of well-being and a genuine thirst for Hashem's wisdom. These qualities can only be found in a true *ba'al midos*, whose finely tuned heart is in concert with the subtleties of Torah wisdom.

Changing Oneself

JUST AS TRUE WISDOM cannot be found in one whose *midos* are wanting, so too, writes the Chazon Ish, genuinely refined *midos* cannot be found in a soul devoid of Torah wisdom. There are those whose drive to help others is remarkable. They engage in acts of benevolence and are truly self-sacrificing. Yet, at the very instant that they are performing an act of kindness, they may quickly react to the slightest offense with rage and even physical reprisal. Why is this? These are people whose actions are not dominated by wisdom; rather, they have an innate tendency toward helping others, be it on an individual or communal level. They enjoy it. But never have they engaged in soul-searching to rid themselves of the negative traits within them.

Not so the scholar, who recognizes that man must strive to conquer his whims and passions and allow his mind, not his desires, to rule. As Shlomo *HaMelech* wrote, *In accordance with his intellect should man be praised* (*Proverbs* 12:8). Praiseworthy is the one whose proper attitude towards others is the result of introspection, not natural inclination.

The Chazon Ish illustrates this idea with an anecdote:

In many European communities, a man would be appointed to find Shabbos hosts for the beggars and wayfarers who had nowhere to go. It happened once that a certain *tzaddik* had understood that he would be having guests for the Friday night meal. The *tzaddik's* family enjoyed welcoming guests into their home and they happily prepared for their company.

However, a misunderstanding had occurred. Following *Ma'ariv* on Friday night, the man in charge mistakenly sent the guest to someone else's home. The *tzaddik* came home alone. His family was crestfallen; all their preparations were for naught. The *tzaddik's* attitude, however, was altogether different. He told his family, "A guest is not an item of merchandise. My sole concern is that his needs be cared for. What difference does it make if this is accomplished through us or another family?" Such was the reaction of a man whose mind ruled over his emotions.

"This would not be the case," writes the Chazon Ish, "with a man bereft of wisdom. He may enjoy helping others, but this will not stop him from begrudging those who carry out that which he had hoped to accomplish."

Indeed, the Chazon Ish was once in the home of an acquaintance as the latter was readying a bed and some food for a beggar who had come to his door. The man appeared happy that this *mitzvah* had come his way.

The beggar, however, was not obliging and refused even to partake of any food. "Why did you put me through all this trouble for nothing?!" the prospective host angrily shouted. The beggar left.

In his soft-spoken way, the Chazon Ish told his acquaintance, "In *Bircas HaMazon* we ask, 'Please, Hashem, our G-d, do not make us needful of the gifts of others...' From observing you, it seems that we should include another request — *that others not be in need of providing us their help...*"

The Torah Personality

THE UNIFYING THEME of the Chazon Ish's *Emunah U'Vitachon* is that in a personality molded by Torah and saturated with its teachings, one's attributes complement each other in perfect harmony. Mind and emotion, *midos* and Torah scholarship, Heavenly fear and trust in Hashem combine to form a symphony that proclaims the greatness of Hashem and the majesty of those who study His Torah and seek to emulate His ways.

The Chazon Ish was such a personality. Those whose lives were touched by his wisdom, sensitivity, kindness and other sublime attributes saw living testimony to Hashem's declaration, *My servant, Israel, in whom I will be glorified* (Isaiah 49:3).

The same meticulousness with which he performed *mitzvos* between man and Hashem was employed in his fulfillment of *mitzvos* between man and man. He wrote, "I take pleasure in gladdening the hearts of others and I feel it a great obligation never to cause discomfort to any man — even for a moment."

THE TORAH COMMANDS US to emulate the ways of Hashem: just as He is compassionate so must we be compassionate . . . (*Sotah* 14a). The Chazon Ish nurtured within himself a feeling for the needs of others that was a semblance of the All-merciful's concern for His creatures.

Boundless Compassion

He was once requested to do something which was totally against his nature. Rather than reject the request, he begged that it be rescinded, saying, "I find it exceedingly difficult to send anyone away empty-handed."

In a letter to a Torah student, he wrote, "I *hunger* to know of your well-being." From his pen flowed words of comfort and consolation. "You are already accustomed to seeing salvation in your hour of need. This should be a source of encouragement and hope in your present situation."

In an appreciation written after the Chazon Ish's death, Rabbi Mordechai Ilai lamented, "Woe! How wondrous was he in helping the fallen to arise, in conquering their weakness of spirit, their depression and despair."

In another letter, we find, "The force of my love for you causes every bit of your sadness to touch my heart."

One writer apologized for any anguish he might have caused the Chazon Ish in pouring out his troubles. "Heaven forfend," responded the Chazon Ish. "You have done the right thing not to conceal your troubles from me. It certainly would be better, though, if I would hear good news from you."

THE CHAZON ISH did not have to be solicited when another Jew's spirits needed bolstering. Dr. Nachman Frei, a member of the administration at *Asusa* Health Facility, once mentioned parenthetically to the Chazon Ish that one of the hospital's patients was an American tourist who had taken ill suddenly. The man was traveling alone and had no relatives in *Eretz Yisrael*. There was no one to visit him and offer moral support, and this was aggravating his condition.

Unusual Concerns

How astounded Dr. Frei was when the next morning he entered the patient's room and found the Chazon Ish at the man's side, offering comfort to someone whom he had never met before.

In 1951, a polio epidemic swept across *Eretz Yisrael*, resulting in the deaths of many children. One day, Rabbi Yitzchak Greenberg of the Lomza Yeshivah told the Chazon Ish of a particularly tragic case: An only child had died and his bereaved parents had few visitors during the week of *shivah*, as people feared contamination from lingering germs. The Chazon Ish asked, "Would my visit be a source of inspiration to them?" Rabbi Greenberg replied in the affirmative. The Chazon Ish immediately rose to leave for the parents' home.

There are those who are truly willing to do for others, as long as their own stature is not compromised. Not so the Chazon Ish — his selflessness was total.

It was his custom to celebrate the Simchas Torah *hakafos* in the study hall of the Ponovezh Yeshivah. One year, on his way home following *hakafos*, he chanced upon a man weeping openly in the street. The man told the Chazon Ish that he was a *ger tzeddek*. He felt that his fellow Jews thought little of him and treated him as an outcast.

The Chazon Ish said, "I invite his honor to sing a *niggun*." The *ger* obliged and began singing in a robust voice. There, in the street, the Chazon Ish danced to the tune in front of the *ger* as one would dance before a bride and groom at a wedding. The man's spirits were revived.

Though he was more than mildly near-sighted, the Chazon Ish often studied without glasses and could have traveled the same way, but he made a point of never leaving his apartment without donning his glasses. He explained, "Without glasses, I might not notice someone's nod or some other form of greeting. Someone might, G-d forbid, be offended."

A reporter for the secularist newspaper *Davar* recounted, "I was curious to meet the Chazon Ish, so I made the trip to Bnei Brak and arrived at his apartment. He left his home to walk somewhere and I accompanied him. He strode slowly, in silence, as I walked at his side. Suddenly, his pace slowed markedly. When I expressed my wonderment, he explained, 'In front of us walks a cripple. It is not proper to pass by with our sure, healthy steps. Better to slow down and remain in back of him.'"

One day, he and Reb Shlomo Kohen entered an apartment building in Bnei Brak. As they mounted the staircase, the loud voices of a husband and wife in the midst of an argument could be heard from within one of the apartments. The Chazon Ish turned and rushed from the building as if fleeing from a fire. He told Reb

Shlomo, "Were they to know that I heard, they would surely be embarrassed..."

Rabbi Serayah Dovlitsky once came to the Chazon Ish asking that he annul a vow (*hataras nedarim*). Annulment of vows requires a *beis din* of three. The Chazon Ish asked a scholar with whom he had been conversing to serve as the second judge and sent someone out to the street to find a third judge. Someone was soon brought in. The Chazon Ish asked the other judges to be seated and presided over the necessary procedure for annulment. Once it was completed, the man who had been called in rose and left. The Chazon Ish then said to those who remained, "Now, we must find a new third judge and run through the entire procedure again. I know that man who just left. He is a wonderful person, but unfortunately is not learned. One who has no understanding of *hataras nedarim* cannot serve as a judge for it.

"But once you called him in, I had to pretend that he was, indeed, serving as a judge. Otherwise, he would have felt humiliated..."

Man of Few Words

AS WE HAVE SEEN in previous chapters, the Chazon Ish was a man of few words. Often, when pressed to speak, he would say, "There are those who know how to speak. I know how to remain silent." On one occasion, when relentlessly urged to address a gathering, the Chazon Ish said, "The Creator endowed all His creatures with natural shields: horns for the ox, scales for fish... silence is my shield."

"Just three words...!" someone once pleaded. "Do you consider three words insignificant?" the Chazon Ish retorted. "With three words, *Harei at mekudeshes* (Behold, you are betrothed), an unmarried woman is transformed into an *eishes ish* (married woman)."*

Yet he never refrained from offering an individual those words which the person needed to hear. He also never failed to greet with a smile anyone he encountered, including small children. In eulogizing the Chazon Ish, Rabbi Shraga Feivel Steinberg said, "Who can forget the first '*Shalom Aleichem*' he was privileged to receive from the Chazon Ish... with such humility... Who can forget how he wished '*Gut Shabbos*' to everyone, including small children, on the last night of his life... with that same humility..."

---

* The specific ramifications of this three-word utterance are discussed in *Even HaEzer*, 27:4.

THE CHAZON ISH once defined true humility to Reb Shlomo Kohen: "People are mistaken in thinking that humility means to think of oneself as an ignorant boor, even when such is surely not the case. Humility means that one realizes his true worth. If he is a *gadol baTorah* he can know this and conduct himself in a manner commensurate with his true standing — but he must not seek honor and glory because of it, for this is his purpose in life. *If you have studied much Torah, do not take credit for yourself, because that is what you were created to do*" (*Avos* 2:9).

The Essence of Humility

Indeed, the Chazon Ish, like the Torah leaders of all generations, was repulsed by honor. When seeking his advice in a difficult problem, one man repeatedly made use of the Talmudic expression "*Yelamdeinu Rabbeinu*" ("Teach us, our teacher"), referring, of course, to the Chazon Ish. Finally, the Chazon Ish could bear it no longer. "Let us leave the '*Rabbeinu*' aside and concentrate on the problem..."

Rabbi Shmuel Wosner cited an incident which epitomized the Chazon Ish's humility:

"It was *erev Rosh Hashanah* of the post-*Shemittah* year. The Chazon Ish appeared at my door and I hurried to welcome him. He said simply, 'I am a resident of the Zichron Meir neighborhood; his honor is the *Rav*. I have therefore come to write a *prozbul*.' *

"He wrote down what was, in his opinion, the correct text of a *prozbul*. Then, he asked that I sit while he stood and read the text aloud. He signed the *prozbul*, 'Avraham Yeshayah, son of my master, guide and teacher, the *gaon*, R' Shmaryahu Yosef.' "

Reb Isser Zalman Meltzer once remarked, "If someone would come and tell me that the Chazon Ish was *Mashiach*, I would believe it." When this was repeated to the Chazon Ish, he could only say, "Ah ... see how badly Reb Isser Zalman wants *Mashiach* to come ..."

IN DEFINING THE HUMILITY of *Moshe Rabbeinu*, whom the Torah describes as the humblest of men (*Numbers* 12:3), *Rashi* writes that to be humble is to be meek and tolerant. In his commentary to *Avos*, *Rabbeinu Yonah* describes a tolerant person as "one who distances himself from anger and responds in a soft tone. Even when he is wronged, he will

Ignoring Affronts

---

* A document by which a creditor can collect debts that otherwise would be lost due to *Shemittah* laws.

tolerate it and no bitter word will escape his mouth."

The Talmudic sage Rav Zeira said that he achieved longevity in the merit of his never having shown irritation or impatience toward anyone in his home (בְּבֵיתִי) (*Megillah* 28a). *Be'er Mayim Chaim* interprets בֵּיתִי, my home, homiletically to mean *within me*. Rav Zeira had conquered his inner self to the degree that he never bore an inner ill will toward another man.

The Chazon Ish, too, possessed this attribute. As he once remarked regarding ill will, "Such merchandise is not found in my store."

Indeed, the Chazon Ish perfected this trait as a young man. When in Minsk during the first World War, he would pray in a *beis midrash* known as "Reb Isserke's *Cheder*," where Torah lectures were conducted throughout the day. The first time he entered the *beis midrash* was on a Sunday afternoon, as a group of men were preparing for a *shiur* that would soon begin. The Chazon Ish opened a *gemara* and, because of his near-sightedness, brought it near his eyes. The sight of this simply attired young man scanning a page from up close struck the others as strange. To some, it seemed that he was searching without knowing what he was searching for.

When the *shiur* was about to commence, the *shamash* went over to the Chazon Ish, took the *gemara* out of his hands and said, "You'd be better off reciting *Tehillim* rather than turning pages of *sefarim*. In any case, this *gemara* is needed for the *shiur*." The Chazon Ish nodded his head without saying a word.

During the Torah reading the next morning, the *shamash* asked the Chazon Ish his Hebrew name in order to call him to the Torah. Upon hearing "Avraham Yeshayah ben R' Shmaryahu Yosef," the *shamash* appeared shaken, for the scholars of Minsk already knew that the Kossowa *Rav's* illustrious son was in the city.

As the Chazon Ish recited the concluding blessing for the Torah reading, the *shamash* was overcome with remorse. Tearfully, he begged the Chazon Ish for forgiveness. The Chazon Ish honestly could not understand what was troubling the man. "You were right to take away the *gemara*; it belongs to the *beis midrash* and was needed for the *shiur*. As for reciting *Tehillim*, you were also correct; a Jew *should* recite *Tehillim*."

When the Chazon Ish was living in Bnei Brak and already acclaimed as a *gadol hador*, a Torah student knocked on his door late one evening to "talk in learning." Receiving no response, the student brazenly climbed up onto a porch and gained entry through an open door. He found the Chazon Ish by his table, studying as usual. The student proceeded to ask question after question in quick succession. The only response he received was silence. Assuming that the Chazon Ish was upset over his brazenness, the student meekly left — by way of the front door.

When the Chazon Ish went for his morning walk the next day, after concluding the *Shacharis* prayers with his *vasikin* minyan*, the student was waiting to ask forgiveness. This time the Chazon Ish responded. "There is one thing for which you have to ask forgiveness — for having suspected me of harboring ill will toward you. I don't know what it means to bear a grudge.

"As for why I did not respond to you yesterday: You came to me in the evening, after I had taxed my strength to its limits in the course of my studies. Your questions were excellent. Answering them would have required deep concentration, something which was beyond me at that point. I did not respond for fear of being drawn into further conversation, thus endangering my health."**

Man of Truth

IN A LETTER of Talmudic discussion, a writer apologized to the Chazon Ish for contending with one of his halachic rulings. In his reply, the Chazon Ish wrote, "Your mention of any possible ill will on my part is simply not understandable to me. What place is there here for ill will? His honor's words are precious to me. Besides, to bear ill will is, to my mind, a most despicable trait."

Another letter reveals both a deep humility and a passion for truth. "Every area of Torah study requires deep concentration. An honest error in no way reflects upon the honor of the student, for such is natural when striving to acquire wisdom. I am always full of errors in the theory or interpretation of the Talmudic text. Yet I am never ashamed. One is required, though, to experience a sense of humility, for if not, it would appear as though he does not adequately evaluate the importance of the *Halachah*" (*Igros*, I:§194).

In his works, we find statements such as, "I retract"; "I have declared impure that which is actually pure"; and "All that which I

---

* Lit., those who are pious and conscientious. *Vasikin minyanim* recite the morning *Shemoneh Esrei* at sunrise, the most preferred time.

** Related by Rabbi Avraham Pollak, *mashgiach* of the Slabodka Yeshivah.

have written here regarding the *Rambam's* view is to be disregarded..."

In a halachic responsum, the Chazon Ish raised the possibility of the *Beis Yosef* having retracted a certain ruling. "Is it not found that a *gaon* retracts a *p'sak*? Was not *Maran* (a reference to the *Beis Yosef*) a *kadosh*? The goal of every sage is truth."

In 1940, after the death of Reb Chaim Ozer, Reb Shmaryahu Karelitz conceived of reprinting the deceased's monumental *Achiezer*. The Chazon Ish endorsed his nephew's idea, adding that he would provide his *ha'aros* (observations and critiques) to the work for publication in the new edition. Later, the Chazon Ish retracted his offer, telling his nephew, "It is no great feat to refute someone when he cannot respond."

In his *Emunah U'Vitachon*, the Chazon Ish writes, "One's manner of speech should be predicated on a firm adherence to truth and a firm abhorrence of falsehood. *Chazal* were unforgiving in their condemnation of falsehood. Its corrosiveness is powerful and its destructiveness is all too prevalent." He would stress that even to alter facts slightly when recounting an incident of no consequence is falsehood.*

On one occasion he said, "It is possible to go through life without uttering a single falsehood. Heaven will assist those who truly desire to speak nothing but truth."

Having overheard a father promise his child a reward for good behavior, the Chazon Ish quickly pointed out the father's obligation to honor his word. As the Talmud states (*Succah* 46b), *Rav Zeira said: A person should not tell a child, 'I will give you something,' and then not give it to him, for he [i.e., the child] will learn to lie, as it is written (Jeremiah 9:4), 'They teach their tongues to speak falsehood.'* The Chazon Ish added that the child will certainly be disappointed when the reward is not forthcoming. To be absolved of any wrongdoing, the father would need the child's *mechilah*, his forgiveness, and a minor's *mechilah* is of no halachic value.

The following anecdote sums up the importance which the Chazon Ish attached to the attribute of truth:

The Chazon Ish's *minyan* would gather in his home for the

---

* In this context, the Chazon Ish pointed out that when *Yaakov Avinu* told his father, "I am Eisav, your first-born" (*Genesis* 27:19), he did so only because of the Divinely ordained nature of his mission. As the commentators explain, even then he strove to stay as close to the truth as possible.

Minchah prayer in the early afternoon. Finding a *minyan* at that time of day often presented a problem. One day, a long time passed before a tenth man was finally found. As the man walked in, Rabbi Shmuel Greineman turned to the Chazon Ish and asked, "What shall I do? I have an appointment with someone at my house at this hour. Shall I *daven* and make him wait for me or should I leave now in order to be on time?"

Said the Chazon Ish, "For a man who cleaves to the attribute of truth, there can be no question as to what to do." Rabbi Greineman left and the search for a tenth man began anew.

Monetary Matters

AS WITH EVERY ASPECT of his service of Hashem, the Chazon Ish demonstrated unusual zealousness in matters of *Choshen Mishpat*, the *Shulchan Aruch's* section of monetary laws.

Once, when visiting an acquaintance, the Chazon Ish would not allow any water he was using to flow down the sink. He explained to his nephew, Rabbi Nissan Karelitz, that the sink's drain emptied onto public property. The *halachah* prohibits such drainage during summertime when the ground is normally dry and would be muddied by liquid flow.

When the electric company issued restrictions on laundering and bathing due to an energy shortage, the Chazon Ish insisted that everyone comply with the request. To ignore it would constitute duress on the seller (i.e., the company providing electricity against its will), which is prohibited by Torah law.

The Chazon Ish walked with a cane. An elderly guest once mistakenly switched canes, leaving the Chazon Ish with a cane not his own. He lost no time in sending the following letter: "Will his honor please be so kind as to permit me to use his cane (which was mistakenly left here) until an exchange can be made."

A request for guidance arrived by mail from Poland. Enclosed was an expensive international stamp for the Chazon Ish to affix on his return envelope. The Chazon Ish chose to respond by way of postcard, the postage of which was far cheaper than the value of the stamp. In his response, the Chazon Ish asked the sender's permission to give the difference in price to *tzeddakah*. In doing so, he went far beyond the requirements of *halachah*, as there is no legal obligation to return unsolicited stamps to a sender.*

---

* See *She'eilos U'Teshuvos Maharsham*, Vol. II:§210-12.

In the attic of his home were sacks of letters that came to him from all across the globe. He once told Rabbi Shmaryahu Greineman, "I cannot bring myself to discard letters and postcards in which lie people's hearts and souls, their pains and sorrows."

One day, a young child made his way up to the attic and rummaged through the sacks. Finding a number of unused return stamps, he tore up the letters in which they came and proudly brought the stamps to the Chazon Ish. Concealing his agitation, he calmly asked the child if he might remember in which envelopes his "treasures" had been found, so that he could write the senders concerning what should be done with the stamps. The child had no recollection of this. The Chazon Ish added up the value of all the stamps and gave that amount to *tzedakah*.

When a doctor absolutely refused to accept payment for services rendered, the Chazon Ish donated the fee to *tzedakah*, in the doctor's merit.

Rabbi Moshe Ilvitzky recalled the following incident from his days in Kweidan:

The Chazon Ish's wife and one of her textile customers, an observant Jew, once became involved in a monetary dispute. The customer said, "Let us ask your husband what the *halachah* is." Off to the Chazon Ish they went. After hearing both sides of the argument, the Chazon Ish sided with the customer. Later, the Chazon Ish sensed that his wife was hurt by his decision. "Tell me, please," he asked softly, "of what value is life if one possesses even a penny that is not his own?"

IN *EMUNAH U'VITACHON*, the Chazon Ish refutes a common assumption regarding character refinement:

Midos and Mitzvos Among existing assumptions is that refinement of *midos* has a bearing only on one's performance of *mitzvos* between man and man, while it is only *yiras shamayim* which affects his fulfillment of *mitzvos* between man and G-d. A result of this misconception is the belief that a person can be wholesome in his performance of *mitzvos* relating to G-d alone, though his *midos* are wanting and he is deficient in his dealings with others.

One who sees to the core of the matter recognizes the hollowness of this belief. A Jew whose *midos* have not undergone refinement through instruction and introspection is in the clutches of his evil inclination. As such, it is inconceivable that he be wholesome in matters between man and G-d. The fact that he fulfills these *mitzvos* in substantial measure is only because their observance does not [usually] run counter to any of his negative attributes. However, when such conflict does occur, his *yiras shamayim* will not be enough to weather the storm.

... It happened once that an individual of this sort extended an invitation to a distinguished guest of his city. The invitation was accepted, the guest promising to visit the man's home on Friday night. The prospective host was delighted, as the visit would bring him honor and pleasure. What did Satan do? He caused the man to forget to add kerosene to his lamp, so that it had but a tiny bit of fuel left over from Thursday night. It was wintertime, when the nights are long. The guest had not yet arrived and the flame was about to die out.

The host envisioned the shame he would experience if his guest would arrive and find his home in darkness. He could not control himself. On Shabbos, he added kerosene to the lamp.

... Such is the way of a man who never purified his soul in the smelting furnace of proper behavior. All his ways are nothing more than sheer habit.

With this insight, the Chazon Ish explained Hillel's statement to the heathen who wanted to be taught the entire Torah as he stood on one foot (as a precondition to conversion). Said Hillel: *"Do not do unto others that which you dislike. This is the whole Torah; the rest is commentary - go study it!"* (Shabbos 31a). One who has perfected himself to the point that he will never do or say anything that will cause hurt to another Jew will undoubtedly have the necessary self-control to properly fulfill all *mitzvos*. This, said the Chazon Ish, was Hillel's intent.

The Case of the Melamdim

TO THE CHAZON ISH, it is *Halachah* which ultimately decides the ethical right or wrong of a given situation. To illustrate this concept, he cites the *halachah* (see *Bava Basra* 21b) that allows local businessmen to prevent strangers from setting up competitive concerns in their area, while prohibiting a similar thing in the case of Torah education. A *melamed* (teacher of Torah) may come from another town and establish a new school, for the interests of Torah education are best served in a spirit of competition. This consideration outweighs the usual concern for the individual's financial loss.

Let us imagine such a situation. A contingent of new *melamdim* come to town and establish a new school. The townspeople are inclined toward exposing their children to new faces and approaches. Many enroll their children in the new school, resulting in severe financial losses for the original *melamdim*.

The *Halachah* determines the ethics of the situation. Had the new *melamdim* done wrong in coming to the city, the first *melamdim* could have insisted that they leave. Had they balked, the *halachah* would have granted the first *melamdim* the use of coercion. They would have been innocent of transgressing prohibitions against causing strife or the like* in their efforts to have the new school closed.

However, now that the *halachah* declares the new *melamdim* to be in the right, any negative reaction on the part of the original *melamdim* would be wrong and even sinful. As the Chazon Ish puts it:

> The newcomers have done no wrong. Those who oppose them are spillers of innocent blood. If they will hate the new *melamdim*, they will have transgressed the commandment against hating a Jew in one's heart. When speaking bad of them, the sin of *lashon hara* will have been violated; when convening meetings to thwart their project, they will have transgressed the commandment that we not follow in the ways of Korach and his assembly; when denying them a favor, they will have been guilty of seeking revenge.
>
> ... Proper ethics dictate that one strive to implant this fundamental principle in his heart: in every situation that involves oneself and someone else, one must judge on the scales of *Halachah* as to who is in the right and who is in the wrong.

Thus, concludes the Chazon Ish, unless the absolute supremacy of *Halachah* is firmly fixed in a person's mind, he will ultimately err and stumble even as he tries to raise himself to an elevated existence. For one's own personal judgment, no matter how well intended, is often not in consonance with what *Chazal* determined as the correct mode of conduct in a given situation.

---

* Provided that their deeds and words did not go beyond that which the *Halachah* permits in such a situation.

THE CHAZON ISH carries the intertwining of ethics and *Halachah* yet further. "Exactness in fulfilling the *Halachah* and subordination to the *Shulchan Aruch* is the simplest road — and may well be the only one — to self-improvement."

The Road to Self-Improvement

Picture the man who has expended great effort and expense to obtain an *esrog* or pair of *tefillin* only to discover that his efforts may have been wasted due to a minor halachic detail that he had overlooked. Laziness, embarrassment, or additional cost could all deter the man from rectifying the problem. However, a man with an unbending conviction as to the centrality of *Halachah* will master his inner self so that no concern or feeling will stand in the way of a *mitzvah*. Such mastery must result in overall refinement of character.

Conversely, the neglect of halachic detail will counteract whatever efforts a person might invest in his quest for self-improvement.

> ... For, generally speaking, one who performs *mitzvos* and avoids transgression by way of habit is aware that numerous halachic details exist; yet he refrains from seeking the guidance of a competent authority. Without a doubt, such an attitude has its roots in negative character traits. When one continuously makes peace with his natural inclination instead of engaging in necessary investigations, strength is lent to the forces of impurity. Any efforts at character refinement are neutralized by an attitude toward *mitzvos* that can only corrupt proper *midos* ...

IN *EMUNAH U'VITACHON*, the Chazon Ish paints a portrait of the ideal man, a "noble soul":

A Noble Soul

Picture a man who yearns to do good for others, whose joy when encountering others knows no bounds; he greets every man with a smiling, luminous countenance. His greatest heartache is when he causes any sort of hurt to someone else, even inadvertently. Therefore, he is forever concerned lest his words miss their mark and have a negative effect. He also takes care not to be guilty of withholding a kindness that ought to be performed.

However, he never takes offense at anything his friends might say, for his heart overflows with love for them and this more than makes up for any iniquities on their part. Moreover, he is prepared to accept with true love any painful words or deeds that are directed his way, for he understands that, indeed, there are few who rise above the lowliness of one's natural inclination, and therefore very little can be expected of them. Even with this in mind, he regards his friends with respect and esteem, never permitting himself to dwell on their shortcomings.

His own shortcomings are another matter. He faults himself for any slight imperfection in his *midos* — while he sees others as totally innocent even when their deeds are caked with sin.

This noble soul will not require a great girding of strength to subdue his own anger, to remain silent in the face of embarrassment. For his soul is already pure and sparkling, incapable of being stained. It is a soul filled with joy and eternal pleasantness.

Were the author of the above word portrait anonymous, one could easily have thought that he was describing the Chazon Ish, the noblest of souls.

CHAPTER THIRTEEN
Everyone's Father

"Every neshamah has its own unique mission ... There are some who are destined to accomplish out in the open. My lot, however, is to sit in my small room and from there, perform kindness for my fellow man" (the Chazon Ish).

"A work unto itself could be written regarding his efforts in these areas ... Every broken heart found in him some sort of remedy. Many of his deeds for others were performed in secrecy; there is no one to lift the veil that still covers them. They are destined to remain hidden forever" (Rabbi Shlomo Kohen).

AS THE CHAZON ISH'S FAME continued to spread, more and more visitors appeared at his humble dwelling in search of help. In his last years, it often happened that more than one hundred people came to see him in a single day. As *Shacharis* commenced in his room each morning, the small hallway of his apartment would already be filled with men and women. This was often true even in summer, when prayers would begin at 4 A.M.

Anyone, Any Time

Some came for advice, especially in the area of medicine, in which the Chazon Ish was incredibly familiar. Others came in search of blessings for themselves or their loved ones. Many offered *kvitlach* on which were scrawled the Hebrew names of those for whom a blessing was sought, a custom more common at the courts of Chassidic *rebbeim*. Scores requested that the Chazon Ish pray for their particular needs. Except in extenuating circumstances, such requests were always granted.*

---

* The Chazon Ish denied requests for a blessing (or prayer) that a litigant be victorious in a *din Torah* against another Jew. Legal disputes should hinge on one thing only — the words

Those that came ranged from *roshei yeshivah* and *rabbanim* to the simplest men and women. The pure faith which the common folk placed in the Chazon Ish's words epitomized the *emunas chachamim* that is unique to the Jewish nation.

Once, a woman in sorrowful straits came to the Chazon Ish to plead that he effect some sort of miracle on her behalf. He listened patiently and shared in her plight, but would not grant her the miraculous assurance that she sought. She repeated her entreaties again and again, weeping incessantly as she begged, while the Chazon Ish listened. More time went by. The woman showed no signs of leaving — and it was *erev Shabbos*. Finally, someone impatiently snapped at the woman, "Enough already! You see that the *Rav* has nothing to add." The Chazon Ish turned to the man and demanded, "Did she perhaps come to see you?" The man's face paled. The woman left shortly thereafter.

On *Motza'ei Shabbos*, the man, who was a close acquaintance of the Chazon Ish, returned to apologize for his outburst. The Chazon Ish greeted him warmly. Before the man could speak, the Chazon Ish said, "I understood your intentions. But that woman was soaking herself in *emunas chachamim*; it was wrong to interrupt her."

Another time, an old woman spent almost an hour in an uninterrupted account of her problems and frustrations. When she finally left, a family member wondered aloud, "From where does one get the patience to listen to all that?" Said the Chazon Ish, "She feels that coming here to talk eases her situation. How can one deny a Jew such a kindness?"

His genuine concern for another Jew's troubles prompted those who initially came for spiritual salvation to return for practical advice.

A woman who had been childless for many years was instructed by the Chazon Ish to change all the *mezuzos* in her house. Not long passed before she was expecting a child. She returned to the Chazon Ish to ask which hospital he recommended for delivery and pediatric care. Here, too, he offered a definitive answer.

Scores of Holocaust survivors found solace in his words of

---

of *Shulchan Aruch*, as understood by its commentators and the *beis din* before whom the case has been presented.

The Chazon Ish also would not offer blessings on behalf of those who sought their partner in life if he had reason to believe that the particular boy or girl would not observe the laws of family purity. To do so would be categorized as helping one to sin, in this case a sin that carries the severe punishment of *kareis*, excision.

comfort, encouragement and advice as they strove to pick up the pieces of their shattered lives. That he lived amid deprivation, travail and physical affliction virtually his entire life — and derived spiritual strength from it all — increased the impact of his words manifold.

Orphaned girls who came to *Eretz Yisrael* at war's end with no family and no hope for the future found an address to turn to for their every need. In caring for these Jewish daughters, the Chazon Ish would settle for nothing less than what he would have wanted for his own. He arranged successful *shidduchim* for many of them, virtually every such match with a *ben Torah*. He ensured that each couple had a proper wedding, apartment, clothing and furniture and, in many instances, financial support after the wedding until they could manage on their own.

A Helping Hand

SCORES OF OTHER poor families were provided with financial assistance by the Chazon Ish. Many of them attempted to conceal their predicament out of shame. Invariably, their situation found its way to the Chazon Ish's door. He invested countless hours garnering the necessary funds and finding the way to supply them in a manner that would not compromise the party's dignity. Once, he was unable to find a way to provide support for a destitute family that absolutely refused any sort of support in any shape or form. Finally, he instructed Rabbi Zvi Kagan of Bnei Brak to wait outside the house until all family members had left for the day and then hurl the money through the window.

It is ironic that a man who subsisted on so little, who did not own a complete *Vilna Shas*, managed to distribute tens of thousands of dollars to others. As his fame increased so did the amounts of charity which others entrusted to him for distribution. In the last years of his life, *tzedakah* funds from around the world arrived regularly at his door. The initial donation for any given cause always came from his personal money. Whenever he was short of funds for some pressing need, the Chazon Ish turned to the generous benefactors among the *Eretz Yisrael* Torah community who responded to his every request with alacrity.

He encouraged others to make proper use of their G-d-given income. In one letter he cites the words of *Shulchan Aruch* (*Yoreh Deah* 247:2), "Never does one become poor from giving *tzedakah*.

No harm or damage can come about through it, as it is written, *And the deed of tzedakah will bring peace (Isaiah 32:17)."* The Chazon Ish adds, "Even if on the surface, with regard to the particular act [of *tzedakah*], this does not seem so, nevertheless, with regard to things in general, whereas all one's provisions and the lack thereof are Divinely ordained, there is no loss, G-d forbid, from giving *tzedakah*. There is only *berachah*."

When projects required raising funds, he would turn to prominent communal activists to undertake the task. On some occasions, he assembled a group of yeshivah students to fund-raise. He would instruct them to involve many Jews in the *mitzvah*, rather than seek the required sum from a few wealthy benefactors.

When this fund-raising was not sufficient, the Chazon Ish would procure personal loans. As time went on, and ever more people in need came to him for help, he was forced to borrow large amounts with increasing frequency. Every cent borrowed was given away to others.

A Double Standard

OF THE SAGE Rabbi Chanina ben Dosa, a Heavenly voice proclaimed, *"The whole world is provided for in the merit of My son Chanina, while My son Chanina subsists on a measure of carob from week to week"* (Ta'anis 10a). Not infrequently, men of wealth pleaded with the Chazon Ish to accept money for his personal needs. He never accepted, managing with whatever the sale of his *sefarim* brought him. Once he was asked, "But from what does one live?" The Chazon Ish replied, "From helping one's fellow Jews."

While he was perfectly content with his lot, he recognized that others needed more. Thus, he writes in one letter, "Since we pray for abundance [with regard to personal provisions], I wish that you be granted income in generous measure."

He was forever alert to the needs of others. When a renowned Torah personage miraculously fled Europe and arrived in *Eretz Yisrael* during the war, multitudes came out to welcome him. But it was the Chazon Ish alone who the very next morning sent an emissary with an envelope containing a generous sum of money.

There were quite a number of poor families whom he sent assistance regularly. Once, an envelope from America containing checks for a number of these families arrived at his door. The Chazon

Ish gave the checks to one of his disciples with instructions regarding their distribution. When the disciple returned from his mission, he parenthetically mentioned the name of one of those to whom he had given a check. A few minutes later, the Chazon Ish casually mentioned the same name and asked whether or not the man had attempted to return the check. The disciple replied that it had been accepted with gratitude. It was then that the Chazon Ish revealed that the disciple had erred. The check was to have been given to someone else. In fact, the Chazon Ish had never offered assistance to the recipient, for, as far as everyone knew, he was not in need. However, from the man's gracious acceptance, it was obvious that his situation was not as it seemed. The Chazon Ish then handed his disciple a new check for the intended individual. And from then on, the other man was added to his list of regular recipients.

HIS *GEMILLAS CHESED* with visitors often went beyond helping them with their problems. Those in his inner circle were amazed at how he would insist that a petitioner who had traveled long and far remain for a meal — often prepared and served by the Chazon Ish himself.

Total Selflessness

One man recalled: "I traveled from Jerusalem to Bnei Brak to discuss something with him, arriving there in mid-afternoon. The Chazon Ish asked me, 'Have you eaten lunch?' I replied, '*Chas v'shalom*! The *Rebbi* should not bother with anything for me. I will eat later.' He retorted, 'What is the *Chas v'shalom*?! Am I not a Jew? Besides, it is not every day that I have such an opportunity — it is lunch-time now, you have traveled some distance, and there is no one here to serve you but myself!' Over my protests, he set the table, brought out some food, gave me a washing cup filled with water and a towel, then sat and related some of his gems of thought as I ate."

His faithful partner in life worried that his activities for others would take their toll on his poor physical condition. Thus, the *Rebbetzin* implored the Chazon Ish's brother, Rabbi Meir Karelitz, to prevail upon him to see visitors only at fixed hours. Though the Chazon Ish always accorded his elder brother's words very high regard, and Reb Meir tried his best, it was to no avail. The Chazon Ish begged that this request not be made of him. "How can the door be closed to those who are suffering and distressed?"

The *Rebbetzin* would do her own pleading — with those who sought his help, asking that they not prolong their conversations longer than necessary. She would explain, *"Er iz mein kroin, ich muz im hitten,* He is my crown; I must protect him [i.e., his health]."

For his part, the Chazon Ish would sometimes tell his petitioners that if they needed him and he was resting, they should not hesitate to bang on his window.

One year prior to *Succos*, the Chazon Ish was standing in his room carefully inspecting the *arba'ah minim* that had been brought for his personal use. A disciple attempted to close the door, so that no visitors would disrupt the inspection. The Chazon Ish stopped him. "The *lulav* can always be inspected later," he said.

His Supreme Sacrifice

"ONE MAY ASK," wrote Reb Shlomo Kohen, "in what way was his self-sacrifice for others most manifest? In that he was prepared to be of assistance to anyone at any moment despite his precarious state of health? In that he allowed himself no rest, even becoming saddled with huge debts in order to help those in financial straits? In that he strained his every mental faculty to unnatural limits as he searched for ways to solve the problems of communities and individuals?

"Yes, he did all of the above. It seems to me, however, that the most precious sacrifice that he offered in order to be *gomel chesed* was his study of Torah. His efforts for others robbed him of most of his time and strained a mind that had been sanctified from the womb for Torah study.

"Torah was his very lifeblood; for it alone did his pure soul yearn. I recall vividly his intense love for Torah, his insatiable thirst for it — and I cannot imagine whence he derived the fortitude to sacrifice so much of his time and thought process on the altar of *gemillas chesed*."

A disciple once lamented that his own involvement with helping a fellow Jew was causing him loss of time for Torah study. The Chazon Ish told him, "You are wrong; this is not *bittul Torah*. Our holy Torah is unlike any other wisdom. Torah is inextricably bound with the Jewish soul. Now, when one performs a kindness for his fellow Jew, his soul is uplifted, thus making it a better receptacle for the absorption of Torah knowledge."

It was common practice for the Chazon Ish to go outside late at night and check if anyone in need of his help was waiting outside, fearful to knock at such an hour. At times when he would be asked in the middle of the night to pray for a sick man in distress, the

Chazon Ish would send someone to awaken yeshivah students living nearby to come join him in reciting *Tehillim*.

Someone related that he once stood outside the Chazon Ish's window after midnight with other members of his family when one of their loved ones was seriously ill. The Chazon Ish awoke to the sound of weeping. Quickly, he dressed and hurried outside. "If a Jew weeps then a Jew must be in anguish," he said softly. Someone in the group explained the situation, including the doctor's prognosis that all was lost. "To whom else could we turn in middle of the night?" the person concluded. "We were sure that the *Rebbi* would not mind."

The Chazon Ish asked for the patient's Hebrew name. Then, he offered words of encouragement, assuring the family that the situation was far from hopeless, contrary to what the doctors had said. He wished them good night and returned to his room to pray.

One evening, a man came to the Chazon Ish's door in search of medical advice. Rabbi Shraga Feivel Steinberg admitted the visitor, then entered the Chazon Ish's room to find him at the sink, washing cup in hand, as he prepared for supper. Seeing this, Rabbi Steinberg began to hurry from the room, saying that he would ask the man to wait. But it was too late. The Chazon Ish would not think of eating while a Jew was waiting for his help. Only after the man had left did the Chazon Ish begin supper, obviously burdened by the weight of the troubles that he had just heard.

That the troubles and trials of others were his own was obvious to all. He once told Rabbi Eliyahu Mishkovsky, *Rosh Yeshivah* of Yeshivah K'far Chassidim, "Digestion [of others' troubles] is one thing, but chewing them over is exceedingly more difficult."

Those who related their troubles to the Chazon Ish in person were exceeded in number by those who communicated with him in writing. After the Chazon Ish's death, Rabbi Aharon Sorasky read through one pile of *kvitlach* that had been sent him. He commented, "Any heart with feeling would be melted — one could almost see the thousands of troubled eyes peering up from those scraps of paper, awaiting salvation."

IN THE MARGIN of one of the Chazon Ish's personal *sefarim*, the following was found scrawled: "The blessing of a *gadol hador* has impact in Heaven and can transform a moment into one of auspiciousness." The efficacy of the Chazon Ish's blessings was vivid proof to this statement. When the Chazon Ish was still a young man in Vilna, Reb Chaim Ozer sent someone in need of salvation to his door — with miraculous results.* Those close to the Chazon Ish in his later years saw, on a day-to-day basis, the wonders brought about by his blessings and prayers.

Urim V'Tumim

Perhaps even more incredible was the counsel he offered for myriads of situations and dilemmas and the often wondrous and unanticipated results of such counsel.

Rabbi Eliyahu Eliezer Dessler, *mashgiach* of Ponovezh and author of *Michtav M'Eliyahu*, referred to the Chazon Ish as the *Urim V'Tumim*** of his generation.

The Ponovezher *Rav* saw in the Chazon Ish the epitome of a Talmudic adage: "*From the day that the Temple was destroyed, although prophecy was taken from the prophets, it was not taken from the wise*" (Bava Basra 12a). Ramban (ibid.) explains, "Although the prophecy of prophets, meaning Heavenly vision, was taken away, the prophecy of the wise, which is ascertained through the paths of wisdom, was not taken. The wise ascertain truth through the Divine spirit that resides within them."

The Chazon Ish never tried to impose his opinion on others. When a petitioner would show displeasure with the advice he had received, the Chazon Ish would say, "I do not decide, I only advise."

The sense of responsibility with which he approached every problem was revealing. Someone once asked his opinion on a *Klal* issue. He replied, "The matter is not currently relevant." His questioner responded with a Talmudic expression, "This [i.e., the Chazon Ish's opinion] is Torah. I wish to be knowledgeable!" The Chazon Ish then said, "People are mistaken when they think that I simply shake my opinions and rulings out of my cuff. In truth, every

---

* See chapter four.
** One of the priestly garments worn by the *Kohen Gadol* (High Priest) in the *Beis HaMikdash* was the *Choshen* (Breastplate). The *Choshen* was adorned with twelve precious stones on which were inscribed the names of the twelve tribes. Inside the *Choshen* was the *Urim V'Tumim* (see *Exodus* 28:30), a slip of parchment upon which the שֵׁם הַמְפוֹרָשׁ, *Ineffable Name*, was written. Heavenly responses to important questions would be seen on the letters of the *Choshen's* stones, which were illuminated through the power of the *Urim V'Tumim*.

decision physically costs me dearly. So long as I am not forced to respond, I must fulfill the commandment to guard one's health."

At times, he would explain the reasoning behind his counsel. There were many occasions, however, when he chose to let the matter remain closed. A simple "yes" or "no" was very often his response to a question of major significance. He was once asked why he had offered different advice to petitioners who had posed identical questions. He responded, "We find that with regard to certain Mishnaic disputes, the Talmud concludes that one may conduct himself according to either opinion. This is not a decision resulting from doubt; rather, it is the precise *halachah* in that particular topic." Similarly, two solutions are sometimes applicable for one problem. To decide which solution should be applied in a given situation sometimes requires the mind of a Chazon Ish.

Over the years, some came to believe that they fully comprehended his method of thought and certain basic principles upon which, to their minds, his opinions were based. Thus, they considered themselves capable of anticipating his decisions in *Klal*-related matters. They were wrong. To arrive at the reasoning of a mind so brilliant and so blessed with *siyata d'shmaya*, one had to be a *tzaddik* and *gaon* of the Chazon Ish's caliber. The Chazon Ish towered over his generation and the workings of his mind forever remained a mystery.

The Chazon Ish himself expressed this point in a letter to a certain *talmid chacham* regarding a *Klal* matter of major significance:

> It pains me that it is impossible for me to explain my position, thus leaving my decision open to questions, doubts and suspicions. What can I do? — Toil in Torah study amid indescribable suffering grants one something unique. No longer does one judge matters on instinct — even instinct that stems from an affinity to *kedushah*. Rather, an intellect nurtured and shaped by Torah prevails over all feelings, which, sublime though they may seem, may actually be tinged with jealousy and anger ...

Once, a religious group attempting to establish a Bais Yaakov school in their settlement was offered the following proposal: If the religious members on the town council would vote in favor of funding for a new *Histadrut* building, then the secularists would cast their votes for funding of a Bais Yaakov building. The religious members approved the deal; rumor had it that they did so upon the ruling of the Chazon Ish.

There were certain *kana'im* (zealots) who were outraged that the Chazon Ish would favor any move that would serve to strengthen the secularist, anti-religious *Histadrut*. One such person presented himself before the Chazon Ish and requested an explanation. The Chazon Ish responded with silence. However, the man would not relent. For quite some time, he repeated his own position again and again, often invoking the Mishnaic adage (*Avos* 1:7), *Do not associate with a wicked person*, as proof. As it became obvious that the man had no intention of leaving, the Chazon Ish felt forced to respond.

"Did you *daven* with a *minyan* today?" he asked the visitor.

"Why, certainly!" came the reply.

"Before you began *davening*, did you check the credentials of each member of the *minyan* to be absolutely sure that none are in the category of *reshai'im* (wicked people)?"

The man did not understand. The Chazon Ish went on.

"What more significant association can there be than to join others in praying to the *Ribono Shel Olam*? Why were you not mindful *then* of the teaching that you persist in quoting? What I mean to say is, one cannot render *p'sak halachah* based on adages of *Chazal*. For every adage that you will cite as proof of your position, I can offer three as refutations.

"My ruling in this matter was based on something else entirely, something which I learned from the Chofetz Chaim. The Chofetz Chaim used to say that one must approach *Yiddishkeit* (Judaism) as one would a business. Will this venture result in a net profit or loss? This is the criterion a businessman uses in deciding on any given undertaking. In *Yiddishkeit*, too, one must always contemplate what the ultimate result of a venture will be. In this particular case, the *Histadrut* would have themselves more spacious quarters, while the religious settlers would have a school which would instill in their daughters Torah values and inspiration. As time went on, some semi- or even non-religious families might be persuaded to enroll their daughters there. Could there be any doubt as to what the ultimate result of this venture would be?"

We may add that just as one must be a businessman to decide on matters of business, so do matters of *Yiddishkeit* often require the expertise of a *gadol* to decide what is actually a profit and what is a loss. Additionally, there are instances where though a given undertaking will surely produce great benefit for the cause of Torah, it may be deemed not permissible because of particular considerations. The Chazon Ish's reluctance to explain his position in this and other instances was precisely for this reason. Let no one feel that familiarity with the opinions of *gedolim* is in itself sufficient qualification for one to decide such matters on his own.

Torah Logic

DELVE IN IT [i.e., the Torah] and continue to delve in it for everything is in it (*Avos* 5:26). In Torah, the Chazon Ish found the answer to every question, the remedy to every problem. He applied Torah logic in ways that one would have never fathomed — and with astonishing success.

A young, childless woman once came to Rabbi Shlomo Yosef Chill, then a *Rav* in Brooklyn, with a harrowing story. She had been feeling ill of late and had seen three respected physicians. Each offered a different diagnosis, none of which were encouraging: according to one doctor, her problem was blood related, according to another she had developed a heart condition, while the third insisted that the source of her problem lay in the nervous system.

Rabbi Chill contacted Rabbi Beinish Finkel, today *Rosh Yeshivah* at Mirrer Yeshivah in Jerusalem, who at that time was a personal attendant of the Chazon Ish.* The Chazon Ish recommended that the woman see a psychologist! She did, and indeed, her problem was emotional. Her symptoms soon disappeared and were replaced by others, as she found that she was expecting — and subsequently gave birth to her first child.

Later, when Rabbi Chill visited *Eretz Yisrael*, he asked Rabbi Finkel if he knew what lay behind the Chazon Ish's opinion. The Chazon Ish had explained himself as follows: Generally, Torah law grants precedence to the majority over the minority. In this case, each opinion offered by one doctor was outweighed by the opinions of the other two doctors. Thus, all were nullified. There remained, then, a real possibility that the problem was not physical at all. Seeing a psychologist was a logical, and indeed correct, first step.

A woman suffering from a kidney ailment was preparing to journey to America for treatment, when she suddenly experienced an attack. A doctor prescribed a pain killer, while a family

---

* Rabbi Finkel is married to a daughter of Rabbi Shmuel Greineman.

member went to the Chazon Ish. The Chazon Ish advised against using the medication. After her arrival in America, a world-renowned specialist successfully treated the woman's condition. The specialist told the woman that it was fortunate that she had not taken the medication, for its use could have interfered with her recovery.

Someone later related all this to the Chazon Ish, conveying the general impression that the Chazon Ish had wrought a miracle. In response, the Chazon Ish explained that his advice was based on nothing more than logic: The woman would soon be under the care of a renowned specialist who was known to have succeeded in curing similar cases. The medication would have eased her pain, but might have produced side-effects. Was it not worth a few days more of pain, rather than jeopardize her recovery?

In another instance, it was the strength of his unshakable *emunah* that prompted the Chazon Ish's counsel. A young woman in the latter stages of pregnancy was experiencing complications. The doctor declared that she would not survive the delivery. The Chazon Ish told the woman's husband not to worry. He said that what the world calls "natural childbirth" is, in fact, nothing short of miraculous. The G-d who performs miracles for every mother in labor would help the man's wife in whatever way was necessary. A few weeks later the man returned to inform the Chazon Ish that the baby had been born; mother and child were fine.

MANY ARE THE STORIES which show that the Chazon Ish was endowed with *Ruach HaKodesh*.

Above and Beyond

He once advised a woman with a heart condition to travel from *Eretz Yisrael* to England so that a certain specialist could perform the surgery she needed. Contact was made with the doctor who told the woman that the journey would not be necessary, as he would soon be visiting the Holy Land and would be able to perform the surgery while there. Strangely, the Chazon Ish ignored this information. The surgery, he insisted, must be performed in England, not *Eretz Yisrael*. The woman heeded his words and had to wait for the doctor to return from his trip before she could undergo the operation.

Routine tests taken prior to the surgery showed a heretofore undetected complication in the woman's condition. The doctor required a relatively new and rare device which was, at that time, available in British hospitals but not in *Eretz Yisrael*. With the aid of that device, the operation was a success.

Another story with a somewhat similar twist has America as the destination. Doctors had been insisting that a Jerusalem woman undergo brain surgery. The Chazon Ish, however, was equally insistent that surgery not be performed. He instructed the family to have the woman taken to America — but he offered no specific solution for the woman's problem. The Chazon Ish provided traveling expenses, arranged for the party to stay with Rabbi Shmuel Greineman, who was then living in New York, and offered but one instruction — no surgery under any circumstances.

Rabbi Greineman brought the woman to a specialist, Dr. Lazarus, who was world-renowned in his field. After hearing the case, Dr. Lazarus said that the case did not fall within his area of expertise, directing the woman instead to his colleague, Dr. Globus.

Normally, appointments with Dr. Globus had to be made at least one month in advance. Rabbi Greineman prevailed upon Dr. Lazarus to gain the woman swift admittance to his colleague. An appointment was arranged for two days hence. After an examination that took more than an hour, Dr. Globus declared the woman to be in need of a specific treatment, not surgery. He directed her to a leading hospital in the area, where the treatment would be administered. The woman and her relatives expressed their gratitude and took leave of the doctor.

As they left the office, Dr. Globus suffered a heart attack. He died shortly thereafter. Providence had allowed him to live long enough to save this woman's life. She responded to the treatments and returned to Jerusalem in good health.

※ ※ ※

A prospective bride sitting in a dentist's chair on the day before her wedding accidentally swallowed a needle which the dentist had inserted into her mouth. She was rushed to a hospital, where doctors expressed concern that surgery would be necessary. While the case was being debated and the woman's condition monitored, the groom telegraphed the Chazon Ish to ask if the wedding should be postponed. He responded, "Do not postpone — the needle will come out by itself before the wedding."

The next day, a four-word telegram arrived at the Chazon Ish's door: "מזל טוב, המחט יצאה, *Mazel tov, the needle came out!*"*

News of the miracle caused a stir in the yeshivah world. The Chazon Ish tried to make nothing of it. "What miracle?" he asked those who expressed amazement. "When as a child I would get a small scratch and bleed a bit, my mother would soothe me by saying, 'Don't worry, it will be healed by the time your wedding day arrives.' So you see, I was only doing as my mother taught me ..."

A woman expecting her first child after thirteen years of marriage was experiencing severe complications in her condition. Leading doctors in the field were unanimous in their opinion that the pregnancy be terminated. The woman's father brought the case to the Chazon Ish. He listened carefully to every detail and asked for some additional information. Then he responded, "Ignore the doctors. Hashem will save her from any mishap and a healthy child will be born." And so it was.

Master of Medicine

INDEED, THE CHAZON ISH'S knowledge of medicine and his counsel in health-related matters was without parallel among the Torah sages of his time. He was as familiar with the human anatomy and its remedies as any professor of medicine and he routinely rendered medical decisions in cases where the patient's life hung in the balance. Day after day, he would be asked whether or not major surgery should be performed, a specialist's advice be heeded, or which curative treatment to undergo. In every such instance, the Chazon Ish either decided the matter himself or directed the party to a physician whom he considered most suited for the case.

His *rebbetzin* once said in jest, "When I married him, I thought that he would one day become a renowned *rav*. Now, it seems that he is more like a physician ..."

It seemed as if his every counsel was Divinely inspired. "Truly incredible," Rabbi Isser Zalman Meltzer once remarked. "His medical advice is on target virtually one hundred percent of the time."

Rabbi Shmuel Wosner once watched in astonishment as the Chazon Ish, after receiving all pertinent information, responded instantly to a life-and-death question. Unable to restrain himself, Rabbi Wosner exclaimed, "Does one decide life-and-death matters instantaneously?" The Chazon Ish nodded.

---

* The Greineman family is in possession of that telegram.

His confidence in deciding such matters was also expressed in his written responses to medical questions. In one reply, he wrote, "The doctor's negative opinion in this matter is of no substance."

Though his advice was offered quickly and confidently, it was never given without a careful analysis of the case. Every symptom, test result and diagnosis had to be explained in full detail. The Chazon Ish's subsequent inquiries were enough to put the petitioner at ease that the case was in the hands of an "expert in the field."

The Chazon Ish was fluent in the strengths and weaknesses of *Eretz Yisrael's* leading physicians in virtually every area of medicine. When directing a party to a particular doctor, he would stress that the patient should go to no one but the doctor whom he named. His nephew, Rabbi Chaim Greineman, related that the Chazon Ish held certain doctors to be diagnostic experts, while others he considered experts only in administering treatments. Thus, he would sometimes send a patient to one doctor for a diagnosis only, then have the person visit a second doctor, diagnosis in hand, to receive the necessary treatment. There were times when he felt that a diagnosis was incorrect and would send the person for a second opinion. Sometimes, he felt it important that a doctor be shown where his error lay. Of course, this depended on who the doctor was and what kind of error was involved.

Once, he contradicted the opinion of a prominent doctor — and his opinion was heeded with successful results. At a physician's conference some time later, the doctor publicly ridiculed the Torah community for heeding the words of rabbis over the "knowledge of experts." He cited the incident with the Chazon Ish as an example. A doctor in the audience raised his hand to speak. He also knew of that case, he said. The Chazon Ish had consulted with him before rendering his decision. One piece of information which the Chazon Ish had sought was the percentage of cases in which the first doctor's diagnosis was incorrect. The second doctor had responded that the doctor was off target twenty-five percent of the time.

The first doctor brought his speech to a swift conclusion.

Eventually, physicians became accustomed to the fact that virtually no Jew from the Torah community would undergo treatment of a serious condition without the Chazon Ish's consent. As time went on, more and more physicians came to revere the Chazon Ish and his medical expertise. Moreover, many of the leading physicians in Israel would consult with him and came to rely heavily on his opinion.

A girl from Bnei Brak suffered a severe leg wound in an accident. Someone quickly raced to the Chazon Ish, who said to bring the girl to Dr. Marcus, chief surgeon at Hadassah Hospital. The Chazon Ish added, "If there is any difficulty in gaining access to him, say that I sent you."

Sure enough, mention of the Chazon Ish to the doctor's secretary gained the girl admittance. While they waited for Dr. Marcus, the girl and her companions talked with the secretary, who expressed awe of the Chazon Ish's medical knowledge.

In fact, the Chazon Ish himself once mapped out the surgical procedure in a complex heart case. Dr. Moshe Rothschild, a pediatrician in Bnei Brak, has in his possession the Chazon Ish's sketch of the procedure.

Dr. Hardan Ashkenazi, a renowned neurosurgeon, was in contact with the Chazon Ish whenever a patient's family desired the Chazon Ish's consent that surgery be performed. In one instance, it was Dr. Ashkenazi who insisted that the Chazon Ish decide whether or not a young boy should undergo brain surgery. The Chazon Ish's note to the doctor read, "It is exceedingly difficult for me to make such a decision. I am hopeful, though, that Heaven will grant the surgery success. *Ish* Karelitz."

In an interview with Rabbi Aharon Sorasky, Doctor Ashkenazi recalled:

> I was always profoundly impressed by the Chazon Ish's inquiries. They revealed a clarity of mind, a penetrating insight into the human anatomy and its cures. Brain surgery was often our topic of discussion. His questions were always on the mark and properly formulated. He attacked the heart of the matter, shedding new light on the situation — causing me, in many instances, to alter my opinion.
>
> In one instance, the patient was critically ill and I was in doubt as to whether or not surgery should be performed. I received a note from the Chazon Ish in which he described two possible reasons for my uncertainty and requested that I inform him which of them it was. That very day, I related his message before a group of physicians and said, "Take note of how the Chazon Ish summarized the various angles of the case in a few concise sentences. Any of us would have needed pages to write what he expressed so succinctly."

Every encounter with the Chazon Ish left me amazed. Virtually no one else made so powerful an impression on me, an impression that can never be forgotten...

There exist today data banks which can provide information on every conceivable scientific question. In my opinion, the Chazon Ish's phenomenal mind had in it much, much more.

In the world of medicine, there are always new problems to resolve. Day after day, I am faced with decisions upon which a patient's future hinges. It is many years since the Chazon Ish's death; yet when faced with difficult decisions, I still often think: If only I could discuss this with the Chazon Ish...

The Source of it All

RABBI YEHOSHUA ZELIG DISKIN, *Rav* of Pardes Chanah, once had a chance conversation with a renowned Israeli physician during which the Chazon Ish was mentioned. The doctor remarked that patients were sent him by the Chazon Ish though he and the Chazon Ish had never met. The doctor asked if Rabbi Diskin could introduce him to Bnei Brak's sage. He explained his desire for the meeting with the following story:

"A young woman had lain ill in a hospital for some time, her doctors unable to determine the source of her illness. Various treatments were tried, all with negative results. The girl's condition was worsening, with no hope in sight. Finally, the matter came before the Chazon Ish. He advised that I be brought in on the case and told the woman's family, 'Though I am not a doctor, it is my feeling that she is in need of surgery to remove...' The Chazon Ish advised the family to respectfully inform me of his opinion.

"I paid heed to his opinion, and subsequent tests proved his diagnosis to be correct. I performed the surgery — only the fourth such surgery in my thirty-five-year career — and the woman fully recovered.

"Now," the doctor went on, "you understand why I want to meet the Chazon Ish. Can you tell me, indeed, how he ascertained a diagnosis which had eluded some of our country's best physicians?"

Rabbi Diskin replied, "The answer to your question is found in a *braisa* in *Avos*: Whoever studies Torah *lishmah* merits many things..."

The above question posed to Rabbi Diskin was asked by scores of people, especially doctors. The Chazon Ish never read medical literature, nor any other secular literature, never entered a medical laboratory, and certainly never attended classes on the subject. His astounding, all-encompassing knowledge of medicine could only have been G-d-given. The Chazon Ish's incomparable dedication to Torah study had unlocked for him the gates to worldly wisdom, all of which are hidden within the Torah's holy and timeless words.

THE FOLLOWING ANECDOTES speak volumes for the man and his spiritual powers:

The Man and His Powers

A few years after the Chazon Ish died, two religious Jews were riding in the back seat of a taxi heading from Bnei Brak to Jerusalem. The men were lamenting the void which the Chazon Ish's death had left. Overhearing the conversation, the driver, who sported an open khaki shirt, Bermudah shorts and no *kippah*, turned to his companion in the front seat and exclaimed, "Did you hear that? They say the Chazon Ish is gone! They don't know what they are talking about!" The driver went on as his intrigued passengers listened.

His daughter had been having a long, difficult labor. Doctors were hovering over her for hours but could do nothing to relieve her agony. There were no signs that birth was imminent. The cab driver was in the hospital's waiting room, anxious to hear that his grandchild had been born and that all was well. An old nurse, aware of the situation and seeing the man's anxiety, went over to him and said, "Why don't you go to the Chazon Ish?"

The man did not know what the nurse was talking about.

"The Chazon Ish," she repeated. "He is a great rabbi and *tzaddik*. His blessings have helped many people. He lives in Bnei Brak. Go there and any child in the street will direct you to his home."

The man jumped into his cab and sped off. It was late at night when he knocked at the Chazon Ish's door. The Chazon Ish answered the knock. In his congenial way, he asked how he could be of help and listened until the man finished his tale. The Chazon Ish smiled and said, "Go back to the hospital. The baby was just born." Warmly, he shook his visitor's hand, wished him *mazel tov* and bade him good night.

The cab driver's heart leaped with excitement, but he found it hard to believe that what he had just heard was true. He dashed back to the hospital. Sure enough, the baby had already been born. Mother and child were doing fine.

Two years later, the man's daughter was again experiencing a difficult labor. This time he did not wait for the nurse's advice. He headed for Bnei Brak. A secularist who was totally out of touch with the religious world, the cab driver was unaware that the man they called "the Chazon Ish" was no longer alive.

The man who answered his knock stared at the cab driver incredulously. Could there really be people in *Eretz Yisrael* who did not know that the greatest Jew of their time was no longer in their midst? The driver recovered from the initial shock and persisted, "It's an emergency. What should I do?"

"People pray at his grave," came the reply.

Directions to the cemetery were given and the cab driver headed there at breakneck speed. Arriving at the cemetery, he vaulted a fence and quickly sought out the grave. Weeping uncontrollably, he prostrated himself on the gravestone and cried out, "*Rebbi*, you saved my daughter once before. Please save her again."

The man was sure that, there in the cemetery, he heard the voice of the Chazon Ish saying once again, "*Mazel tov*, the child has been born." He returned to the hospital. The child had been born.

❦ ❦ ❦

In the settlement of Rishon L'Tzion there lived a non-observant Jew who had emigrated from Europe after the second World War. Born from parents who were devoutly religious, his observance of *mitzvos* had slackened from the time he had left his father's home as a young man in Hungary to earn a livelihood. Weak in faith, he did his best to conceal any vestige of Jewishness when the Nazis invaded his country. It did him no good; when the deportation of Jews began, he was herded aboard a train bound for Auschwitz. He survived the war and made his way to the Holy Land. Unfortunately, the Land's spiritual blessings had little influence on him: he had drifted so far that even Yom Kippur was to him a day as any other.

On the eve of Yom Kippur 5713 (1952), the man returned home from work as usual. That night, his late father appeared to him in a dream wearing a *kittel* and *tallis*. The father admonished his son to repent, for if not his life would be shortened.

The man tried to shrug off the dream, but this became increasingly difficult as the same dream appeared to him on seven consecutive nights.

Distant as he was from religious life, the man *had* heard of the

Chazon Ish. He traveled to Bnei Brak to discuss his dreams. No sooner had the man entered his study then the Chazon Ish declared sternly, "Alas! You perform forbidden labor on Shabbos, on Rosh Hashanah ... even on Yom Kippur! Your father has no peace in the Upper World. *Kareis* (excision) has been decreed upon you!"

Having spoken, the Chazon Ish rested his head on his arms as if dozing. The man stood before him open-mouthed, dumbfounded by what he had just heard. He had yet to speak a word to the Chazon Ish.

After a few minutes, the Chazon Ish opened his eyes and said, "In the merit of which great *mitzvah* that you performed in your youth have you been granted new life? ... now that you will return to the proper path and go in the way taught you by your father ... Do you recall the great *mitzvah* which you performed in your youth?"

The man regained his composure somewhat and collected his thoughts. He replied that he had always behaved properly toward his fellow man and was always charitable toward the poor.

"This is not sufficient," responded the Chazon Ish, "Not for this alone did you merit having the Heavenly decree against you be rescinded."

Then the man remembered. He had been about fourteen at the time. A woman informed his father that in a village some distance from theirs, a young Jewish boy lay dead with no one to care for his burial. And so, as a fourteen-year-old lad, he had set out alone on a holy mission. Times were dangerous; the roads were filled with roving bands of plunderers. Under constant fear of death, he had made his way through a forest. His mission proved successful.

Hearing this, the Chazon Ish nodded in approval.

From that day on, the man was fully observant.

In 1961, the man related his story to Rabbi Elazar Klein of Be'er Sheva, who included it in his work, *Kiryas Arba*. When Rabbi Klein took ill in the spring of 1977, his family sent a copy of his *sefer* to the Steipler, along with a request that the Steipler pray for his recovery.* Later, the Steipler told Rabbi Moshe Mordechai Shulsinger, "There is a story about the Chazon Ish in this *sefer* that is truly amazing ... an awesome tale, the likes of which one does not hear ...

---

* The Steipler not only prayed for Rabbi Klein's recovery but also studied the *sefer* as a source of merit for its author.

"... As is known, *neshamos* (souls from the Upper World) would appear to the Chazon Ish. The father of this man came from the World of Truth to the Chazon Ish and told him about his son, asking that the Chazon Ish set him on the right path. This is what transpired in that story."

❧ ❧ ❧

One morning, the Chazon Ish appeared unusually happy. He related the reason for his joy to a close relative. On the previous night, the *Vilna Gaon* appeared to him in a dream and they had become engaged in Talmudic debate. *"This time,"* the Chazon Ish told his relative, "I won."

CHAPTER FOURTEEN
Apple of His Eye

"The Chazon Ish restored the crown of Shemittah to its original glory, as he did with other Land-related mitzvos. He strengthened the generation's faith in Torah sages ... and much more. And his primary accomplishment was the b'nei Torah whom he set on their feet" (the Brisker Rav).

"A youth who toils diligently in Torah brings warmth to my heart and captures my soul ... I am bound to him with chains that can never be undone" (from a letter of the Chazon Ish).

THE CHAZON ISH DEVOTED much of his time for the sake of individual *b'nei Torah* throughout the Land. His efforts in this area were far reaching. There were boys whose parents had to be convinced to enroll their son in a yeshivah; there were students whose poor performance in yeshivah demanded careful analysis and sagacious decision-making; and there were scores of *b'nei Torah* who thirsted for the Chazon Ish's advice as they strove to scale the heights of Torah wisdom and Heavenly fear. The Chazon Ish gave selflessly of himself for the sake of any Jew, all the more so for the students of Torah to whom he referred as "the Nation's soul and its light."

Guiding Light

As noted in a previous chapter, the concept of the *beis midrash* being the province of all Jewish boys was not widely understood in *Eretz Yisrael* of the 1930's. Times were hard and parents were concerned both for the present and for their son's financial future. The Chazon Ish rose to the challenge of inculcating his generation with the awareness that the future hinged on the growth and development of a yeshivah movement in the Land.

A father and son once came before him for litigation. The father insisted that his son, then seventeen, had spent enough years studying in yeshivah; the time had come for him to learn a trade. "I want my son to earn a livelihood with dignity," were his words. The son bashfully insisted that studying Torah was all he desired.

The Chazon Ish turned to the father and quoted a *braisa* in *Avos* (6:4): *This is the way of Torah: Eat bread with salt, drink water in small measure, sleep on the ground, live a life of deprivation — but toil in Torah! If you do this, you are praiseworthy and all is well with you.* "You are praiseworthy" — in this world; "and all is well with you" — in the World to Come.

"Now," the Chazon Ish went on, "we can readily understand that the study of Torah in this world will bring one eternal bliss in the Next World. But how can one derive satisfaction in his present existence when he is living a life of deprivation? Also, the words *If you do this* seem superfluous.

"In truth, those words hold the key to the *braisa's* message. Deprivation is a relative concept: one person can be ecstatic over his material situation, while someone else may be miserable with the same. Your son has already tasted the sweetness of Torah study. To him, any material sacrifice for Torah is drowned in a sea of spiritual delight. Whatever his situation, he will truly feel that he is lacking nothing — and indeed he will be correct! To insist that he leave the *beis midrash* is to deprive him of a life of true fulfillment."

❀ ❀ ❀

In Tel-Aviv, there lived a teenage yeshivah student of average scholastic ability whose neighborhood friends had convinced him to leave yeshivah to work on a religious *kibbutz*. The boy's *rebbeim* were dismayed by his decision; they felt that he had not yet reached the stage in life where he had to think about a livelihood and they were convinced that he should remain in yeshivah at least for the near future. However, their efforts to persuade him to abandon his plans proved fruitless.

One of the boy's classmates went to the Chazon Ish with the story. Though the Chazon Ish had never met the boy, he took the time to write him the following letter:

> The *Mishnah* [*Avos* 3:18] states: *Beloved is man, for he was created in G-d's image; it is indicative of a greater love that it was made known to him that he was created in G-d's image* ... I speak now for my own benefit. An exceptional love is found in the heart of one who toils in Torah for he who chooses to study Torah, which was given to the Jewish nation as an inheritance. From this insight, my dear one, you can well understand the joy I shall experience in seeing you delight in the joy of Torah as you continue your studies — and the sadness that will envelop me should you, G-d forbid, choose the opposite. It is self-love that urges me to inform you, my precious one, of all this in the hope that you will take pleasure in bringing joy unto me.
>
> I close with a blessing and await your response, איש (*Ish*)

The boy was deeply moved by the letter. He traveled to Bnei Brak to explain his decision to the Chazon Ish in person. He was certain, he explained, that his future lay in working on a religious *kibbutz*. He had given serious consideration to learning in yeshivah full time for another year, but certain considerations, which he now delineated, convinced him that he should not pass up the present opportunity.

The Chazon Ish extended his hand as he wished the boy *hatzlachah* (success). He said not another word. The boy went home confident that his explanation had satisfied the Chazon Ish. Little did he know that he would soon be receiving a second letter:

> I wish to explain my position regarding your decision to join the *kibbutz* now ... It is my feeling that nothing in the world can compare with the value of a year's Torah study. Moreover, one should not forsake the study of Torah because of concerns for the future (see *Rashi* to *Deuteronomy* 18:13*).
>
> My precious one, I did not want to hurt your feelings while you were here — but I also did not want you to think that your explanation met with my approval. It is my obligation to apprise you of this ...

The boy remained in yeshivah.

NO YESHIVAH CAN CATER to the needs of every type of student. It takes wisdom and a good measure of *siyata dishmaya* to discern

---

* To the verse *Be wholesome with Hashem, your G-d*, Rashi explains: "Walk with Him in wholesomeness, depend upon Him and do not delve into the future; rather, accept whatever comes upon you with wholesomeness. Then, you will be with Him and His lot."

For One and All

precisely which place of learning, which grade level and which *rebbi* is best suited for any given *talmid*. Though he had never attended a yeshivah, had no children of his own and had never held a teaching or administrative position in a yeshivah, the Chazon Ish was often consulted when such advice was needed. He had only to speak briefly with a *bachur* to understand his strengths and weaknesses, his potential for success and his negative inclinations.

His letters in this regard speak for themselves:

> He possesses a gifted mind and is personable. He is also distracted by his inclinations ... as are many bright fellows. He therefore needs constant guidance. But these are the ones who are destined for greatness ... (*Igros*, I:§75).
>
> A student by the name of ... came to me with his bitter story. Due to family problems, he cannot remain in Jerusalem. Therefore, he came to your yeshivah — but it is already a week that he is wandering about there. I am told that the administration feels he has no place there and refuses to accept him.
>
> I cannot possibly give him the positive answer he expects from me; that is for your administration to do. And for me to tell him that matters are outside my realm — this response was long ago disqualified, as has been said: "Is that a way to answer a bitter soul?" I therefore told him that I would try [to gain him admission], but could not guarantee anything definite. I am keeping my word to him with this letter, and because the situation of this student is such a difficult one — and especially in our days when those attending *yeshivos* are so few ... If you can answer affirmatively please do not keep the good news from me (II:§53).
>
> In our days, the rescuing of a boy to provide him a Torah education is no less urgent than rescuing him from drowning. Because of his age ... [he] can be developed and elevated to the level of a scholar in a very short time, but he needs special attention. Perhaps private tutoring can be arranged mornings and evenings. This could be handled by one of the older boys ... (II:§57).

In a discussion regarding Torah education, the Chazon Ish said that people are often greatly concerned with the fate of a community but not so concerned with the fate of an individual. The proper way, he insisted, is to view every Jew as a world unto himself. The Chazon Ish saw a boy's potential failure as a yeshivah student as someone else might view the possible loss of Torah to all of *Klal Yisrael*, ר״ל.

Someone close to the Chazon Ish once presented him with the following question: He had just been hired as a principal of a yeshivah. He had the option of assuming his post immediately, at the tail end of a semester, or waiting until the start of the new school year. He was presently working as a fund-raiser for Torah causes and would, in any case, be utilizing his time for the sake of Heaven.

The Chazon Ish replied, "Start immediately! Perhaps in these remaining days you will draw even a single *talmid* close to you and set him on a proper path — this is more precious than fine gold!"

❧ ❧ ❧

A Torah educator informed the Chazon Ish that circumstances had forced him to seek another means of livelihood.

"Which field do you propose to enter?" asked the Chazon Ish.

"Diamond polishing."

"But you *are* a diamond polisher!" he exclaimed. "What could be more precious than a Jewish child!"

HE TOLD Rabbi Ben-Zion Bamberger of Ponovezh, "Instill in your *talmidim* a firm belief in *hashgachah pratis** ... this has a profound impact on a tender young heart ... that nothing is left to chance, all is through *hashgachah*, therefore nothing is beyond the power of *tefillah* ... this is the proven road to success, for through proper outlook one is transformed into a different person ... *In all your paths, be cognizant of Him, and He will set your ways straight* (Proverbs 3:6) — this is a verse on which all of Torah hinges ..."

Instilling Faith

In an essay made public during his years in Vilna, the Chazon Ish called for "education toward absolute commitment" with regard to matters of faith. The *Rambam's* well-known advocacy of moderation applies to character traits, such as anger as opposed to indifference, frugality as opposed to squandering — areas where one should avoid extremes. By contrast, commitment to *emunah* and *bitachon* must not be lukewarm or moderate; it must be absolute. Thus, those who bear the responsibility for teaching fundamentals of

---

* The concept that Heaven takes note of and is involved in man's day-to-day affairs and that the nature of this Providence is relative to each man's worth, specifically with regard to *emunah* and *bitachon*, faith and trust in Hashem (see ch. 10).

Greeting young Torah students in the new yishuv

faith must exercise great caution in how they transmit these principles.

The following is drawn from that essay:

> ... Absolute commitment is the ultimate development of a subject, as opposed to mediocrity. One who abhors commitment has his share among the falsifiers or those who simply lack understanding. If there is no commitment there is no completeness and without completeness there can be no beginning. Beginnings are fraught with difficulties. Completeness is the sharp response which places everything in its proper perspective.
>
> We are accustomed to hearing various circles proclaim that their share is not among the "extremists" [i.e., ultra-religious]; they leave themselves the [title of] a loyal Jew with sufficient faith and [submission to] the Torah viewpoint. We permit ourselves to say ... that just as a lover of wisdom does not love but a bit of wisdom and despise it in large measure, so too does a lover of Torah not desire the middle of the road [with regard to matters of faith] and reject absolute commitment.
>
> The Thirteen Principles of Faith* are in sharp conflict with simplistic ideas and the accepted way of life under the sun. The clear recognition which [leads to] conviction with regard to these principles is the love for absolute commitment.
>
> A middle-of-the-road existence has justification when one

---

* As delineated by *Rambam*.

admires absolute commitment, allows his soul to be drawn toward it and [allows his] offspring to be brought to the soaring heights of commitment. However, the middle-of-the-road existence which scorns absolute commitment is shameful.

Our obligation is to teach absolute commitment! ... Those who have established middle-of-the-road schools were not successful in [combating the] forgery inherent in this attitude. Their education breeds a righteous attitude toward one's turning his back on those religious laws that he finds difficult and those beliefs that he finds contrary to the accepted way of living. He has been robbed of the secret of absolute commitment, because his parents and teachers have scoffed at it.

A Positive Approach

THE CHAZON ISH held firmly that love and a positive approach toward one's *talmidim* are an educator's keys to success. When Rabbi Eliyahu Eliezer Dessler was serving as *Mashgiach* of the Ponovezh Yeshivah, there were some who felt that he demonstrated an overabundance of love and a shortage of sternness in guiding and monitoring his students' discipline. The Chazon Ish brushed aside this critique with a play on Talmudic terms: "*Meshichah* (drawing close) is more powerful than *chazakah* (force)!"*

In a discussion with a yeshivah principal, the Chazon Ish stressed the importance of emphasizing a *talmid's* strengths and playing down his flaws. Making a person feel good about himself is often what inspires him to improve. The Chazon Ish elaborated, "In all my days, no one ever deceived me into believing he was better than he actually was. However, there were times when I intentionally allowed someone to think that he had succeeded in this ... this gave effectiveness to my words of instruction as the person strove to live up to the standards that he was portraying."

He stressed the need for *talmidim* to be infused with a sense of accomplishment, "for this will increase their diligence and dedication to study." Conversely, he cautioned against demoting a student as a means of inducing him to improve his scholastic performance. Demoralizing a child can often have detrimental impact on the ultimate goal — that his love for Torah grow as he grows and that he develop into a true *talmid chacham* and G-d-fearing Jew.

Once, a young student was caught stealing. The yeshivah

---

* *Meshichah* and *chazakah* are both *kinyanim*, halachic acts of acquisition.

administration was inclined to have the boy expelled. The Chazon Ish intervened. He asked the principal, "Has a student ever been expelled for speaking *lashon hara*? That is also a sin, but its transgression does not warrant expulsion from yeshivah — neither does stealing."

Like His Own

THE CHAZON ISH had only to hear that a *ben Torah* was in need of assistance and he acted immediately. He concerned himself with providing clothing, proper food and other material items for needy students. Once, he learned that an ill student attending a yeshivah some distance from Bnei Brak was suffering from a throat ailment and was not being properly attended to. Without wasting a moment, the Chazon Ish purchased a jar of honey, hailed a taxi, and, accompanied by his confidant Reb Zelig Shapiro, was on his way. His visit to the boy's bedside caused quite a stir. From then on, the dormitory personnel made sure that ill students were properly cared for.

He stressed the need for students to guard their health and he kept a careful watch on those who had been neglectful of this: "I am concerned for your health ... Do not abstain from the fish-oil remedy. I have heard that kosher oil can be obtained. It would be good for you to pursue the matter ..." (*Igros*, II:§7).

The Chazon Ish, surrounded by b'nei Torah

"I greatly desire that you allow your body to return to its normal condition" (II:§98).

"I hunger to learn of your physical well-being . . ." (II:§98).

"Perhaps you can spend a month at a summer resort . . . ask your soul to do kindness with your body" (II:§100).

Over the years, a number of young boys and teenaged students were taken in to live with the Chazon Ish. One such case involved a young boy attending Tiferes Zion. The boy's family situation required that he live in the school's dormitory. When he developed a stomach disorder that made caring for him an unpleasant task, the Chazon Ish had him brought to his apartment where *Rebbetzin* Kanievsky nursed him back to health.

In the preface to his *Sha'arei Orah*, Rabbi Meir Tzvi Bergman*expressed his appreciation to the Chazon Ish, ". . . who brought me near to him. For two years, I slept in his room; he taught me Torah and inspired me toward its study." Orphaned at a young age, he was one of a number of boys whom the Chazon Ish took under his wings and nurtured into students who eventually became outstanding *talmidei chachamim* and disseminators of Torah.

Rabbi Mordechai Shlomo Berman writes in his *Asher L'Shlomo*, "Our great teacher . . . the Chazon Ish, took me into his home; like a father, he reared me and taught me. I was with him for six years, day after day . . ."

SCORES OF TORAH STUDENTS sought to discuss Torah with the Chazon Ish and see if their own *chiddushei Torah* met with his

Crucial Factors

approval. Young *talmidim* would come excitedly to relate a good question or answer which they had propounded. He found time for them all, as he strove to hone their skills and inspire them toward greater love of Torah.**

One student related a relatively simple *chiddush* and then lamented the length of time it had taken for him to formulate it. The Chazon Ish responded that propounding *chiddushei Torah* requires *siyata dishmaya*. The degree of *siyata dishmaya* one merits is

---

* *Rosh Yeshivah* of Yeshivah Rashbi in Bnei Brak. Among his published works is *Mavo She'arim* (Gateway to the Talmud).

** Conversely, the Chazon Ish would as a rule refrain from commenting on the *chiddushei Torah* related to him by established *talmidei chachamim*. Once, during his later years, a visiting American *rav* related a *d'var Torah*. Unsure as to what the Chazon Ish's silence meant, the *rav* asked, "May one say such a *p'shat*?" Replied the Chazon Ish in jest, "Why certainly! Did you not just say it?"

dependent on many factors, not the least of which are diligence and dedication to study. Thus, a *chiddush* that one person propounds in hours might take another only minutes to originate.

On another occasion, he said, "Without *yiras shamayim*, it is impossible to truly succeed in Torah study. However, even *yiras shamayim* alone is insufficient: to ascertain the truth in Torah one must acquire the 'forty-eight qualities.' "*

"Abilities for Torah study," he said another time, "are not always apparent in one's youth. Sometimes, intense desire to succeed can reveal hidden strengths that have been lying dormant ... A student can walk to a street-corner with a mind that has been unable to understand — then turn the corner to find that the channels of wisdom have suddenly been opened to him ... I recall how, as an eighteen-year-old, one of our generation's *gaonim* would turn to me with questions in *Gemara* that revealed a lack of elementary understanding. His mind could not grasp a thing — and yet he developed into something great."**

In guiding individual *b'nei Torah* along the road to success in their studies, the Chazon Ish did more than encourage diligence and total immersion in learning. To a student who aspired to Torah greatness, he sent the following list of recommendations (*Igros*, I:§20):

> (1) Scrupulously avoid indulgence in food ... an exceedingly low mode of conduct and a hindrance to learning. As the *Midrash* states, *Before praying that words of Torah become assimilated in oneself, one should first pray that delicacies not*

---

* *Avos* 6:6. See chapter one of this book.

** In his *Chayei Olam* (pg. 82), the Steipler writes, "In truth, every student of Torah succeeds in large measure, each according to his own level. Every page of *Gemara* that one studies and knows, every *Tosafos* that one understands, is an acquisition and an achievement of itself; moreover [with each successive *daf* or *Tosafos* learned] one has succeeded that much more in opening his mind to understanding a *sugya* and to proper Talmudic reasoning. If he will pursue his studies diligently, then his small successes will accumulate until his Torah knowledge will proclaim his stature and his seat among the learned will be established.

"It is known that in their youth, many *talmidei chachamim* were considered by their peers to be failures and of inferior intellectual ability. As they grew older, however, it became apparent that they had acquired a fundamental knowledge of most of *Shas* and were, in fact, superior in the give-and-take of Talmudic debate. They became experts in rendering *p'sak halachah*.

"Above all, it is important that one study diligently, that he toil to ascertain the truth. Our Sages have taught that if one claims to have toiled in Torah study and has not succeeded, do not believe him (*Megillah* 6b). I have been apprised that the *Meiri* (*Mishlei* 13:11) has already stated: 'We have often seen men who encountered difficulties in their studies at first, but who succeeded in the end.' "

enter oneself [see *Tosafos* to *Kesubos* 104a]. Also, it is said, *Withdraw your hand from a pleasurable feast* (*Gittin* 70a).

(2) Become accustomed to praying that you be rescued from your evil inclination. Express this prayer in any way you wish, so long as it flows from the heart.

(3) Avoid performing any act that is driven by a desire for honor, G-d forbid. Abstain from anything that will result in your being honored.

(4) Scrupulously avoid any act deemed strange by everyone else.

(5) Delve into the words of *Maharsha*.* When asking others to explain *p'shat* (a text's basic meaning), do it modestly, without any trace of arrogance. Our Sages have taught, *Be exceedingly humble in spirit* (*Avos* 4:4). On the heels of humility comes fear of Hashem. Possession of true humility assures a student of success in Torah study.

To one *ben Torah* he wrote, "One who strengthens himself in Torah is performing an act of *chesed* for *Klal Yisrael.*" As always, he based his statement on the words of *Chazal*, including their assertion that were it not for the Torah study of *David HaMelech*, Yoav ben Tzeruah could not have led his armies to victory (*Sanhedrin* 49a).

In another letter, the Chazon Ish writes:

One must strengthen himself in the study of Torah; this will be a source of merit for both the *klal* and the individual.** This [i.e., Torah study] ... should be with the intent of living by what one learns; I am referring to the observance of negative commandments, which people are more in the habit of treading upon — particularly with regard to *mitzvos* relating to one's fellow man.

---

* Rabbi Shmuel Eliezer Eidles (1555-1631), whose Talmudic commentary is considered the most basic among all *Acharonim*.

** In Manchester, there lived a scholarly businessman named Rabbi Gedaliah Rabinowitz. Rabbi Rabinowitz' knowledge of Torah was vast and profound; he delivered a *Daf Yomi shiur* every day to more than one hundred participants.

Rabbi Rabinowitz took ill with a serious stomach ailment and journeyed to the Holy Land in advance of the surgery that he was to undergo. It was then that he paid his first visit to the Chazon Ish. He introduced himself as a British businessman, told of his problem and requested a blessing. The request was granted. Before taking leave of the Chazon Ish, Rabbi Rabinowitz asked if he could relate a Torah thought. It soon became apparent to the Chazon Ish that his visitor was much more than a businessman. When Rabbi Rabinowitz concluded his *d'var Torah*, the Chazon Ish turned to him and said, "Do not have surgery." These words were heeded with positive results. The Chazon Ish never explained why he had offered this counsel when he did. Ostensibly, it was the merit of Rabbi Rabinowitz' Torah study that prompted the Chazon Ish's words. It is also possible that the Chazon Ish perceived that this man was a disseminator of Torah.

One must exercise caution not to cause his friend hurt through words even for an instant; to do so is to transgress a Torah prohibition* (I:§211).

Purity leads to holiness which, in turn, makes its bearer a more fitting receptacle for the study of Torah. The Chazon Ish would tell yeshivah students that even a laxity in such rabbinically mandated laws as morning *negel vasser* or the required washing of hands for other reasons** can cause one's Torah study to suffer.

A *bachur* once came to the Chazon Ish lamenting his lack of achievement in learning. What the Chazon Ish had to say was not what the *bachur* had expected to hear. "Were your *tzitzis* spun with proper intent? Did you purchase them from a G-d-fearing Jew [whose word can be trusted]? Is your *tallis katan* of at least minimal length and width? Who wrote the *parshiyos* of your *tefillin* and who prepared their *battim* and *retzuos*?"

Finding One's Match

AS THEY DID WHENEVER in need of sagacious advice, yeshivah students sought the Chazon Ish's counsel regarding *shidduchim*. Concerning what to look for in a prospective mate, he would often say, "The prime requirements are that she be of pure heart, possess a love of Torah and a personality that is pleasant and refined. Such a woman will, no doubt, be a fitting helpmate to one who strives for Torah knowledge and Heavenly fear."

A student whose family was poor was offered a match with an equally poor girl. Seemingly, the lack of means on either side would limit if not eliminate post-marriage full-time study. Should the *bachur* consider this *shidduch*? Said the Chazon Ish, "There are three partners in the creation of every human: Hashem, the father and mother (*Kiddushin* 30b). When a couple establishes its home upon the foundations of Torah, then Hashem, as it were, enters into their partnership.

"So what if the first two partners have no means of which to speak? The third Partner owns heaven and earth. He will provide you with all that you need."

In response to a letter which centered on the dowry agreement of a prospective groom, the Chazon Ish wrote:

---

* See *Leviticus* 25:17. An entire book devoted to this prohibition, entitled *The Power of Words* (by Rabbi Zelig Pliskin), has recently been published.
** See *Orach Chaim* 4:18.

> Your excessive exactness in matters which our Sages placed at a distance — as stated clearly in *Rama* (*Even HaEzer* 2:1) — is not understandable to me. The *Rama* concludes, "Whatever the bride's parents give should be accepted with a 'good eye' (i.e., regardless of the amount); then he will succeed." The *Rama's* assurance of success is surely worth more than one's personal efforts. As I am accustomed to being influenced by the *Rama's* opinions, with regard to both myself and others, it is difficult for me to comprehend his honor's feelings in this matter (*Igros*, I:§167).

Regarding qualities that should be sought in a prospective husband, the Chazon Ish had this to say, "Aside from scholarship and piety, one should be certain that the *bachur* will be caring and concerned toward his spouse."

He once told Rabbi Chaim Kreiswirth, *Rav* of Antwerp, "One should approach *shidduchim* with a broad perspective. For example, a *bachur* may be a scholar and a descendant of a long, unbroken chain of *talmidei chachamim*. Torah has continuously returned to 'its place of lodging' and one would expect this to continue — but such is not always the case. If the boy's *midos* are wanting, the chain will end.

"The converse is true as well. Picture a *bachur* who is not a *lamdan*, but is G-d-fearing, serious about his studies and of sterling character. In the merit of his qualities, he may well have children who will be the first link in a chain of *talmidei chachamim* that will span generations."

The Chazon Ish suggested and helped arrange dozens of matches involving yeshivah students. The young women whom he suggested were usually daughters of his acquaintances or orphans with whom he had been involved. His grasp of personalities was keen and swift; a conversation, a letter, or a brief description of an individual was often all the Chazon Ish needed to perceive that person's strengths and weaknesses and what he or she needed in a mate.

His insight into the human psyche was sometimes crucial in steering an individual toward his or her correct match.

A *bachur* seemed on the verge of becoming engaged. His friends were concerned for they knew that the girl's religious observance was wanting. A close friend succeeded in convincing the *bachur* to consider another girl, whose reputation was impeccable. Some time elapsed and the *bachur* seemed ready to marry the second girl. Then, he became filled with doubts, telling himself that perhaps the first girl really was more suited to him. He was in a dilemma, at a loss over what to do.

Again, the *bachur's* friend came to his aid. "Go to the Chazon Ish," he advised. The *bachur* was apprehensive. He had never been to the Chazon Ish, but had heard enough about him to know that he was both fearful and embarrassed to discuss such a matter with him.

"You are mistaken," the *bachur* told him. "I have been to the Chazon Ish many times. One does not feel ashamed or ill at ease when speaking to him. He is warm and considerate and you will feel perfectly comfortable in unburdening yourself to him."

The *bachur* soon found himself in the Chazon Ish's small study. As his friend had predicted, he was able to calmly relate the entire episode in detail as the Chazon Ish listened with rapt attention. As was his custom, the Chazon Ish did not interject; only after the *bachur* had fallen silent did he speak.

The Chazon Ish's words took the *bachur* by surprise. First, he asked that the *bachur* recall both girls' manner of dress. After thinking a while, the *bachur* realized that the two were quite similar. The Chazon Ish then said that this was probably the source of the *bachur's* confusion; the second match was a subconscious reminder of the first. He continued, "It is for you to decide whom you wish to marry. If you feel that the first girl is the right one, so be it. However, do not break off with the second girl until you meet the first girl again, propose to her and your proposal is accepted."

The *bachur* heeded the advice. At his meeting with the first girl, the unexpected occurred. He found himself unable to propose. It suddenly dawned upon him that of course this girl was not suited for him. The Chazon Ish had been right. The manner of dress was at the root of his perplexity. But now that the opportunity was at his doorstep, he realized with certainty that this girl was not for him. He married the second girl.

Letters of Inspiration

THE SCORES OF LETTERS to *b'nei Torah* collected in *Kovetz Igros Chazon Ish* comprise a treasury of guidance and inspiration. Thoughts on diligence, joy, *tefillah*, faith, guarding one's health, the value and rewards of study and more are penned in a manner that plainly conveys the author's love of Hashem, His Torah and those who dedicate themselves to its study. These letters reveal a unique ability to size up an individual and address the person's needs in a manner most suited to him. To one student, he portrayed the sublime merits of Torah study; to another, he derided the futility of pursuing earthly pleasures; to a third, he extolled the student's G-d-given abilities, while to a fourth, he wrote of the pleasure the boy would bring his parents by dedicating himself to Torah. His words to those struggling to find themselves as *b'nei Torah* are particularly poignant:

> ... It is not easy to dedicate oneself to diligent Torah study — however, the difficulty is but fleeting. When one has firmly committed himself to Torah, all difficulties vanish. There is no delight in the world like diligent Torah study ... But what can I do if your ears are shut and your heart is closed. Woe to the precious time that you are wasting, woe to the wonderful *midos* that you are forsaking ...
>
> Know that it is a deeply rooted love and compassion which impels me to offer you reproof against my nature. I beseech you: Change your ways, son of man, change your ways! Tomorrow you will regret the laughter of today. The days of your youth will pass by swiftly; the world is like a stormy sea; the fruits of life are but to take pleasure in the toil of Torah study, whose benefit is eternal ... (I:§8).
>
> You already know that I am your adversary. Basically, our dispute is as follows: I desire that you choose life — and as for yourself? I desire that you dominate your evil inclination, rather than your being dominated by it — and as for yourself? I desire that you despise evil — and as for yourself? I desire that you find the money of others utterly contemptible and that you reject transitory earthly pleasures, which leave one with nothing once they are over — and as for yourself? I desire that you seek a good name for yourself, that you choose a correct path which will earn you the esteem of your fellow men — and as for yourself?
>
> You are still in your youth: it is in your hands to cast your lot among exalted men of distinction. It is in your hands to acquire the wisdom of Torah which is the power of life upon this earth. Instead, you are engulfed in the futilities of a lazy life without responsibility, forsaking the source of flowing waters. *What profit does man have from his labor for which he toils beneath the sun?** Man's days on this earth are limited; they pass like a fleeting dream. It will not be long before you are

---

* *Ecclesiastes* 1:3.

middle aged, a little longer and you will be among the hoary. Son of man, please forsake your futile ways, please forsake your sins ... or today's laughter shall give way to tomorrow's weeping.

Do not consider yourself beyond hope, or imagine that it is simply too difficult to change. True, all beginnings are difficult, but nothing stands in the way of resolve. One who seeks to purify himself is granted Heavenly assistance. What is most needed is firm resolve in one's heart and that one not be thrown back by obstacles that appear at the start of the purifying process.

Know that wisdom is a thousand times more sweet to the wise than are honeycomb drippings to the palates of fools. *Wisdom excels folly as light excels darkness** (I:§17).

Know, my precious one, that ... many *gedolim* first began learning after they had matured. They clothed themselves in a spirit of strength and decided with absolute resolve to dedicate themselves to Torah and to throw the tumult of this world behind them ...

The pleasures of lusts give way to shame and despondence. Conversely, withstanding a test infuses one with strength and joy.

Now, my precious one, do it for your sake if not for mine. Dedicate yourself to the diligent study of Torah and you will discover vitality and pleasure which has no equal upon this earth.

I await the news that you have dedicated yourself to Torah. What is man and of what value is his life if he does not acquire a knowledge of Torah and come to know his Creator, and recognize the purpose for which he was sent to this world, rather than live a life of emptiness (I:§44).

---

* *Ibid.*, 2:13.

CHAPTER FIFTEEN
The Chazon Ish and the Steipler

In the Shadow of Greatness

WHEN THE CHAZON ISH passed away in 1953, his leadership, along with its uniquely unassuming style, was passed on to his illustrious brother-in-law, Rabbi Yaakov Yisrael Kanievsky, the Steipler *Gaon*. The Steipler's greatness in Torah, as evident in his multi-volumed *Kehillos Yaakov*, and his incredible *tzidkus* are legendary. His brother-in-law's junior by some twenty years, the Steipler considered himself a disciple of the Chazon Ish and was totally submissive to his *da'as Torah*. As he himself once expressed it, "Whatever the Chazon Ish did not forbid is permitted, whatever he did not permit is forbidden."

As long as the Chazon Ish was alive, the Steipler kept an extremely low profile, first as *Rosh Yeshivah* of the Novaradok Yeshivah and then as an administration member and *maggid shiur* (lecturer) at what would later be called *Kollel Chazon Ish*. However, with his brother-in-law's passing, the Steipler emerged as a veritable giant of his generation. To his small apartment on Rechov Rashbam 10, countless multitudes of Jews streamed for advice on *Klal* and personal matters, blessings, and prayers in times of distress. Like the Chazon Ish, the Steipler's oneness with Torah gave him the ability to solve every sort of problem that came to his door. Like the Chazon Ish, the Steipler possessed a degree of *Ruach Hakodesh*, an ability to see beyond the visible. This ability is the subject of numerous amazing anecdotes.

From the time of the Chazon Ish's death, the Steipler would not hesitate to make known his *da'as Torah* on issues affecting the Torah community. Everyone knew that his word was that of Torah, and that his thinking reflected the outlook of his predecessor, the Chazon Ish.

The Steipler Gaon

The Steipler's Torah

IT WAS THE CHAZON ISH who arranged the match between his sister Miriam and the Steipler.* In 1925, while studying in the Novaradok Yeshivah in Bialystok, the Steipler published his first work, *Sha'arei Tevunah*. When the *sefer* came into the hands of the Chazon Ish in Vilna, he decided that its author was eminently suited for his sister. Many years later the Chazon Ish told someone that from reading *Sha'arei Tevunah*, he was able to deduce the level of the author's *yiras shamayim*. "It was on this basis," the Chazon Ish concluded, "that I selected the *Rosh Yeshivah* (as he always referred to the Steipler) to be my brother-in-law."

Following his marriage, the Steipler became a *maggid shiur* at the Novaradok Yeshivah in Pinsk. Often, he would send his *chiddushei Torah* to the Chazon Ish for his comments. The cover letter** to a collection of *chiddushim* sent in 1927 reads:

---

* The Chazon Ish's father had died by that time.
** Published in *Kreina D'Igresa*, a collection of the Steipler's letters (Bnei Brak, 1986).

> To the crown and splendor of Israel, the eminent and great *gaon, tzaddik* — foundation of the world ... our guide, *HaRav* Avraham Yeshayah, *shlita*,
>
> Having inquired as to his honor's well-being [and] as it has been many days since I have sent a letter containing *chiddushei Torah*, I have decided to send the enclosed monograph. Now, I know with certainty that it contains many items that are only fit to be said in the way of *pilpul*, which in the opinion of his eminence, the *gaon, shlita*, is of no value. However, I have no other copies, as I record my thoughts for my own benefit, solely so that I can refer to them and be aroused [to further thought]. As it is exceedingly difficult for me to record them again and sift out that which is near to truth, I therefore ask forgiveness in advance.
>
> In any case, I feel that there are to be found herein at least some observations which are fit to be pondered ...
>
> I close with a blessing, and a wish for peace and all the best,
>
> One who awaits the Redemption and who knows the poverty of my lowly worth,
>
> Yaakov Yisrael Kanievsky

In another letter, penned in 1931, the Steipler wrote:

> ... Reb Moshe,* *shlita*, has asked me many times to send him *chiddushei Torah*; [therefore] I have sent him the enclosed monograph. In my opinion, it is something wondrous, thank G-d, and is not far from truth. I have now rewritten it with additions and deletions. Please examine it to see if it is worthy of being published ...

A Sublime Abode

THE STEIPLER'S LIVING QUARTERS when he first came to Bnei Brak were little different from those of the Chazon Ish in his first years there. Eventually, the Steipler, his *rebbetzin* and their three children were forced to leave their dwelling. It was then that the Chazon Ish invited his brother-in-law to share with him the modest structure built for him by Mr. Baruch Meyers (see ch. 5). The house was intended for a single family, but the Chazon Ish solved this problem by having a closet built in the middle of the largest room to divide the house in half. This arrangement proved to be a blessing for the Chazon Ish for, in his later years, when it became difficult for his own *rebbetzin* to

---

* Reb Moshe Karelitz, brother of the Chazon Ish and editor of the *Knesses Yisrael* journal.

Rabbi Chaim Kanievsky

care for him, his needs were attended to by his sister, *Rebbetzin* Miriam Kanievsky.

An additional benefit for both families was the nearness of the Chazon Ish to the Steipler's son and two daughters. To the Steipler's children, the Chazon Ish was much more than an uncle. He cared for them deeply, involving himself in their development and their every concern. In fact, the Chazon Ish had a hand in the *shidduchim* of all three children.

One *Simchas Torah* toward the end of his life, the Chazon Ish wished the members of his *minyan* "*Gut Yom Tov,*" then made his way to his study. *Hakafos* had ended only minutes earlier. He entered his study to find the Steipler and his son, Reb Chaim, already learning together. The Chazon Ish looked at his brother-in-law and nephew admiringly. He remarked to someone who was with him, "*Der zun's beki'us is m'ein dem Rogatchover's* — The son's [i.e., Reb Chaim's] breadth of knowledge is a semblance of the Rogatchover's."*

For the Steipler, living together with the Chazon Ish provided him with an unusual opportunity to observe his brother-in-law's

---

* Related by Reb Shmaryahu Karelitz. The Rogatchover *Gaon*, Rabbi Yosef Rosen, was acclaimed as a genius among Torah geniuses in the early part of this century. Today, Rabbi Chaim Kanievsky is renowned as a *gaon* of rare distinction.

personal conduct and his manner of dealing with the myriad questions and problems that came before him. One wonders if the Chazon Ish, who surely knew that his brother-in-law was destined to emerge as a leader of his generation, had this in mind when inviting him to share his home.

Indeed, the Steipler made good use of this opportunity, as is evident from a letter which he wrote to Rabbi Aharon Sorasky. When Rabbi Sorasky was compiling *P'eir HaDor*, the five-volume encyclopedic work on the Chazon Ish, he frequently consulted with the Steipler, who advised him on what to specifically include or omit, and as to how certain points should be expressed. When asked if a certain opinion attributed to the Chazon Ish merited inclusion, the Steipler responded in writing:

> ... Heaven forfend to include any of this! ... In truth, we saw many times that petitioners had no understanding at all of what our master (of blessed memory) had responded. The matter could sometimes hinge on a motion of his, on an inflection, etc.
>
> There were times when, knowing that a definitive response would serve no purpose, he would give an answer that could be understood more than one way.
>
> In my estimation, our master did not in this instance rule permissively, Heaven forfend; rather, he saw that they would not obey him and so he answered in a manner of abstention. This he did many times, for reasons which cannot be elaborated on at this time.*

Recalling the Chazon Ish

IN THE YEARS FOLLOWING the Chazon Ish's death, the Steipler would often speak of his brother-in-law's greatness, especially of his Torah genius. The following was heard from the Steipler by Rabbi Moshe Mordechai Shulsinger:

> It was the Chazon Ish's custom that on the respective *yahrtzeits* of his father and mother, he would study *Masechta Chullin* (141 folio) in its entirety as a source of merit for his parents' souls. The Steipler remarked, "He was able to do this because the entire *masechta* was firmly etched in his mind,

---

* Published in *Peninei Kehillas Yaakov* by Rabbi Moshe Mordechai Shulsinger (Bnei Brak, 1986). Rabbi Shulsinger writes that the Steipler had high regard for Rabbi Sorasky and for his writings and would encourage him to carry on his "honored endeavors of creating authentic religious works."

which allowed him to review the *Gemara* along with *Rashi* and *Tosefos* in a matter of hours."

With typical humility, the Steipler then added, "And we find it hard to continue after learning four or five *blatt*."*

The Steipler was once present when a renowned *talmid chacham* came before the Chazon Ish and spent a full hour reciting an original exposition on a most complex topic, adducing proofs to his *chiddushim* from far-flung areas in *Shas*. When he had finished, the Chazon Ish removed a *gemara* from his bookcase, opened to a certain page, and, pointing to a particular line, asked, "But how will you explain this?"

After a few moments of thought, the visitor retracted his entire thesis.

Once, the Steipler came across an interesting explanation for the *halachah* which forbids a witness to alter or retract his testimony once he has spoken. The explanation was based on the Torah's describing testimony with the word *yagid* as opposed to the apparent synonym *yomar*. Using Scriptural verses, the author attempted to prove that *yagid* means to relate all that one has to say, which would be the basis for not allowing the witness to say any more once he has spoken before the court.

The Steipler related the explanation to the Chazon Ish, who immediately began citing verses in which *yagid* clearly had the meaning which the *sefer* had attributed to *yomar* and vice-versa. The Steipler told Rabbi Shulsinger, "It was amazing to see him cite verse after verse from places in *Tanach* which are generally unfamiliar."

The Steipler then lamented, "It is a shame that I did not write down all the verses cited by the Chazon Ish. Do you know why I didn't? Because as long as he was alive, there was no need to write anything down. He was always there to ask and everything was revealed before him, as when asking through the *Urim V'tumim*; and if what he said was forgotten, then we would ask again and retrieve

---

* The humility with which this was said can be better appreciated in light of the following story: During his first encounter with his future wife Miriam, the Steipler dozed off. The Chazon Ish, who had arranged the match, later asked him why this had happened. The Steipler explained that his current routine was to study for thirty hours at a stretch and then to sleep for six. Since he had to travel to Vilna by train for this encounter, and the journey would make learning difficult, he decided to complete his thirty hours before the trip and then sleep on the train. When he had boarded the train, he saw the upholstered seats and was afraid that they might contain *sha'atnez*, so he stood the entire way. He had arrived without having slept in well over thirty hours.

what we had lost. As for later — we did not want to think that he would ever be taken from us..."

The Steipler sighed deeply.

He once told Rabbi Shulsinger, "We saw something wondrous in the Chazon Ish: Until his last day, he forgot nothing. When discussing any topic with him, in any area of Torah, it seemed as if he was then in the midst of studying it. He knew everything with a clarity, the *sugyos* with opinions of all the *Rishonim* and the conclusions according to the *halachah*, as if he was then totally engrossed in the subject. I am speaking of *sugyos* of which I knew that some thirty or forty years had gone by since he had last studied them [in depth]. Everything was written upon his pure heart and engraved upon his holy mind with a full recall and a powerful and exalted understanding. This is how he was until his very last day."

Rabbi Shulsinger then asked, "With what did the Chazon Ish merit this? Was it because he reviewed his studies incessantly?"

Said the Steipler, "Certainly one cannot recall without a lot of review. However, the *Gemara* states that one needs *siyata dishmaya* in order to retain the Torah he has learned (*Megillah* 6b). The Chazon Ish had this *siyata dishmaya*, in the merit of his incredible *tzidkus* and his awesome *yiras shamayim*. The awe of Hashem's glorious greatness hovered over him all his days... never did he make a move without first consulting the *Shulchan Aruch*. He hearkened to fulfill the particulars of *halachah* as would those of earlier generations.

"It was in the merit of such incredible *tzidkus* that he earned this *siyata dishmaya*, so that all his learning remained with him without the slightest forgetfulness. His learning was as joyous and illuminating as at Sinai."

A Lesson In Humility

FAR BE IT FOR US to compare these two luminaries. However, one should bear in mind that the praises which the Steipler lavished upon the Chazon Ish are echoed by those said of the Steipler after his own death in Av 5746 (1986). He too was described as an *Urim V'tumim*, one who had the perfect response for any sort of problem put forth to him. His fear of Heaven is the subject of countless stories, beginning with his days in the Russian Army, when he spent a sub-zero night on guard duty without the benefit of an overcoat, for fear that the heavy army overcoat provided him might contain *sha'atnez*.

The Steipler's immense awe of the Chazon Ish and his lowly

The Steipler (far left) at Kollel Chazon Ish on the yahrzeit of the Chazon Ish

opinion of himself never changed. After the Chazon Ish's death, the Steipler assumed leadership of *Kollel Chazon Ish*. He said *shiurim* regularly, until advancing age made this impossible. From that time, he would deliver a *shiur* but once a year, on the *yahrtzeit* of the Chazon Ish. The last year of the Steipler's life, the *shiur* was attended by an unusually large crowd. When someone mentioned this to the Steipler, he replied, "They probably came to honor the Chazon Ish."

CHAPTER SIXTEEN
The State

THE CHAZON ISH LIVED for only five years after the State of Israel was founded. His presence during that period was indispensable in molding a Torah stance toward the secularist government and its policies for his and future generations.

Clarity Amid Confusion

The very creation of the State caused a wave of confusion in Torah circles. How was a Torah Jew to understand this earth-shattering event? After two thousand years of exile and persecution, the Jewish nation seemed to have reached a turning point. What sort of turning point was it?

The Chazon Ish's opinion was unequivocal: "We are not witnessing the *aschalta d'geulah* (beginnings of redemption), but the conclusion of the *galus*." To Rabbi Shlomo Wolbe he said, "Perhaps it [i.e., the State] is the final test before the coming of *Mashiach*."

He saw no possibility for coexistence between the Torah community and the secularist government. Torah and the nation's rich heritage had no place in a secularist system which preached that ours should be a nation like any other. Truth and falsehood must inevitably clash.

Just as his condemnation of secularism was total, so was his love and compassion for the individual who had been led astray. In his writings, the Chazon Ish clearly differentiates between secularism as a movement and as a way of life for the *tinok shenishbah*,* the Jew whose environment has caused him to reject Torah. Of our wayward brethren, the Chazon Ish writes, "It is incumbent upon us to draw them to us with bonds of love, so that the light of truth will illuminate their ways to whatever degree possible" (*Chazon Ish, Yoreh Deah* §13).

---
* Lit., a child taken captive; denoting a person who is a victim of circumstance with regard to his religious beliefs.

IN FALL OF 1952 (5713), Prime Minister David Ben-Gurion visited the Chazon Ish in his small Bnei Brak apartment. At that time, the

Ben-Gurion's Visit

Torah community was in an uproar over the issue of compulsory national service for girls.*
Ben-Gurion knew that the Chazon Ish sanctioned Orthodox participation in the Knesset as a means by which the Torah community could secure its needs. He thought his visit might achieve a more positive relationship between the government and its religious adversaries.**

While many viewed this meeting as a momentous occasion, the Chazon Ish placed little hope in it. He made it clear to Ben-Gurion that there was no room for compromise on any of the issues affecting Torah life. At one point, Ben-Gurion asked, "The majority of our country's people are irreligious. You are in the minority. Who should conform to whose way of life?"

The Chazon Ish replied by citing the Talmudic law (*Sanhedrin* 32b) that when two ships, one laden with cargo and the other completely empty, travel toward each other down a strait scarcely wide enough for one, the empty ship must back up and allow for the full one to pass. The Chazon Ish continued, "Our ship is laden with three thousand years of history, heritage and tradition. Yours, however, is empty, devoid of any real substance. Confrontations are inevitable. Who, then, should step back for whom?"

Ben-Gurion challenged the Chazon Ish to say if there was really a better way to run the country. For example, was not the existence of a well-equipped, well-trained army crucial to the State's survival, or would the Chazon Ish propose to arm the land's soldiers with *gemaras*?

The Chazon Ish replied with a parable: A peasant was driving his cart in the bitter cold of winter. As the frost dug deeper into his bones, the peasant jumped to the ground, desperately scooped up

---

* See further in this chapter.
** Ben-Gurion also sought a meeting with the Brisker *Rav*, but was refused. Earlier, Reb Chaim Ozer Grodzensky had succinctly expressed the *Rav's* approach. It happened that a delegation of religious activists from Europe were refused an audience with the *Rav*, who held some of their philosophies to be contrary to Torah. These same people had never been refused entrance to Reb Chaim Ozer in Vilna. When questioned about the *Rav's* position, Reb Chaim Ozer replied, "And what is wrong if there is still one Jew who cannot tolerate falsehood?"

Before the meeting between the Chazon Ish and Ben-Gurion took place, someone close to the Brisker *Rav* expressed apprehension that such a meeting might produce damaging results. The *Rav* replied with genuine amazement, "Can there be any such fear when the Chazon Ish is involved? He is greater than us all, both in wisdom and in Heavenly fear . . ."

some snow and rubbed it into his hands, bringing them some warmth. The peasant thought, "How wonderful it is to have winter and snow. Why, without them, there would be no hope of getting warm!"

The message was obvious: Certainly a well-trained army was now a necessity, but it was the bankrupt policies of secular Zionism that had brought the country to its current situation.*

Contending with the Secularists

HE SAW THE PHILOSOPHY of secularist Zionism as leading to eventual religious oppression. It was with this in mind that he worked unsuccessfully during the days of the British mandate at securing some degree of autonomy for the religious community. This would have set a precedent for the Jewish state soon to be established, thus improving the religious position under a secularist government. During those first years of statehood, he was heard to say that only the country's preoccupation with the military situation prevented his fears from becoming a reality.

He was convinced, though, that secularist antagonism could never jeopardize the existence of Torah life in *Eretz Yisrael*. Throughout the millennia, religious persecution never caused the Torah Jew to abandon his resolve. To the contrary, it was only in the enlightened, emancipated world of Western Europe where there had been a real possibility of the Torah becoming completely forgotten, ר"ל.

In 5712, the saintly *Rebbe* of Satmar, Rabbi Yoel Teitelbaum, came to the Holy Land where he visited the Chazon Ish. As is well known, the Satmar *Rebbe* was steadfast in his opposition to dealing in any shape or form with the secularist regime. The *Rebbe* asked why the *Rambam's* ruling that one must flee to caves and wilderness in order to escape a sinful society was not applicable to the current situation. Replied the Chazon Ish, "The holy *yeshivos* are the places of refuge in our generation."

Rabbi Shmuel Wosner was present at that historic encounter. He

---

* On another occasion, the Chazon Ish expressed a similar thought with a different parable. In the Chofetz Chaim's town of Radin (Poland), an aged Jew fell into an open pit and broke his leg. One of the town's Jews brought the infirm man to his home where he nursed him back to health. The Chofetz Chaim was deeply impressed by this kindness and told the man, "May my lot be the same as yours." Replied the Jew, "I deserve no praise. It was I who dug that pit and left it uncovered."

The Satmar Rav

recalled, "... Those two *tzaddikim*, our master, the Chazon Ish and the holy *admor* of Satmar, met. They discussed and debated the generation's situation at length. The Chazon Ish reiterated more than once that the only hope was to build one yeshivah and then another, to establish one *cheder* and then another, to organize one study group and then another, to arrange one Torah lecture and then another. We must bring close to Torah all who can possibly be brought close. Ultimately, these candles will join together to form a huge flame which will dispel much of the darkness."

The Chazon Ish kept abreast of developments in the highest echelons of government so that steps could be taken to head off any potential threat to Torah observance. He saw political activism as an obligation; thus it was necessary for the Torah community to be represented both in the Knesset and on the local level. He was unmoved by the argument that such representation implied acceptance of the secularist government. "If I am attacked by bandits in the forest and they threaten me with their weapons, should I not attempt to initiate a dialogue in order that my life be spared? Does this imply that I am legitimizing banditry?" he challenged.

On another occasion, he made reference to *Rashi's* comment (*Genesis* 32:25) that the Hebrew word וַיֵּאָבֵק, *and he wrestled*, is related to the word וַיִּתְקַשֵּׁר, *and he became intertwined. For this is the manner of two who struggle to overthrow one another, that one clasps [the other] and knots him with his arms* (*ibid.*). This sort of embracing is certainly not a recognition of the other's legitimacy.

He was adamantly opposed to the use of violence as a means of accomplishing the Torah community's goals. Aside from being ineffective — the government certainly had the ability to respond with far greater force — such tactics enraged the secularists, thus posing a danger to every observant Jew. The Chazon Ish likened the status of those who engage in violence to that of the Jewish counterfeiter in a gentile land whose actions pose a threat to the entire Jewish community. *Taz (Yoreh Deah* 157:8) rules that he is to be considered a *rodef* (one who pursues with intent to harm) who forfeits his right to protection by the community and should be handed over to the authorities.

WORKING THROUGH SUCH ACTIVISTS as Knesset member Rabbi Yitzchak Meir Levin (Agudath Israel), he accomplished much.

Chinuch Atzmai Once, the Chazon Ish asked when the next Knesset recess would be, explaining, "When they recess, I can breathe easier, knowing that no new laws will be passed until they return."

Torah education and military service were two areas of particular concern. At the State's founding, there existed four educational systems which were fully funded by the government and consequently fell under its jurisdiction. The network of Agudath Israel elementary *yeshivos* for boys and Bais Yaakov schools for girls comprised one of these systems. The Chazon Ish was not opposed to the *yeshivos* accepting government funding — as long as the government had absolutely no say in the running of the schools. However, with the government providing full funding, autonomy was impossible. The Chazon Ish considered it vital that Torah educational institutions be granted full autonomy whatever the price.

Thus, the system of *Chinuch Atzmai* (lit., independent education) schools came into being. It was — and still is — a thriving network of Torah schools whose administration is free of any government involvement. A heavy price was paid for this independence, as the government grants the system only a portion of its operating costs.

Chinuch Atzmai schools offer some degree of secular education. The Chazon Ish also sought government recognition of *chadarim* which teach virtually nothing but Torah, as had been the way of Torah education for centuries. Rabbi Yitzchak Meir Levin secured such recognition; every parent thus had the legal option of dedicating his child to a life of pure Torah learning. These *chadarim* (such as *Tashbar* schools*) receive no government funding.

---

* Aside from a short daily period for the teaching of writing and mathematics, *Tashbar* schools teach only Torah. At one point, the government offered *Tashbar* a one-time financial grant. Upon the directive of the *gedolei Torah*, this offer was refused for fear that some sort of change in curriculum would later be demanded in return.

Though *Chinuch Atzmai* schools offer secular education, the Chazon Ish saw in them the primary means of perpetuating *emunah* and Torah observance in the Holy Land. It is certain that in the absence of such schools, countless numbers of parents would instead enroll their children in schools with religious standards vastly different from those of *Chinuch Atzmai*.

Rabbi Aharon Kotler was a dynamic proponent of *Chinuch Atzmai*. He served as President of the system's American fundraising organization and worked tirelessly for it. When Reb Aharon visited *Eretz Yisrael* soon after the system's founding, the Chazon Ish took the opportunity to express his deep appreciation to him. It was then that the Chazon Ish remarked, "Without *Chinuch Atzmai* it would be impossible to live in the Land."

Giyus Banos

THROUGH QUIET BUT EFFECTIVE diplomacy, religious freedom for soldiers was secured and kosher food was provided them. Full-time yeshivah students were granted deferments from military service. Then came the explosive issues of *giyus banos* (conscription of women) for military service and *sheirut leumi* (compulsory national service for women).

Even before the founding of the State of Israel, the secularist leadership did not hide its intention to draft girls for military service. In talks held before the State's inception, religious parties were assured that observant girls would not be coerced into such service.

During the War of Independence in 1948, a number of religious girls were forcibly taken from their homes and brought to induction centers. The Chazon Ish immediately contacted Rabbi Yitzchak Meir Levin, who succeeded in bringing these practices to a halt. At the same time, the *beis din* of the *Eidah Chareidis* issued a proclamation stating that army service would compromise the *tznius*, modesty, characteristic of religious Jewish girls. It declared that *giyus banos* was forbidden by the Torah's prohibitions against immorality and came within the category of sins for which the Torah demands *yeihareig v'al ya'avor*, one should be killed rather than transgress.

The Chazon Ish, as well as other Torah luminaries throughout the world, concurred with this opinion. Ashkenazic Chief Rabbi Isaac *HaLevi* Herzog and his Sephardic counterpart, Rabbi Ben-Zion Meir Chai Uziel, issued a joint ban against *giyus banos*.

In 1949, a proposed law calling for conscription of all girls ages eighteen to twenty-two, regardless of their religious convictions, was brought before the Knesset. At the directive of the Chazon Ish and the *Moetzes Gedolei HaTorah* (Council of Torah Sages) of *Eretz Yisrael*, the Agudah representatives sought to have the measure killed in totality. Conscription of girls for military service was virtually unheard of among other nations,* was contrary to the attribute of modesty which distinguished the Jewish woman throughout the ages and should not be imposed on any Jewish girl, regardless of her religious commitment.

Negotiations at that time produced positive results. *Giyus banos* legislation was signed into law, but with the restrictions that any girl who cited religious *or personal* objections would be exempted from military service. Thus, army service was in fact a matter of choice for all Israeli women. The case, however, was far from closed.

IN THE WINTER OF 1951, a proposed amendment to the existing *giyus banos* legislation was put forth in the Knesset. Current law permitted a girl to be exempt from service through a simple declaration of objection on religious or personal grounds. The proposed amendment would do away with the "personal objections" exemption and would require observant girls to provide proof of their religious convictions. Moreover, any girl exempted from military service would be required to fulfill two years of *sheirut leumi*, national service. The nature of this service would be either agricultural training on a religious settlement or service in any of a number of government agencies. Jurisdiction over such service would be in the hands of the Defense Ministry.

Sheirut Leumi

Some were inclined to draw distinctions between army service and national service. To the Torah leadership, however, it was all the same: a clear threat to the modesty and morals of Jewish daughters. Rabbi Zvi Pesach Frank, Jerusalem's revered Chief Rabbi, articulated the Torah viewpoint**:

> ... Who would have imagined that Satan would bring about the conscription of Jewish daughters, something unheard of in the annals of our people's history — even the nations of the world have not breached the fences of morality in so blatant a manner — to forcibly distance the Daughters of Israel from the homes of

---

* At that time, only Chile, Afghanistan and Turkey conscripted women for military service.
** In his preface to *Hilchos Medinah* by Rabbi E.Z. Waldenberg.

their parents, who yearn to rear them in the spirit of Torah and tradition.

... I am not prepared, at this moment, to enter into discussion and offer proofs regarding the halachic aspects of this issue. We have already seen the bitter results of *giyus banos*. The majority [of female recruits] have been ruined through their service in the army. Parents weep endlessly for their daughters who have been given over to *shmad*,* blemished by corruption and thoroughly shorn of their Jewish faith. How can there be any room for debate when it is certain that these girls will ultimately be left with no vestige of Jewishness? We are dealing with the impurity of immorality!

Rabbi Zvi Pesach Frank

... Recently, the government has issued what they consider to be a concession, saying that instead of military service, the girls will be taken for *sheirut leumi*, meaning service on *kibbutzim* or government agencies. In truth, this is nothing more than deception, so that they will be induced into thinking that *sheirut leumi* is less harmful ...

In another instance, Rabbi Frank said the following: "Even if they will recruit young women for the recitation of *Tehillim* and arm them with *Korban Minchah siddurim*, the prohibition would remain intact! The determining factor is the forced conscription [resulting in their coming under the government's jurisdiction], not the nature and purpose of the conscription." The Chazon Ish expressed similar sentiments: "Any dominion over a woman, in any form, aside from that of her father or husband, falls within the bounds of immorality."

---

* Lit., *destruction*; a reference to religious persecution.

NEW ELECTIONS WERE HELD in Israel during late summer of 1951. Ben-Gurion invited Agudath Israel to join his new coalition and offered the party's leading representative, Rabbi Yitzchak Meir Levin, a ministry post. At that time, Rabbi Levin was assured that the *sheirut leumi* issue would not be brought before the Knesset for debate for at least a year. With that understanding, Torah leaders advised Rabbi Levin to enter into the coalition.

Consensus of Sages

However, during the coming year a number of religious issues, including *sheirut leumi*, again dominated the agenda. In the summer of 1952, Rabbi Isser Zalman Meltzer met with Agudah members of the Knesset and informed them in the name of the *Moetzes Gedolei HaTorah* of *Eretz Yisrael* (which he headed) that should *sheirut leumi* become law, the party would be required to leave the coalition and relinquish any government post without delay. A letter from the *Moetzes Gedolei HaTorah* of America bore the same *p'sak*.

On 15 Elul, 5712 (1952), a proclamation regarding *sheirut leumi* was issued by four of the Land's most revered *rabbanim*: Rabbi Zelig Reuven Bengis of the *Eidah Chareidis*; Rabbi Zvi Pesach Frank, Rabbi Isser Zalman Meltzer and Rabbi Dov Beirush Weidenfeld, the Tchebiner *Rav*. It read:

> As we have already made known our opinion, which is the Torah's view, regarding *giyus banos*, that it falls within the guidelines of the Three Cardinal Sins,* for which the Torah requires *yeihareig v'al ya'avor*; and as the government stands ready to enact legislation forcing Jewish daughters to be conscripted for *sheirut leumi* outside of military service, we therefore make known our opinion that our ruling regarding *giyus banos* for army service applies fully to *sheirut leumi in all aspects*.
>
> We turn to all Jewish daughters and require of them through the power of our holy Torah to gather and stand ready to protect their souls, to be a wondrous example for the Jewish nation, in the way of Chanah and her seven sons and in the way of the four hundred boys and girls who were taken captive for matters of disgrace and chose to throw themselves into the sea [*Gittin* 57b],** and to resist with every means those who wish to snatch you away.

---

* Idol worship, adultery, and murder.

** During the days when the Syrian-Greeks ruled the Land of Israel, Chanah and her seven sons were brought before the evil Emperor Antiochus. One by one, from oldest to youngest,

It is required of you to suffer imprisonment and accept persecution and to sanctify the Holy Name, as is written, *Because for Your sake we are killed all the time* [Psalms 44:23].

With the help of Hashem, we will merit the fulfillment of: *For the rod of the wicked shall not rest upon the lot of the righteous* [Psalms 125:3].

We, the undersigned, 15 Elul 5712, Jerusalem.

Reuven Zelig Bengis   Zvi Pesach Frank
Isser Zalman Meltzer   Dov Beirush Weidenfeld

Two months later, thirteen prominent Sephardic *Rabbanim* issued their own ban against *sheirut leumi*.

When someone suggested that stoppage of the *sheirut leumi* legislation might spur the secularists to press instead for the drafting of yeshivah students for army service, the Chazon Ish replied, "Is one permitted to offer one of his children to be killed in order to save his remaining children?"*

A Time to Act

THE INTRANSIGENCE of Ben-Gurion and his government forced Rabbi Yitzchak Meir Levin to resign his post as Minister of Welfare and Agudath Israel to leave the ruling coalition. The impact of this move should have been profound, as it demonstrated the sense of values of Torah Jews, who

---

each child was ordered to break Hashem's covenant and worship an idol. Proudly, they all refused, choosing death instead. According to some accounts, Chanah then stood over the bodies of her children and movingly expressed her exultation over her children's sacrifice. She then asked that Hashem gather in her soul. Her soul soared Heavenward and she was reunited with her children.

When the Second Temple was destroyed, four hundred Jewish boys and girls were seized and transported by ship to Rome for immoral purposes. When the youths realized what awaited them, they asked the oldest and wisest of the group, "If we drown ourselves in the sea, will we still merit a portion in the World to Come?"

The wise youth cited the verse, *My Lord promised, "I will bring back from Bashan* [i.e., those threatened by immoral disgrace], *I will bring back from the depths of the sea"* [i.e., those who drown themselves to preserve their purity and to sanctify Hashem's name] (*Psalms* 68:23). Upon hearing this, the maidens all leaped into the sea without hesitation. The youths immediately followed their example.

* When the same question was posed to the Brisker *Rav*, he replied, "Heaven forfend that we permit that which is forbidden, for the sake of Torah study. We can do nothing but follow the dictates of *Halachah*.

"At the time of the destruction of the first *Beis HaMikdash*, the *Kohanim* ascended to the roof of the Temple and cast the keys of its doors heavenward, as if to say, 'We can no longer fulfill our obligations; let Hashem do that which He sees fit.' A hand reached out from Heaven and accepted the keys, signifying that the *Kohanim* had acted correctly [*Pesikta Rabbasi* to *Lamentations*]. Similarly, we dare not insure the survival of Torah through permitting the forbidden. If faced with such a situation, then we will have to leave to Hashem the fulfillment of the assurance, *For she* [i.e., the Torah] *will not be forgotten from his children"* [Deuteronomy 31:21].

Rabbi Yitzchak Meir Levin addressing the Knesset during the debate over sheirut leumi

relinquished political gains for the sake of their religious beliefs. Unfortunately, all this was dulled by the refusal of the Knesset's other religious parties to heed the call of the *gedolei Torah* not to seek compromises in this matter. Instead, compromises were offered, accepted — and Agudath Israel remained alone in its condemnation of *sheirut leumi*. The government delighted in its "divide and conquer" success and had no intention of bending to the demands of the Torah leadership.

Until this point, the Chazon Ish had maintained his usual active but behind-the-scenes posture. Now, with the situation becoming ever more grim and the Knesset heading toward a vote, he saw the urgency for the kind of activism that he so abhorred. A disciple recalled:

"Not to leave his place was for him the rule. Public appearances were foreign to him, his pure soul detested open letters and

Chapter 16: THE STATE / 247

proclamations ... yet, in this instance, the unimaginable occurred: Letters were written to all who had the potential to damage the cause, requesting their compassion so that they not cause damage; letters to all who might be of help, asking that they help. In short, he now entered a world that had previously been distant and abhorrent to him. Why did he do all this? *To rescue from sheirut leumi, one may desecrate the Shabbos* [if absolutely necessary]. This was not mere rhetoric, but a *p'sak* which was implemented by those who asked the question.

"The personal *sefer Torah* for which he waited seventy-five years to write was secondary. His entire being was dedicated toward the rescue of the Jewish daughter. He could not be occupied with the writing of the *sefer Torah* even in the final months of his life. 'I cannot give time for anything, including the *sefer Torah*,' he said, when asked to set a date for the bringing of the scroll into his *beis midrash*."

In his eulogy of the Chazon Ish, Rabbi Shraga Feivel Steinberg lamented, "Our master was wont to say in the name of the Chofetz Chaim that man is indolent regarding the use of all his organs, save for the tongue. Our master would add, 'People do not realize that I am indolent even with regard to my tongue.' However, with regard to the rescue of Jewish daughters, we all saw that his tongue gave no sign of indolence. He did not pause nor rest, nor did he divert his holy mind from the matter for an instant. The pain of the *sheirut leumi* decree affected him deeply. On one occasion, he wrote that the heart of a *gadol hador* grows steadily weaker each day because of this decree. Because this matter would affect the foundation of the Jewish home, he wrote letters, communicated orally, sent declarations to communal activists — all of this out of *ahavas Yisrael*, to rescue the Jewish daughter who is the foundation of the Jewish home ... His intentions were always pure and holy, stemming from a love for his fellow Jews that was not dependent on anything. He had no day and no night, no eating and no drinking; nothing but *ahavas Yisrael*."

Impassioned Reproof

WHEN ONE OF the religious parties officially made known its intentions of remaining in the coalition and supporting the new legislation, the Chazon Ish penned a searing letter to a party representative with whom he was well acquainted. The letter, in part, read:

The great love that I feel for you, my dear one, does not allow me to stand idly by while your blood is spilled like water; it is being spilled not by your enemies, nor by your friends, but by your own hands. You have become swept up by a spirit of madness which is driving you toward spiritual suicide, to ruin your soul in the eyes of all who truly fear Hashem and in the eyes of the generation's sages and to leave a remembrance of yourself that will be for eternal shame.

The viewpoint which divides the Torah in two, questions of *issur v'heter** on the one hand and guidance in everyday life on the other; and which holds that for *issur v'heter* one should subjugate himself to the sages of his time, while leaving other matters to his own free choice — this is the viewpoint held by the heretics of old in [enlightened] Germany who drove their brethren to assimilate with the other nations until they could not be rescued. Now, you have risen to conduct yourself as those sinners.

Your heart has not been deeply pained by this law because you are far, far removed from the sages of Torah who toil in its study day and night and who are akin to Heavenly angels. It is difficult to convey the nature of this pain to one who is insensitive to it. Think of these girls of ages eighteen to twenty-two ... of their mothers and fathers whose concern for them is constant ... how fearful must these modest young women be of a society as irreligious and immoral as the one which surrounds us. Any sort of compulsory service at this age would surely frighten them ... Their parents have not ceased from trembling ever since these proposals were first set forth — and you now plan to be an accomplice in this decree?! Your influence can, with a single stroke, lead to the law's passage over the tears of the oppressed ...

To distinguish between instruction regarding *issur v'heter* and with regard to matters of legislation is a distortion of Torah, a disgrace to *talmidei chachamim* and places one in the category of those who have no portion in the World to Come and who are unfit to offer testimony [in a Jewish court of law].

The disgraceful course on which you have embarked will bring about a hatred in your heart toward the chosen ones among our people, according to the principle that hearts are reflective of one another ... this will have a bearing on your descendants, distancing them from a love for *tzaddikim* — is the way in which you have chosen to rear your offspring ...?

---

* Lit., forbidden and permissible; a reference to questions pertaining to *kashrus*, marital laws and the like.

Attempts at Persuasion

IT WAS IN MARCHESHVAN 5713 that the meeting between the Chazon Ish and Ben-Gurion took place. While Ben-Gurion made known his intentions to keep the discussion away from specific issues, the Chazon Ish would not allow the opportunity to go by without bringing up the issue of the day. He told the Prime Minister, "It is obvious that democratic countries must have recourse to force in establishing adherence to its laws. However, a law which attacks the very essence of one's beliefs is destined for failure. There will always be people of spirit who will stand in defiance of such laws, and no amount of coercion will be able to sway them. The law will fail and the government will stumble along with it. Thus, any government concerned for its own and its country's self-esteem will not enact such laws."

Later, the Chazon Ish summed up. "Your weapons have potency only as long as the *gedolei Torah* have not ruled *yeihareig v'al ya'avor*. The moment they issue this ruling, all your weapons are useless."

The visit did not alter Ben-Gurion's position. The Chazon Ish, who had not placed much hope in the visit, continued his efforts on all fronts.

It became known that Ben-Gurion was in the process of forming a new ruling coalition that included only one religious party — Mizrachi. He no longer needed Agudath Israel's votes. The Chazon Ish judged the moment psychologically right for one final attempt at persuasion. In a letter to Ben-Gurion dated 19 Kislev, 5713, he wrote that, to his mind, the Prime Minister must surely be experiencing misgivings over having caused distress to so many with his proposed legislation. Until now, a change of heart on his part might have been seen as a capitulation to political pressure, something which any prime minister sought to avoid. However, now that he had been able to form a coalition without the participation of the law's opponents, his retraction would be viewed as a sensitive response to the anguish of the Torah community and a recognition of its right of conscience.

Ben-Gurion was unmoved. His reply was extremely cordial and respectful. He referred to the Chazon Ish as the *gadol hador* and described their encounter as a "momentous occasion for me, one which I will never forget." Still, he insisted that *sheirut leumi* had the support of the entire secularist population, a significant percentage of the religious population, and was necessary for national security.

The Chazon Ish's letter to Ben-Gurion

Ben-Gurion acknowledged that the halachic aspects of the issue were beyond him; he continued, however, "I know that among those knowledgeable in *Halachah*, there are divergent views [regarding *sheirut leumi*]." This statement was, of course, predicated on the conflicting stands of the respective religious parties.

While Ben-Gurion's contention carried no weight in the yeshivah community, it was important that the broad religious population know the facts. On 20 Kislev of that year, a meeting of Torah leaders was held in Jerusalem. Among the participants were: Rabbi Isser

דעת תורה

של מרן הגאון החסיד

בעל **החזון איש** שליט״א

בנידון גזירת גיוס בנות ישראל לשרות לאומי

שמסר לתלמידיו :

הרב ר' שרגא שטינברג
הרב ר' גדלי' נדל

ואלה הם דבריו סלה במלה :

גיוס בנות ישראל לשרות לאומי
בכל צורה שהיא
הוא איסור גמור ואין בזה שום צד היתר
חובה מוטלת על כל איש מישראל
למנוע גזירה איומה זו

Public announcement bearing the Chazon Ish's *p'sak* on *sheirut leumi*

Zalman Meltzer, the Gerrer *Rebbe* (Rabbi Yisrael Alter), Rabbi Eliezer Yehudah Finkel (Mirrer *Rosh Yeshivah*), Rabbi Yechezkel Sarna (Chevron), Rabbi Shabsi Yogel (Slonimer *Rosh Yeshivah*), Rabbi Meir Karelitz, Rabbi Zalman Sorotzkin, Rabbi Y. Adler, Rabbi D. Sperber and the Boyaner *Rebbe*. The conclave reiterated the rabbinic ban against *sheirut leumi*.

For the first and only time in his life, the Chazon Ish permitted a *p'sak* in his name to be displayed throughout the length and breadth of *Eretz Yisrael*.

WHEN THE CHAZON ISH learned that elements in the Mizrachi Party were pressuring the Chief Rabbinate to issue a ruling on which they could hang their endorsement of *sheirut leumi*, he wrote Chief Rabbi Isaac *HaLevi* Herzog in an attempt to dissuade him from such a step:

The Letter to Rabbi Herzog

> It is well known that as the end of this exile draws ever closer it becomes increasingly difficult to perceive Hashem's Providence over man's affairs. While nothing that occurs can be ascribed to chance, not even the painful striking of a small finger,* all this is cloaked in obscurity and concealed in darkness. People are mired in the quicksand of disbelief, chained in the dungeons of heresy; their deeds evolve from this sorry state. They tread upon the Torah's most stringent edicts, with nary a pang of conscience or moral reflection.
>
> Amidst a climate so grave, there remains a remnant still faithful to Hashem and His Torah. How can we guide our young ones and disseminate Torah, while, with fearful hearts and a broken spirit, we are preoccupied with erecting protective walls to shield our precious ones from a society where falseness and abominable lusts are plainly revealed?
>
> How awesome is the pain, how cruel is the wound, of our daughters who have been reared with the glorious modesty of Jewish womanhood, now threatened with being thrust into this alien environment. They are to be exposed to a lifestyle of indulgence and self-gratification, shown pleasures that excite the eyes, and offered the fragrance of foreign incense. They will hear mockery and derision of the precious attribute of *tznius*, of *emunah*, and of *mitzvos* in general. The thought of this breaks one's heart and brings one to tears.
>
> ... Those who will cast their gaze upon these young women are to them like a beast of prey which lies in wait. These girls — and their mothers and fathers — will have been denied their free choice. They will be forced to meet up with young men who make their very souls tremble and forced to tread a path whose every turn is permeated with a spirit that is totally alien to them.
>
> Our hearts are torn asunder by this decree!
>
> Our eyes are turned heavenward in the hope that events will somehow lead to the law not being passed and that they will abandon their evil intentions. Praiseworthy is he who will merit being the one through whom this will come about ...

---

* See *Chullin* 7b.

> I express my heartfelt gratitude to his glorious honor, if I have found favor in his eyes that he contemplate and endorse my words and do all that is in his power for our salvation.

Following Rabbi Herzog's receipt of the letter, the Chief Rabbinate ruled definitively against *sheirut leumi*. Nevertheless, Mizrachi was prepared to cast its vote with the government. The Chazon Ish tried one final attempt at persuasion. He penned the following to Mizrachi's Knesset representatives:

> To my beloved and dear members of Knesset of the *Poalei HaMizrachi*,
>
> I feel obligated to inform you, my dear ones, that voting in favor of *sheirut leumi* is forbidden by *Halachah*; nothing in the world can alter this fact. I am confident that you will fulfill your obligation in this matter.
>
> From the depths of my heart, I offer my blessings that the Holy Name be sanctified through your actions. I pray that we will soon merit the fulfillment of the prophecy that all the earth be filled with His wisdom, that those distant will come near and that peace shall reign in the Land.
>
> I extend my blessings for well-being, with love and respect.

The recipients of the letter responded with a visit to the Chazon Ish. During the course of their discussion, the Chazon Ish was challenged to cite the paragraph in *Shulchan Aruch* which prohibits national service for women. He replied, "It is found in the fifth section of *Shulchan Aruch*, one which is not written and is the province of only true *talmidei chachamim*."*

The Chazon Ish failed to persuade his guests. When the final vote on *sheirut leumi* was taken, all but one Mizrachi representative voted for the law's passage.

Showdown

A PRELIMINARY VOTE on the issue was scheduled for 10 Av, 5713 (1953). That day, thousands of men, women and children from the Torah community gathered in Jerusalem. Gracing the assemblage was the *Moetzes Gedolei HaTorah*, the *beis din* of the *Eidah Chareidis*, Sephardic rabbinic leaders, the Tchebiner *Rav*, the Belzer *Rebbe* (Rabbi Aharon Rokeach), and the Brisker *Rav*. It was the first time that the Brisker *Rav* had ever participated in a public gathering. The Chazon Ish, too, would have

---

* When asked where there is reference in the Torah to such a ban, the Brisker *Rav* replied, "In the Ten Commandments," an allusion to the prohibition against immorality.

joined had his deteriorating health not prevented him.

Not one address was sounded. In calling this assemblage, the generation's leaders had one purpose in mind — *tefillah*. Tearfully, the throngs beseeched Hashem to save them from the impending decree.

The vote was cast. A majority of the Knesset voted in favor of *sheirut leumi*. A final vote was scheduled for 15 Elul of that year. On the fourteenth of Elul, another mass *tefillah* gathering took place in Jerusalem; other gatherings were held in Torah settlements throughout the Land. The next day, the *sheirut leumi* amendment won final confirmation.

The Chazon Ish was deeply grieved, but he would not despair. "They have done nothing more than spoken," he insisted, meaning that the law would never be carried out. When asked if he said this with certainty, the Chazon Ish responded, "I am not a prophet; my words were uttered in the way of a bequest, an utterance that will hopefully be fulfilled." History attests to its fulfillment, as no religious girl has ever served the State against her will.

Of the thousands of *tefillos* that had been offered, the Chazon Ish said, "They were not for nought. A *tefillah* that is not immediately answered hovers in the Heavenly spheres, retaining its full potency until the proper moment . . ."

IN THE FALL OF 1953, word spread that the government was preparing to draft all able-bodied young women for national service.

His Duty Fulfilled

It was only two days before the Chazon Ish's death. A failing heart left him dangerously weak. The Chazon Ish summoned Rabbi Avrohom Wolf, dean of the Bais Yaakov Seminary for Girls in Bnei Brak. He told Rabbi Wolf that any girl receiving a draft notice was required to ignore it. He then told his sister, *Rebbetzin* Miriam Kanievsky, "You are a mother of daughters. Know that they must accept martyrdom rather than allow themselves to be drafted."

A few days earlier, the Chazon Ish rested on a porch bench outside his apartment as he discussed the *sheirut leumi* situation with his disciple, Rabbi Shraga Feivel Steinberg. Suddenly, the Chazon Ish sat upright, lifted his hands heavenward and declared, "Now I can come before the Heavenly Court and say that I have fulfilled my duty. I have done all that I could have done!"

His reference to the Heavenly Court left Rabbi Steinberg deeply troubled. Not long passed before its meaning became painfully clear.

CHAPTER SEVENTEEN
Final Days

AS THE CHAZON ISH neared his seventy-fifth birthday, in early fall of 1953 (5714), he carried on as the generation's leader while his failing heart was further strained by the ongoing battle against *sheirut leumi*.

Premonitions During the soul-searching days between Rosh Hashanah and Yom Kippur, hundreds of Jews streamed to his door in search of his advice, halachic viewpoint and blessings. The unusual number of petitioners seemed to suggest a sense of foreboding that the Chazon Ish's days were numbered.

As always during that season of the Jewish calendar, one could perceive the Chazon Ish to be gripped by the awe which the time demanded. Still, the Chazon Ish had the ability to "temper the attribute of justice with compassion," as he greeted each visitor with genuine love and concern.

It had long been the custom of Rabbi Avraham Menachem Gelanti, an aged scholarly *tzaddik* from Tel-Aviv, to join the Chazon Ish's private *minyan* on Yom Kippur. Each year at the fast's conclusion, Rabbi Gelanti would turn to the Chazon Ish and request, "Would our master please bless me that I will merit joining him next year for Yom Kippur." The Chazon Ish always responded warmly, offering the blessing that had been sought.

This year, however, the Chazon Ish would only say, "*Shanah tovah, g'mar chasimah tovah* — may you have a good year, may you be sealed [in the Book of Life] for the good." Rabbi Gelanti was visibly shaken.

THE FESTIVAL OF SUCCOS arrived. Following the time-honored custom of visiting one's Torah teacher during the three major festivals, masses came to wish "*Gut Yom Tov*" to the teacher of all Israel. From morning until night, well-wishers filed past him.

Z'man Simchaseinu

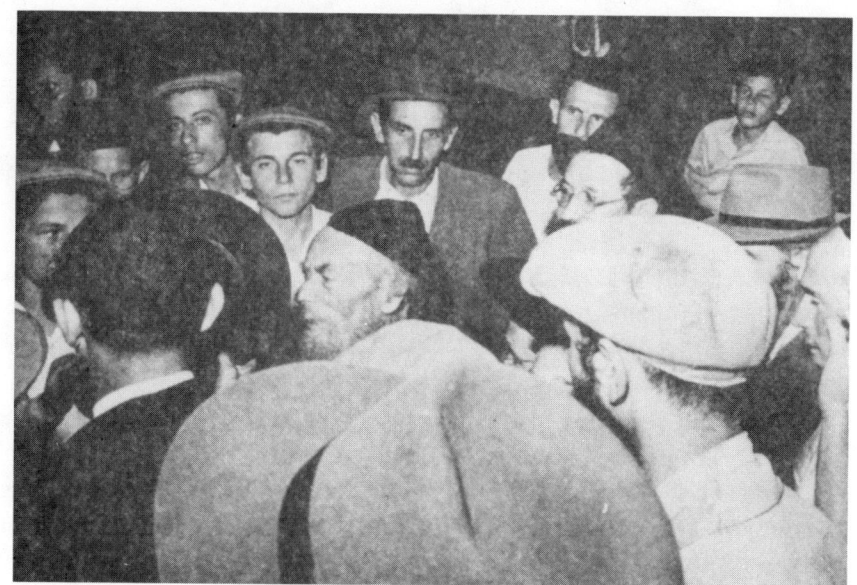

Simchas Beis HaSho'eivah celebration in the succah of the Chazon Ish (center) during his final years

Succos is *z'man simchaseinu*, the season of our gladness, and the Chazon Ish was always particularly joyous during those days. He would sing and dance with the men of his family and with members of his *beis midrash* and would exhort those close to him to maintain a joyous spirit. Each year during *Chol HaMoed*, a small group of young men and boys from *Zeirei Agudath Israel* would gather in his *succah* for a *Simchas Beis HaSho'eivah* celebration. As in the days of the *Beis HaMikdash*, when the generation's scholars were the primary performers at such celebrations,* the Chazon Ish was the center of the festivities. A circle would form around him as he danced alone, singing and waving his hands to the delight and excitement of all as they clapped and sang along.

This year on the night designated for the celebration, hundreds

---

* The unlearned people could not actively participate in *Simchas Beis HaSho'eivah*; they could only observe and marvel. It was the sages — heads of *Sanhedrin* and *roshei yeshivah* — who were permitted to perform.

It is with regard to these celebrations that *Rambam* (*Hilchos Lulav* 8:15) writes, "The celebration of a *mitzvah* and the joy one expresses as a result of his love of Hashem — such a celebration is an extraordinary form of Divine service. Whoever holds himself aloof from such festivity deserves to suffer punishment ... but, whoever humbles himself on this occasion and takes himself lightly, it is he who is a truly great and dignified personage and it is he who demonstrates that he serves Hashem out of a sense of adoration."

gathered outside the Chazon Ish's apartment, leaving his family with no choice but to direct those assembled to a nearby *beis midrash* to celebrate, while the Chazon Ish remained at home.

The Chazon Ish did attend the *Simchas Torah hakafos* at the Ponovezher Yeshivah, as he did every year. It was the last public gathering he attended. At one point, the students danced on and on as the study hall reverberated with the words יִבָּנֶה הַמִּקְדָּשׁ עִיר צִיּוֹן תְּמַלֵּא, *May the Mikdash be rebuilt; the city of Zion replenished*. Someone complained that the dance had lasted long enough. The Chazon Ish disagreed. "Why, it is they who are building the *Mikdash* of the future!"

After the final *hakafah*, a large crowd accompanied the Chazon Ish home. A young child observing the scene asked within earshot of the Chazon Ish, "Why are they walking him home? Doesn't he know the way?" The Chazon Ish smiled and said, "I had the very same question."

Completing His Mission

WHEN THE FESTIVAL ENDED, the Chazon Ish returned to his usual routine, though he was experiencing occasional chest pains and was noticeably weaker. Communal activists converged on his apartment as always, individuals came with their personal requests and yeshivah students came to discuss their studies. The Chazon Ish found the time and strength to peruse and comment on a manuscript of a budding young *talmid chacham*, well aware of the encouragement this gave the author.

He studied with typical freshness and intense concentration. To Rabbi Shmuel Greineman, he handed over a manuscript for publication on the laws of *Choshen Mishpat*. Twelve days before the end came, the Chazon Ish studied and annotated the inaugural volume of *Divrei Mordechai* by Rabbi Mordechai Mann of Bnei Brak. He also completed recording his own *chiddushim* to the laws of *tzitzis*, an accomplishment from which he derived particular satisfaction. "*Hilchos tzitzis* was for me a treasure," he remarked. "*Ich hob areingechapt* (I managed to squeeze it in)!"

On Thursday, 5 MarCheshvan, the Chazon Ish was scheduled to meet with Rabbi Yitzchak Gershtenkorn, Bnei Brak's communal leader. Rabbi Gershtenkorn was returning that day from an extended visit to the United States. His flight was delayed, and when it finally touched down at Lod airport, it was almost midnight. Rabbi

Gershtenkorn hailed a taxi and directed the driver to Bnei Brak's Rechov Ezra where the Chazon Ish lived. When the car pulled up, the Chazon Ish was standing outside his apartment, awaiting Rabbi Gershtenkorn's arrival.

Over the years, the two had conferred countless times. This meeting, however, was unlike any other. In previous meetings, Rabbi Gershtenkorn would report on various communal projects and issues, with the Chazon Ish interjecting with questions and comments that were sharp and concise. On this night, the Chazon Ish did most of the talking, touching on a variety of all-important topics: Shabbos, *kashruth*, Torah education, *mikvaos*, the municipal council, relations with local secularists. It seemed as if the Chazon Ish was delivering his parting testament for the city whose unique spiritual fiber he had woven and protected for two decades.

Pain of Another Sort

ONE WEEK LATER, his strength decreased alarmingly. After hearing the doctor's prognosis, the Chazon Ish's family implored him to stop accepting visitors, at least for the time being. "How can one admit people at a time like this?" a relative demanded. The Chazon Ish responded with a question of his own, "How can one *not* admit them? Some of them have come from afar... their hearts are mournful... it is not for nothing that they have come here."

The next day, the Chazon Ish was confined to bed, too weak to speak. Petitioners were told that he could not be seen. Many men and women chose not to leave, on the chance that he might later feel well enough to accept visitors.

In the early afternoon of that day, the Chazon Ish forced himself out of bed in order to recite the *Minchah* prayer with his *minyan*. As the *tefillah* drew to a close, a line of petitioners formed in front of the lectern where the Chazon Ish sat. The physical pain which he was then experiencing was outweighed by the emotional pain he felt for those who had come to him with their troubles. He excused himself for a moment, went into another room and downed some medication. Then he returned to bed, with strict instructions that the petitioners be shown to his bedside.

Thursday evening, 14 MarCheshvan, a large flow of visitors were admitted to see the Chazon Ish. In addition to petitioners with personal requests, Rabbi Binyamin Mendelsohn, *Rav of Moshav Kommemius*, and Rabbi Avraham Wolf were there to discuss *sheirut leumi*. The Chazon Ish summoned Rabbi Shraga Feivel Steinberg to discuss the progress of some younger students at *Tiferes Tzion*, where Rabbi Steinberg served as a *Rosh Yeshivah*. When their discussion had ended, the Chazon Ish handed his disciple a letter from America and asked that he read it to him. "I have no strength to read," he apologized.

That night, the Chazon Ish was visited by a young student from *Tiferes Tzion* who sought an answer to a question on *Gemara*. The boy's appearance infused the Chazon Ish with new strength as he listened intently and with obvious delight to the question. Then, with his usual "come, let us think into this," he entered into a discussion which resolved the student's query.

Later, the Chazon Ish went out for a short walk, hoping that the crisp nighttime air would do him good. Before he could return indoors, some new petitioners had appeared. He lay down on a porch bench to accept the visitors. By the time the last one had left, it was close to midnight.

Final Hours

THE NEXT MORNING, *erev Shabbos*, the Chazon Ish prayed *tefillas Shacharis* with his *vasikin minyan*. As soon as the prayers had ended, petitioners came forward on behalf of the sick. The Chazon Ish was in great pain, and when necessary he bit down on his lip so that no groan would escape him. The pain made it extremely difficult for him to speak. Nevertheless, he gathered the strength to write down each patient's Hebrew name, while nodding that he understood the situation.

While this was going on, someone burst into the room, saying that a child who had been sick from birth had died in Kfar Saba and doctors were preparing to perform an autopsy in defiance of Torah law. Now the Chazon Ish spoke, as he summoned two young men and dispatched them to Rabbi Eliyahu Moshe Ganchovsky, a member of the Knesset. "Tell him," said the Chazon Ish with emotion, "that he is not to *daven* or do anything else until the body is released." Then, he added, "Tell him that the child's mother is not well; she will not be able to withstand the tension should there be any problems, G-d forbid . . ."

The body was released and brought to Bnei Brak for burial. Shortly before the onset of Shabbos, the Chazon Ish, experiencing some relief from his earlier pains, fulfilled the *mitzvah* of *levayas hameis* as he accompanied the child to its final resting place.

Shabbos was ushered in. The Chazon Ish recited *Ma'ariv* with his *minyan*. As he wished his fellow congregants "*Gut Shabbos,*" he seemed perfectly tranquil. This too was the impression of those who joined him for the Shabbos meal that night.

After the meal, he strolled a bit outdoors. It was near midnight when he retired for the night. A short while later, before he had fallen asleep, the Chazon Ish experienced severe chest pains. He asked the young

Rabbi Eliyahu Lopian

boy who shared his room to bring him a pill and some tea. Before the boy could fulfill the request, the Chazon Ish's soul had been returned to its Maker. The angels had bested the mortals and taken possession of the holy ark.

That night, Rabbi Eliyahu Lopian,* legendary *tzaddik* and *Mashgiach* at Yeshivah Knesses Chezkiah in Zichron Yaakov, dreamt that a Torah scroll was going up in flames. He awoke shaken. When Shabbos ended, he learned the meaning of his dream.**

When the Brisker *Rav* heard the tragic news, he exclaimed, "The world has been stricken! Yesterday, *Klal Yisrael* had the Chazon Ish

---

* Reb 'Elya' emigrated from England to *Eretz Yisrael* in 1950. He was then nearing eighty and planned to dedicate his remaining years toward self-improvement (as he put it) after having inspired *talmidim* for decades. However, soon after arriving in the Land, he was implored by the administration of *Knesses Chezkiah* to assume the post of *Mashgiach*. Reb Elya asked the Chazon Ish to decide the matter for him. The Chazon Ish replied unequivocally that Reb Elya should accept the position.

Reb Elya countered, "But I am already old..."

The Chazon Ish responded with a citation from *Tehillim*: עוֹד יְנוּבוּן בְּשֵׂיבָה, דְּשֵׁנִים וְרַעֲנַנִּים יִהְיוּ, לְהַגִּיד כִּי יָשָׁר ה׳, *They will still be fruitful in old age, vigorous and fresh they will be — to declare that Hashem is just . . .* [Psalms 92:16-17]. He said, "In the merit of your 'declaring that Hashem is just' (i.e., through instruction to *talmidim*), may you be vigorous and fresh in your old age."

Reb Elya served as *Mashgiach* of the yeshivah for close to twenty years.

** *Chazal* compare the death of a *tzaddik* to the breaking of the *luchos* (tablets bearing the Ten Commandments; see *Rashi* to *Deuteronomy* 10:6) and the destruction of the *Beis HaMikdash* (*Eichah Rabbah* 1:39).

— now, we are without him. Darkness has descended upon the world."

Farewell

NEWS OF THE CHAZON ISH'S death was announced on *Kol Yisrael*, Israeli state radio, soon after the conclusion of Shabbos. Throughout that night, thousands from all across *Eretz Yisrael* streamed to Bnei Brak's Zichron Meir neighborhood to attend the funeral the next morning. The Chazon Ish's private *beis midrash* was jammed as never before for the daily *vasikin minyan*, while in the adjacent room where he had studied Torah and offered counsel, mourners tearfully recited *Tehillim* near his body.

At the funeral, scores of mourners wept openly. Rabbi Shmuel Greineman expressed their feelings: "Woe! Our father has left us!" Among the tens of thousands who had converged around the Chazon Ish's home were many who were non-observant but who nevertheless sensed that they too had suffered a tragic loss.

Rabbi Meir Karelitz delivered the first eulogy. "It was not his desire that we eulogize excessively," he said amidst sobs. "I wish to relate but one thing. When he reached the age of thirteen, he accepted upon himself to study Torah *lishmah*. I can bear witness that he did just that for more than sixty years."

One half hour later, the procession to the cemetery began from in front of the Chazon Ish's home. As his body was laid to rest in Bnei Brak's *Shomrei Shabbos* cemetery, the sounds of anguished outcries seemed to reverberate across the Land.

His Legacy

IN CONCLUSION, the following excerpt from an eulogy delivered by Rabbi Shmuel Greineman during the week of *shivah* is cited:

... We saw awesome products of his deeds and deeds that were awesome of themselves. There were times when his blessing brought immediate cure to the sick. He sent critically ill patients overseas for dangerous surgeries along with the assurance that they would return cured — and they did.

No longer will we merit his sweet recital of the *Shema*, his lengthy *Shemoneh Esrei* in which each blessing was said so intently. During [the blessing of] *Refa'einu*, his eyes would flow with tears for the many sick for whom he prayed... During his last week, his strength diminished drastically. The doctors exhorted him to rest but he refused to close his door to those who needed him.

He was well aware of his stature; he knew full well that he was the generation's leader. Yet, when a Jew desired to come close to him for precisely this reason, the Chazon Ish told him, "It would be far better for you to come close to the Torah itself."

Who will shield us with his prayers and supplications, now that our crown has been taken? To whom will all the world turn with their halachic inquiries? Every day, a pile of mail concerning matters of *Halachah* arrived at his door. All of Torah was open before him. His *chiddushim* remain, but his unique way of study has gone with him. Torah, Torah, gird yourself in sackcloth!

The Chofetz Chaim would say that in Torah lies the answer to every problem, only that one must know where in Torah to

A recent photograph of the Chazon Ish's tombstone. Top of stone is blackened from the many memorial candles lit there since his death.

find a particular answer and then approach the matter with pure *da'as Torah* which is absolutely free of any foreign attitudes or personal interests ... It is for this reason that so many people, among them scores of *roshei yeshivah*, sought his counsel. Always, they came away with the definitive Torah view ...

He sought to conceal his awesome ways: he revealed an inch and concealed two more. So much remains hidden forever. Who will replace his thousands of hidden acts of charity? At the funeral, one yeshivah administrator wept, saying that without the Chazon Ish he sees no way to maintain his institution. His deeds were so concealed that even his attendants were unaware of them. How can one refrain from weeping over the loss of such a man?

Rabbi Chaim Volozhin once said that his *rebbi*, the *Vilna Gaon*, was akin to the *Rishonim* who lived centuries earlier. Rabbi Elchonon Wasserman asked the Chofetz Chaim to explain why Heaven decreed that a soul such as the *Gaon's* descend to a generation in which it did not belong. The Chofetz Chaim explained as follows: In every generation, the presence of Torah leaders serves to impede that generation's spiritual decline. However, in certain generations, the risks of spiritual decadence are particularly great. Heaven may then deem it necessary to send to this world a soul that actually belongs to an earlier, more sublime period. Such a soul can singlehandedly uplift an entire generation and raise its spiritual sights. Such a soul was that of the *Vilna Gaon*.

Such was also the soul of the Chazon Ish. A soul that belonged centuries ago was sent to preserve Torah life in our time. He planted the seeds of Torah throughout the Holy Land, combated ignorance and secularism, illuminated the world with his Torah wisdom, and raised the sights of an entire generation. As long as he lived there were no doubts, for his word was definitive.

Though he was my brother-in-law, I was overcome by awe and fear each time that I approached him. He was, after all, a veritable angel.

It is incumbent upon us all to strive to emulate his ways in at least some small way. In this merit may he shield us from Above just as he did during his years on this world. Let us pray that he intercede in Heaven on our behalf, and that in his merit the Land be saved from all harm. May Hashem have mercy on the remnants of our Nation and may we soon merit the Redemption, amen.

Glossary
Bibliography

Glossary

All Entries are Hebrew unless otherwise indicated.

Admor: title of leader of a Chassidic sect

agunah (pl. *agunos*): woman whose marital status is uncertain because she has neither a divorce nor evidence of her missing husband's death

ahavas Yisrael: love for one's fellow Jew

aishes chayil: woman of valor; based on *Proverbs* ch. 31

aleph beis: Hebrew alphabet

ameilus baTorah: diligent toil in Torah study

Amoraim (Ar.): authority quoted in the Gemara

arba'ah minim: four species used during Succos services

Arizal: Rabbi Yitzchok Luria (1534-1570); legendary kabbalist

Avos (*Pirkei Avos*): Chapters of the Fathers, part of *Mishnah*

ba'al tokei'a: person designated to blow the shofar on Rosh Hashanah

bachur: unmarried man

Baruch Hashem: "Thank G-d"

batim: the cases for the scrolls of phylacteries

beis din: rabbinical court

Beis HaMikdash: the Holy Temple in Jerusalem

beis midrash (pl. *battei midrash*): study hall

ben Torah (pl. *bnei Torah*): one who studies and adheres to the teachings of the Torah

berachah: blessing

Bircas HaMazon: Grace after Meals

bittul Torah: wasting time from Torah study

blatt (Yid.): one full leaf (two pages) of the Talmud

braisa: a Tannaic teaching not included in the *Mishnah*

chametz: leavened products forbidden during Passover

chas v'shalom: "G-d forbid"

chasid: 1) pious individual; 2) follower of Chassidic movement founded by R' Yisrael Baal Shem Tov

Chazal: (acronym for Chachameinu, Zichronom Livrachah) our Sages, of blessed memory

cheder (pl. *chadarim*): Torah school, elementary level

chesed: kindness

chiddush (pl. *chiddushim*), *chiddushei Torah:* original analyses and interpretation of difficult points of Torah

chilul Hashem: desecration of Hashem's Name

Chol HaMoed: intermediate days of Passover or Succos

Choshen Mishpat: section of *Shulchan Aruch* dealing with monetary matters

Chumash (pl. *Chmashim*): Five Books of Moses, or a volume thereof

da'as Torah: Torah viewpoint

daven, davening (Yid.): to pray, prayers

din Torah: case before a *beis din*

drashah (pl. *drashos*): sermon or discourse

dveikus: state of heightened closeness to G-d

Eidah Chareidis: lit., Assembly of Those who Hearken [to Hashem's word]; Torah community founded in Jerusalem during the 1920's
emunah: faith in Hashem
emunas chachamim: belief in the pre-eminent wisdom of Torah scholars
Eretz Yisrael: the Land of Israel
erev: the eve of (a Sabbath or Festival)
eruv (pl. *eruvin*): structures which make it permissible to carry in an otherwise restricted area on Shabbos
esrog: citron, one of the *arba'ah minim*

gadol baTorah: one exceptionally knowledgeable in Torah
gadol hador: the prime Torah leader of the generation
galus: exile
gaon (pl. *gaonim*): brilliant Torah scholar
gedolei haTorah: the Torah leaders of the generation
Gemara (Ar.): the part of the Talmud that elaborates on the *Mishnah*; [not capitalized] a volume of the Talmud
gemillas chesed: loving-kindness
ger tzeddek: righteous convert to Judaism
giyus banos: conscription of females to the (Israeli) Army
gomel chesed: one who does acts of loving-kindness
Gut Shabbos (Yid.): Sabbath greeting

hadasim: willow branches, one of the *arba'ah minim*
HaKadosh Baruch Hu: The Holy One, Blessed is He; i.e., G-d

hakafah (pl. *hakafos*): circuits around the bimah on Simchas Torah
Halachah: the body of Torah law; [not capitalized] a Torah law
HaMelech: the King
Hashem (lit., "the Name"): G-d
hataras nedarim: absolving of a vow according to *Halachah*
heter: lit., permit; halachic ruling permitting a given act
hishtadlus: effort

igros: letters
issur: lit., ban; halachic ruling forbidding a given act
Ivrit: Hebrew

Kabbalah: the esoteric teachings of Torah
Kaddish: prayer recited by mourners
kadosh: holy person
kareis: excision; Divine punishment causing premature death
kashrus: the laws defining Kosher food
kedushah: holiness
kiddush: blessing recited over wine on Shabbos
kiddush Hashem: sanctification of G-d's name; martyrdom
Klal Yisrael: the Jewish people
klal: a group, especially the Jewish people
Kohanim: male descendants of the priestly family of Aharon
kollel: post-graduate yeshivah
Korban Minchah: a siddur with Yiddish translation widely used by women
kvitl (pl. *kvitlach*) (Yid.): note bearing a request of a tzaddik

lashon hara: evil speech

GLOSSARY / 267

Levi'im: descendants of the tribe of Levi

levayas hameis: escorting the dead to their final resting place

lishmah: for its own sake

lulav: palm branch, one of the *arba'ah minim*

Ma'ariv: evening prayer service

ma'aser (pl. *ma'aseros*): tithe, often referring to that required of Israeli-grown produce

maggid shiur: Torah lecturer

masechta: Talmudic tractate

mashgiach: spiritual mentor of students in a yeshivah of higher learning

Mashiach (lit., 'Anointed One'): the Messiah

maskil (pl. *maskilim*): follower of *haskalah*, so-called Enlightenment movement which began in the late 1700's and preached the assimilation of Western culture into Jewish life

mazel tov: congratulations

melamed (pl. *melamdim*): Torah teacher of children

Melaveh Malkah: meal eaten Saturday night in honor of the departure of the Sabbath

mesiras nefesh: self-sacrifice; devotion to the point of risking one's life

mezuzah (pl. *mezuzos*): small parchment scroll affixed to doorpost (see *Deuteronomy* 6:9)

midah (pl. *midos*): character trait

Midrash: classic anthology of the Sages' homiletical teachings on the Torah

mikveh (pl. *mikvaos*): ritualarium

Minchah: afternoon prayer service

minyan (pl. *minyanim*): quorum of ten men required for communal prayer

Mishnah: Tannaic dicta compiled by R' Yehudah HaNasi; together with *Gemara* comprises the Talmud

mispallel: one who prays

mitzvah (pl. *mitzvos*): Torah commandment

Moetzes Gedolei HaTorah: Council of Torah Sages

mussar: ethical and moral Torah teachings

Nach: acronym for *Nevi'im* and *Kesuvim*, (Scriptural) Prophets and Writings

negel vasser (Yid.): ritual washing of hands upon arising in the morning Rabbinically ordained to remove spiritual impurity

neshamah: soul

Netziv: acronym for R' Naftali Tzvi Yehudah Berlin (1817-1893), a leading Torah Sage and author in his generation

niggun: tune

nu (Yid.): "so?"

Orach Chaim: section of *Shluchan Aruch* dealing with matters pertaining to everyday life

pashtus: simplicity

Pesach: Passover

Pesukei D'Zimrah: Psalms recited as part of *Shacharis*

pilpul: a Talmudic discourse which weaves together various statements of the Oral Law

posek (pl. *poskim*): halachic authority

p'sak, p'sak halachah: decision of Torah law

p'shat: basic textual interpretation

Rabbeinu Yonah: R' Yonah of Gerona [Gerundi] (1180-1263); Talmudist and author of classical ethical work, *Sha'arei Teshuvah*

Rabbeinu: our Teacher

Rambam: R' Moshe ben Maimon [Maimonides] (1135-1204); codifier, commentator on *Mishnah*, and seminal figure of Jewish philosophy

Ramban: R' Moshe ben Nachman [Nachmanides] (1194-1270); Talmudist, Kabbalist, and author of classical commentaries to *Chumash* and *Gemara*

Rashba: R' Shlomo ben Aderes (1235-1310); famous Halachist and Talmudist

Rashi: R' Shlomo ben Yitzchak (1040-1105); most famous and widely studied commentator on Scripture and Talmud

rav (pl. *rabbanim*): rabbi

rebbe (pl. *rabbeim*): leader of a Chassidic sect

rebbetzin (Yid.): Rabbi's wife

rebbi: teacher or master

Refaeinu: blessing in *Shemoneh Esrei* praying for the sick to be healed

retzuos: straps of *tefillin*

Ribono Shel Olam: Master of the Universe, G-d

Rif: R' Yitzchak al-Fasi (1013-1103); classic Talmudist and codifier

Rishonim: early Talmudic commentators and codifiers (10th to 15th centuries)

rosh yeshivah (pl. *roshei yeshivah*): dean of a Torah institution

ruach hakodesh: Divine Inspiration

seder: ritual festival meal eaten on first two nights of Passover

sefer (pl. *sefarim*): book, especially on Torah subject

sefer Torah: Torah scroll

sha'atnez: Biblical commandment prohibiting use of garment containing both wool and linen

Shach: R' Shabsi HaKohen (1621-1662); author of famous commentary to *Shulchan Aruch*

Shacharis: morning prayer service

Shalom Aleichem: 'Peace unto you'; traditional Jewish greeting

Shalosh Seudos: third Sabbath meal

shamash: synagogue caretaker

Shas: the Talmud

sheirut leumi: national service (for Israeli women)

Shema: Jews' declaration of faith beginning with the words *'Shema Yisrael'* and recited at morning and evening prayer services

Shema Koleinu: sixteenth blessing of the *Shemoneh Esrei*

Shemittah: the Sabbatical year, during which the Torah commands that land in *Eretz Yisrael* be left fallow and its fruits be treated with sanctity

Shemoneh Esrei: the Amidah prayer recited three times daily

shidduch (pl. *shidduchim*): marriage match

shiur (pl. *shiurim*): Torah lecture

shivah (lit., seven): seven days of mourning following death of a close relative

Sh'lah: acronym for *Shnei Luchos HaBris*, classic work by seventeenth-century Talmudist and Kabbalist Rabbi Yeshayah Horowitz

shlita: acronym for "May he live a long and good life," appended to the name of a particularly righteous person

shochet (pl. *shochtim*): ritual slaughterer

Shulchan Aruch: Code of Jewish Law, compiled by R' Yosef Caro (1488-1575)

siddur: prayer book

Simchas Beis HaSho'eivah: celebration held during Succos reminiscent of the Temple festivities during that festival

Simchas Torah: last day of Succos festival marking the completion of the reading of the Torah during the weekly public reading of that year

siyata dishmaya (Ar.): Divine assistance

succah: booth in which the Jew is commanded to dwell during Succos

Succos: Feast of Tabernacles or Booths

sugya (pl. *sugyos*) (Ar.): topic in Talmud

tallis: a large fringed prayer shawl

tallis kattan: small *tallis* usually worn beneath a man's outer garments during the day, to whose corners are attached *tzitzis*

talmid (pl. *talmidim*): student

talmid chacham (pl. *talmidei chachamim*): Torah scholar

Tanach: Scripture

Tannaim: teachers of the *Mishnah*

techias hameisim: resurrection of the dead, a cardinal belief of Judaism

tefillah (pl. *tefillos*): prayer

tefillin: phylacteries (see *Exodus* 13:16)

Tehillim: Psalms

terumah (pl. *terumos*): one of the tithes of Israeli produce

Torah: the Bible

Tosafos: Twelfth century Talmudic commentary printed in all editions of the Talmud

Tosephta: Tannaic teaching not included by Rabbi Yehudah HaNasi in the *Mishnah*

tzaddik (pl. *tzaddikim*): exceptionally righteous individual

tzedakah: charity

tzidkus: piety

tzitzis: fringes worn on a *tallis kattan* (see *Numbers* 15:38)

tznius: personal modesty

Va'ad HaRabbanim: rabbinic council

vasikin: lit., those who are exceptionally pious; usually referring to those who pray the morning service at sunrise, the most preferred time

yahrtzeit: commemoration of deceased's day of death

yarmulka (Yid.): skullcap

yeshivah (pl. *yeshivos*): Torah school, usually high-school age and up (as opposed to *chadarim*)

yiras shamayim: Heavenly fear

yishuv: settlement

Yom Tov: Festival

Yoreh Deah: section of *Shulchan Aruch* dealing with *kashrus*, family purity and other laws

z'chus: merit

Zeraim: first section of *Mishnah*, dealing primarily with laws relating to the produce of *Eretz Yisrael*

Bibliography

PRIMARY SOURCES

HaChazon Ish B'Dorosav. Rabbi Aharon Sorasky; Bnei Brak, 1984.
Kovetz Igros Chazon Ish. compiled by Rabbi Shmuel Greineman, Bnei Brak (no pub. date).
Pe'er Hador — Chayei HaChazon Ish. Rabbi Shlomo Kohen, editor (with Rabbi Aharon Sorasky); Bnei Brak, 1966.
Rabboseinu. Rabbi Y.A. Wolf, editor; Bnei Brak, 1977.
Sefer Chazon Ish — Emunah U'Vitachon. Tel-Aviv, 1954.

SECONDARY SOURCES

B'Derech Eitz Chaim (The Life of Rabbi Isser Zalman Meltzer). Rabbi Yedael Meltzer; Jerusalem, 1986.
Dinim U'Minhagim Chazon Ish; compiled by Rabbi Meir Greineman; Bnei Brak, 1988.
Guardian of Jerusalem [Ha'Ish al HaChomah]. Rabbi Shlomo Zalman Sonnenfeld; New York, 1983.
Hisorerus (collected writings of the Chazon Ish). Bnei Brak, 1989.
Kreina D'Igresa — Kovetz Igros Maran HaRav Yaakov Yisrael Kanievsky. Bnei Brak, 1987.
Marbitzei Torah U'Mussar. Rabbi Aharon Sorasky; Bnei Brak, 1989.
Mishnas Rabbi Aharon: Ma'amarim V'sichos Mussar (Vol. III). Lakewood, 1988.
P'ninei Rabbeinu Kehillos Yaakov. Rabbi Moshe Mordechai Shulsinger; Bnei Brak, 1986.
The Maggid Speaks. Rabbi Paysach Krohn; New York, 1987.
The Story of the Steipler Gaon. Hanoch Teller; New York, 1986.
The Torah Personality. Rabbi Nisson Wolpin, editor; New York, 1980 [*The Chazon Ish* by Rabbi Aaron Brafman].
The Torah Profile. Rabbi Nisson Wolpin, editor; New York, 1988 [*The Steipler Gaon* by Rabbi Eliyahu Meir Klugman].

PERIODICALS

Digleinu. B'Mechitzaso shel Rabbeinu by Rabbi Shlomo Kohen; MarCheshvan 5714 (Part I), Kislev 5714 (Part II).
The Jewish Observer. Living Valiantly Keeping the Shemittah by Rabbi Hanoch Teller (Dec. '79). *Shemittah in Israel Today* by Rabbi Nisson Wolpin (Apr. '87).

This volume is part of
THE ARTSCROLL SERIES®
an ongoing project of
translations, commentaries and expositions
on Scripture, Mishnah, liturgy, history,
the classic Rabbinic Writings,
biographies, and thought.

For a brochure of current publications
visit your local Hebrew bookseller
or contact the publisher:

Mesorah Publications, Ltd.

4401 Second Avenue
Brooklyn, New York 11232
(718) 921-9000